RETHINKIN

ANWAR IBRAHIM

Rethinking Ourselves

Justice, Reform and Ignorance in Postnormal Times

HURST & COMPANY, LONDON

First published in the United Kingdom in 2025 by
C. Hurst & Co. (Publishers) Ltd.,
New Wing, Somerset House, Strand, London, WC2R 1LA
© Anwar Ibrahim, 2025
All rights reserved.

Distributed in the United States, Canada and Latin America by
Oxford University Press, 198 Madison Avenue, New York, NY 10016,
United States of America.

The right of Anwar Ibrahim to be identified as the author
of this publication is asserted by him in accordance with the
Copyright, Designs and Patents Act, 1988.

A Cataloguing-in-Publication data record for this book
is available from the British Library.

This book is printed using paper from registered sustainable
and managed sources.

ISBN: 9781805264194

www.hurstpublishers.com

Printed in Great Britain by Bell & Bain Ltd, Glasgow

For Azizah

CONTENTS

PROLOGUE

EYE OF THE STORM

Change is, more often than not, a tropical cyclone. And in the waning days of the twentieth century, we knew that we were not only at the mercy of one of history's greatest cyclones of change, but perhaps the first convergence of multiple simultaneous mega-events. The post-Cold War world triggered a realigning of geo-politics, technology was advancing communication, information, and efficiency by quantum leap, and the World Wide Web had arrived heralding phenomenal change. Along came disruptive shifts towards globalisation, a neoliberal economic order, and the ebbing crises in energy and global warming. At the centre of the tropical cyclone is the eye of the storm, the calm and tranquil epicentre of the event. The winds and rains cease as clouds eagerly swirl around. In the latter half of 1998, the eye of this storm was firmly fixed on the country I call my home, Malaysia.

The sun went down on 20 September. Yet, the usual twilight cooling of temperatures did not follow. The tension between the people and the government was thick and a coup de grâce from the powers that be could come at any time. Beneath the surface, this day was the culmination of weeks of orchestrated campaigning that had built up a vile media blitz to assassinate my character. Surrounding the eye of the storm, the point of least intensity, is the eyewall, a ring of towering thunderstorms representing the most intense zone of the storm, where storms are most severe and the winds are at their highest. Eighteen days prior, on 2 September,[1] I was unceremoniously and summarily sacked from my posts as deputy prime minister and minister of finance. I was relegated as a political outcast to face the overbearing might of the state.

The storm began with an opportunity. In 1997, I assumed the office of acting prime minister. The reform I had long sought after could finally be implemented. Working with what was then called the Anti-Corruption Agency (ACA), we looked into some glaring loopholes in the agency's existing structure. We even conducted a detailed study of the Hong Kong Anti-Corruption Commission as a point of comparison. One of the more glaring finds in all this research was that the ACA, as it stood then, would allow corrupt officials to be shielded from the law once they were no longer in office. To rectify this deficit and pave the way for the contemporary iteration of the ACA, the Malaysian Anti-Corruption Commission (MACC), an amendment was drafted. The amendment was first discussed in a cabinet meeting where my fellow ministers seemed to suggest that it was not the right time for such changes. If not now, when? So, I threw caution to the wind in spite of the exhortations and earnest advice from close colleagues of the repercussions of my actions. I pushed the amendment through parliament where it was voted into law. My actions were seen not just as a threat against the holders of power but as an audacious attack against the beneficiaries of the kleptocrats—families, cronies, and captains of industry. Soon after, the knives were out against me. The storm was in full gale.

The average eye of a tropical storm can be between twenty and forty miles wide, but the experience can last for around thirty hours. The eye I was in lasted for eighteen days. Prior to this relative calm, the ferocious eyewall of the 1997 Asian Financial Crisis gave its worst. On 2 July 1997, a heavy clap of thunder rolled across the financial markets of East Asia. The Bank of Thailand, having run out of international reserves, threw in the towel and floated its currency, the Thai baht (฿), in order to sustain its US dollar value. Unsurpassed since the Great Depression of 1929–39, this turmoil started to brew, eventually unleashing a raging tempest from Thailand, throughout Southeast Asia. It first went to the Philippines, then to Indonesia, Singapore, and Malaysia, before taking off for the shores of other Asian countries. The chaos erupted with such rapidity and force that it also spread to Russia and Latin America and threatened to engulf the entire world with its pernicious impacts.

In the financial history of the world, no capitalist country has ever demonstrated immunity from one kind of financial crisis or another. It is the nature of the free market that sometimes overshooting takes place and the economy becomes susceptible to external shocks. But on the whole, governments that built strong institutions would command the confidence of the people. When a financial crisis breaks out, swift and decisive measures must be taken by responsible governments to stabilise the situation. Under these circumstances, the use of public funds may be the only means possible to turn the economy around. When I was finance minister in the 1990s, we called this the Keynesian doctrine of pump-priming, a device not entirely free from misuse or abuse. Depending on who was doing the pumping and who was on the receiving end, collecting the fruits of priming, such an undertaking can be open to gross malfeasance. When the issues of governance, transparency, and accountability are left neglected, even the tried and tested toolkit for economic woes could prove to be ineffective. Between the implementation of sound policy decisions and the realisation of a government's true objectives lies a deep and widening chasm. Between saving billions for the nation's coffers and rescuing friends and cronies, falls the shadow of shady decisions made by those in power. The voices of hawkers and rural farmers fall on deaf ears, drowned out by the pleas of the sons of cronies.

On reflection, this was a time of financial euphoria where Malaysia was among the Asian Tiger economies, hailed as the Asian Miracle. The World Bank published a special report entitled 'The East Asian Economic Miracle', which analysed the economic achievements of the region. While many Asian leaders basked in the glory of this accomplishment, I took it with cautious optimism. I was mindful that the success could be transient if we were not alert to the pitfalls that lingered, primarily related to issues of abuse of power and corruption. On one occasion, in my welcoming remarks to the World Bank President James D. Wolfensohn, I said that while we rejoiced at our success, we should not forget the plight of the poor and the marginalised. Further, I highlighted the imperative of good governance and accountability as a bastion against the temptation and risks of corruption and abuse of power. This would warrant the necessary checks and balances that could come about with proper commitment and legislation.

As a nation, Malaysia had managed to weather that crisis, but only just so. This financial crisis served as an ominous warning for global financial crises to come. The 1997 crisis also nearly snuffed out the 'Tiger Cub' economies of Malaysia, Indonesia, Thailand, the Philippines, and Viet Nam in their cradle and threatened the endangered 'Rising Tiger' economies of South Korea, Taiwan, Hong Kong, and Singapore. The recovery placed a shadow on the hopes for the dawn of what many were speculating would be the 'Asian Century'. And Malaysia had no time to rest if it did not want its then forty years of progress from colonial servitude to have been in vain.

PROLOGUE

The calm of the eye collapsed along with the front door of my house—which was unlocked, by the way. It was kicked in by masked, armed men with automatic weapons. My sacking and defamation had been only the beginning. Now I was under arrest.

Hours that could well have been days later, I awoke in a cell on an infernal level of Bukit Aman, the Royal Malaysian Police Headquarters in Kuala Lumpur. Months of stress and struggle, especially from the last few weeks before I was dramatically arrested at home, had caught up with me all at once. Awake, I was exhausted.

Only one thing was allowed to me in my more or less immobilised condition. I turned to the jailer and asked in which direction was the *qibla*, the direction towards Mecca in which Muslims pray. A small spigot in my cell granted me the ability to perform my *wudu* or ablutions, the sacred washing Muslims undergo prior to doing their five daily prayers. It was the most difficult *wudu* I have performed to date. As I stood in the direction of Mecca, the sacred city, I took a deep breath, clearing my mind, and I did the one thing still allowed to an incarcerated man. I prayed.

On the other side of the eye of the storm a great deal of change stood before all of us, beyond the then all-consuming fear of the Y2K virus.[2] While technological advancement was expected to go the only way available, few would have been able to anticipate the impacts of the digital transformation and revolution on our doorsteps. Indeed, even in 1999, a US presidential election had consequences for the rest of the world. But few could have foreseen the stakes of the showdown between George W. Bush and Al Gore, especially in light of the terrorist attacks and 'war on terror' that were to follow. Meanwhile, much of the world had not come to terms with the trauma of colonialism or properly critiqued the postcolonial experience. Justice was not as easily accessible a commodity as our post-war, human rights aware contemporary world might have suggested. I was engaging this fact at first hand. Democracy had been taken for granted and nefarious people were taking advantage. Islam, the world's second largest religion, was a matter of deep ignorance for many around the world and it was about to be thrust into the spotlight on the world's stage. But that light was to be of a most unfavourable hue to those of us who were Muslim. And prior ignorance continued to arc towards further ignorance, even towards hate, xenophobia, and especially Islamophobia. All the norms and ways of thinking we had taken as given were also evaporating and would need to be replaced by novel and innovative approaches to what was increasingly becoming a postnormal world.

The famous black eye I received in prison became a symbol of *Reformasi*—reform.[3] It was a new storm of long-overdue change for Malaysia. As storms in Malaysia and beyond gathered and raged outside the prison walls, personally I too faced protracted incarceration, but I could not allow it to eclipse the significance of the bigger picture: the struggle against the deep-rooted corruption and the abuse of office, between freedom and tyranny, in pursuance of justice, has punctuated the much longer story of my career. Its genesis lay in my scholarly pursuits which moulded my intellectual growth, initially focussed on the issues of poverty and societal welfare. This led to my first 'dalliance' with the draconian Internal Security Act (ISA)[4] following demonstrations way back in 1974.

Hence, while my infamous 1998 sacking and imprisonment are well known, the fact is that 1998 was not my first time in detention. At the centre of an earlier gathering storm was the abject poverty of rural farmers in Baling, in the northern Malaysian state of Kedah. It was a cause with mass appeal to college and university students of the 1970s, like us. Baling's economy was made or broken on the rubber industry. The year 1974 was not fortuitous as harsh weather conditions hit the rubber harvests, tanking the market globally. Inflation was on the rise and the price of basic goods had rocketed outside the capacity of many of Malaysia's rural poor, most of whom were of Malay ethnicity. By November, farmers took to the streets. Adding fuel to fire, the parliament of the day saw fit to raise its own salaries. Then, the protests escalated. In Tasek Utara, a village in the southern state of Johor, farmers were protesting eviction from their homes and the price of basic goods. The protests escalated into December, when our coalition of students brought the demonstrations to such a level that the authorities felt a police crackdown was necessary. It was fast and furious. The upshot was my two years of detention without trial. I found myself at Kamunting Detention Centre, in the company of my compatriots, including the noted academic Syed Husin Ali.[5]

When I was released in 1976, only two years had passed but things had changed significantly. The administration that had seen to my detention had been dissolved. After the demise of Abdul Razak, his successor Hussein Onn became the third prime minister of Malaysia. Malaysia was under its third premiership. Saigon had fallen and the US had abandoned Viet Nam; the country was now fully communist. The first iteration of ASEAN held its first summit in Bali, Indonesia, in February, signifying a regional force to be reckoned with that pushed the ideals of peace and non-alignment. The leader of the People's Republic of China, Mao Zedong, had died a week before my release. Change had come to Malaysia, to Asia, and to the world. It even came for me personally. I was no longer a student. There could be no innocence of youth after my dance with the ISA. I returned to leading ABIM (Muslim Youth Movement of Malaysia) with renewed vigour and firm determination. I had to change the way I was thinking. We all did. It would not suffice to allow change to be something that just happened to us, ready or not; change could be a force that we could usher in through agency and derive power from. Over the next few years, I took on my job with gusto, attending conferences and participating in international engagements. And while I came into my own during my activist days, the recollections of those lost along the way weighed on me. Those who had fought hard against the powers that be consistently arrived at two possible outcomes: either they capitulated along the way through one miscarriage of justice or another, or were pacified and put out to pasture in a dead-end university posting. The naivety of youth quickly justifies the noble fight. I no longer had that excuse. There had to be a different way. I worked hard to polish my intellectual acumen. I travelled the land, engaged with students, religious and community leaders, and built a large, close-knit network. Eventually, this network was broadened to an international arena of Muslim scholars and included noted academics such as Seyyed Hossein Nasr, Ismail al-Faruqi, Fazlur Rahman, and leaders of Islamic movements. At the same time, I engaged with representatives of the Vatican, the World Council of Churches, World Fellowship of Buddhist Youth, and Hindu intellectuals. These conversations and discourses led to a simple realisation: while ideals must form the fundamental basis and rationale of our struggles, they will come to nought unless translated into actions. Eventually, I also reasoned that the best chance for true, substantial change and reform was to come from within, not from outside. So, I joined the ruling political party, the United Malays National Organisation (UMNO) in 1982; and proceeded to sink my teeth into the job of bringing change to my country.

In the 1980s and 1990s, change was shifted into top gear. My rise was a great education. While I had garnered a lot of conventional knowledge from my days as an activist, I was educated further, election by election and ministry by ministry. I am not a technocrat, but learned to heed the advice of those wiser on various matters. And beyond that, I always stayed connected to the people, eager to hear their desires and grant them access to their needs. The core principle of justice was always there. And where so many had been denied it, we needed new ways of getting it to the masses. I also learned the incredible power the state and education had in enabling us to take a stake in the change all around. And I had made true friends and taken many pages of wisdom from some of the brightest luminaries of our age. And although I had come so close, after my capricious removal from office, the option of change from within was no longer available to me. But I was not alone.

While the system which saw me plucked from the high offices of government and condemned to the bowels of prison could be described as being complicit in a perverse miscarriage of justice, the powerful elite of my country had become a parody of itself. A combination of greed and fear saw Malaysia become an international embarrassment of the hope once placed in our postcolonial project. The party that I lead, the People's Justice Party (PKR) or Keadilan, was established on 10 December 1998. After my release from prison in 2004, and equipped with a party of my own, I was confronted with a political scenario that was completely different.

'Cash is king'[6] was the mantra of the ruling kleptocrats, celebrating with glee and gusto the looters of the state, as the then prime minister himself noted with hubristic pride. Corruption not only thrived, but it was also on full, blatant display. It was our gilded age of opulence, paraded unashamedly. Elites walked around as if they were demigods, untouchable, and answerable to no one. Cronyism, nepotism, favours had in spades. The 1Malaysia Development Berhad (1MBD) humiliation, which became the subject of an international corruption scandal in 2015, was a symptom of the disease.[7] The nineteenth-century British historian Lord Acton was correct in his assessment of the corruptibility of power, but it also blinds inasmuch as the allure of riches and bounty are concerned.[8] To be sure, this pervasive corruption would not have seen the light of day but for the complicity or sheer abandonment of moral rectitude of the elites. Meanwhile, the powerful ratcheted up innumerable skeletons from their closets and safely swept them under the carpet until they were uncovered by a series of exposés.

Through the 2008 and 2013 elections, we made great strides, as a united opposition, in spite of the overwhelmingly lopsided playing field. The entire machinery of the state was mobilised to suppress dissent and silence the voice of truth. Realising that these machinations did not yield the desired effect, they resorted to even more insidious subterfuge. The kleptocrats returned to their old bag of tricks and pulled out trumped-up charges. A media blitz was organised to display scurrilous allegations, utterly devoid of truth. All subtlety was abandoned as they set in motion the exact same measures that were used against me in 1998. The full force of the organs of the state rained down on me, culminating in my inevitable conviction. Undoubtedly, this was an upshot of the state powers working hand in glove with the judiciary. They might have wanted my career to end 'not with a bang but a whimper', as T. S. Eliot put it.[9] But providence had other plans.

It was déjà vu all over again, but in a warped sense. There I was, in 2015, flying high in a wave of public support with bright prospects of attaining the highest office of the land, only to find myself hurled back to the position of 1998 and consigned within the walls of incarceration once again. Certainly, I did not expect prison to be a bed of roses. But neither did I expect it to be a bed of concrete. Quite apart from the unpalatable food and unhygienic living conditions, there was the psychological and emotional torture of being deprived of the one thing that could really sustain my sanity, let alone my intellectual well-being.

When I was in prison, deprivation of reading material was one of the chief attempts to inflict mental torture. Throughout my prison years, books were my constant companions. Reading was solace in a world that made little sense, denied the company of other people, of course beyond what company a prison guard can afford. In solitary confinement, rereading the Qur'an brought me great peace. But I am a voracious reader and, at the time, believed I had all the time in the world. It is not difficult to imagine the sorts of things that are often smuggled into prisons, but perhaps not very high on that imagined list are books. The twentieth-century philosopher Isaiah Berlin tells us that freedom is essentially the absence of constraints imposed by others.[10] I am free to the degree to which no man interferes with my activity; political liberty in this sense is simply the area within which a man can act unobstructed by others. But viewed behind the walls of incarceration, shorn of philosophical abstraction, freedom takes on a completely different dimension. Thus, for me, freedom was simply the day my lawyer placed on the table before me my own copy of the Riverside Edition of *The Complete Works of Shakespeare*. Friends would regularly send books which would then be smuggled in for me. Over time, I had built up quite a library in my prison cell. While works from the canons of world literature gradually accumulated around me, my most intimate companion and chief source of comfort came from the Bard himself. *Hamlet, King Lear, The Winter's Tale*—the list may look predictable, even hackneyed, but only if we see it from the frigid perspective of academia. In the stony silence of the night, when I had no one to talk to, Shakespeare's characters become more than mere *dramatis personae*.[11] They spoke to me and allowed me to speak to them.

During my incarceration in 1998, books on social justice, freedom and democracy, development and progress, were at the top of my reading list. From there, I moved on to the works of philosopher and poet Muhammad Iqbal, the Iranian thinker Ali Shariati, the Indonesian intellectual Muhammad Natsir, as well as Frantz Fanon, John Locke, Thomas Paine, and Alexis de Tocqueville.

And there was an assortment of books of all shapes and ideas at the time of my first imprisonment in 1974. For us, the impressionable pupils of a new age—the supposed inheritors of the future—the 1970s were a confusing time. Ideas about development, how the 'Third World' and 'developing countries' could catch up with the West, were buzzing in every direction, and thousands of words written lay in wait for us to read them. I recall ploughing through the American scholar Daniel Lerner's *The Passing of Traditional Society: Modernizing the Middle East*, the Malaysian sociologist Syed Hussein Alatas's *The Problem of Corruption*, and the Swedish Economist Gunnar Myrdal's *Asian Drama*. The concept of postcolonialism—that is, we were now supposed to be in a postcolonial period—was prevalent. We expected to be free from colonial control and oppression. But we soon discovered, as Edward W. Said posited in *Culture and Imperialism*, that the West perpetuated colonial domination through art, literature, and culture.[12] This intellectual capture extended even to politics and economics. Alatas argued that wide-ranging Western dominance in the humanities, including development studies, is manifested in what he called the 'captive mind'—an imitative susceptible and uncritical attitude bereft of independent thinking.[13] Hence, it becomes vulnerable and easily surrenders to the onslaught of Western economic and social paradigms. But emancipation from Western cultural domination is not akin to rejection of the basic universal values of justice, freedom, and democracy.

For me, these are the navigational tools that could take us to a future of progress, social harmony, and prosperity. We should not conflate these values with the history of European colonialism, which was characterised by carnage, racism, and the plunder of the economic resources of colonised peoples. The values of justice, freedom, and democracy are not incompatible with eastern precepts of how societies ought to be governed. In Malaysia, which is multicultural and multireligious, these values intersect and are moulded into Asian values. Values of paramount importance in Islam, such as *ihsan* (virtue), *rahmah* (compassion), and *adl* (justice), have built civilisations of great import and influence throughout the world. But those left behind by the colonial masters as surrogate rulers, as well as the newly emerged class of nationalist elites, have uncritically rejected these values—falling prey to the toxic nature of the 'captive mind'.

While in prison, I made copious notes on books that I had read, and my own reflections. When I was again incarcerated in 2015, I resolved to keep a journal of my intellectual forays with a view to writing a book. With this journal and earlier prison notes, I embarked on an initial draft. But after considering the approaches taken by Antonio Gramsci, the renowned Italian Marxist, and Nelson Mandela, I decided to produce a work of reflections on both my political and intellectual journeys. Between 1929 and 1935, Gramsci wrote around thirty notebooks during his imprisonment by the Italian fascist regime under Benito Mussolini.[14] My own notebooks came to dozens of 'exercise books', which the prison guards allowed me to have, one by one, each stamped with a unique number. By their very nature, prison diaries tend not to be orderly, even less lucid, prose. Mine turned out to be as unsystematic and random as those of Gramsci, plus written in English, Malay, and sometimes a combination of the two, in a handwriting that has been described as notoriously illegible. Just as Gramsci drew inspiration from a string of writers and philosophers, from the left as well as the right, I too drew my inspiration from a wide range of thinkers, authors, essayists, and critics.

However, there is something about being confined to a small cell that forces you to focus on yourself and to think about the world outside. Gramsci reflected on the plight of the working classes, their educational and intellectual development, as well as cultural hegemony.[15] In *The Gulag Archipelago*, Aleksandr

Solzhenitsyn looked at the lives of prisoners around him and examined the history of the Gulag.[16] During my enforced sojourn in Sungai Buloh Prison between 2015 and 2018, my mind too was firmly focussed on the nature of oppression and tyranny, the fragile state of democracy and freedom, the moral upheaval of our times—the perilous state we find ourselves in! The world has changed, and is changing rapidly. Many things we took for granted are in a state of unrest—from the economy to democracy, politics to the sustainability of our environment. Climate change is set to wreak havoc throughout the globe. Indeed, the very notion of what it means to be human is being questioned, thanks to the rapid-pace developments taking place in bioengineering and artificial intelligence (AI). It is not one or the other, this or that, that we need to rethink, but everything that we might otherwise consider normal in our contemporary existence. Indeed, we need to rethink ourselves.

This book has its genesis in my prison jottings. The pandemic left a context that could not be ignored and necessitated a re-evaluation of the analysis, criticism, and my initial ideas. A piece of graffiti spray-painted onto the walls of a subway station in Hong Kong during the pandemic has stuck with me. Roughly translated, it read, 'we can't return to normal, because the normal that we had was precisely the problem'. In that normal, there is confounding poverty, mean-spirited discrimination, grave injustice, unbridled corruption, cheating, lying, and stealing. That normal gave us our political woes and our economic pains, took the people's mandate and threw it back in their faces, and demanded mindless addiction to development and progress for progress's sake. Meanwhile, our technology becomes our crutch as we stand unable to cope with the normal we so desired, and the machines do our thinking for us. I think we have surpassed the most horrifying scenarios that George Orwell or Ray Bradbury or the other great science fiction and speculative writers could imagine. It is time for us to revive our creativity and our imaginations. To read more and think about what we read. To rethink our world and to rethink ourselves. As the British science writer Colin Tudge advocates, we need to rethink everything that we do and that we take for granted.[17] This is tantamount to nothing short of a renaissance. It is only here that we can attain the reform and revision we have dreamed of for generations. And it is here that we can begin taking on the issues that have plagued us in the past to prevent them, along with other crises we might anticipate, from occurring tomorrow and for future generations.

We just might manage to navigate our way out of the numerous existential predicaments with firm resolve and commitment to see our hopes for the future become reality.

One

POSTCOLONIAL ANGST

I

The most precise description for my generation, those born generally between the late 1940s and early 1960s, is found in the local moniker: the Merdeka Generation. *Merdeka* being the Malay word for independence, ours coming in 1957, only about a decade later than the post-war wave of various other colonial dominions that declared independence from Great Britain. Our first prime minister, Tunku Abdul Rahman, heroically declared 'Merdeka!' seven times on the last day of August in 1957, as the Union Jack was lowered, and the new Malayan flag was raised. And so, we walked confidently into the interregnum born out of the wake of World War II and Japan's occupation—which would require expert level navigation to transcend. To Tunku's great credit, this was a period of immense challenge, requiring both strategic vision and keen statesmanship to bring to fruition and, in so doing, birth a new nation founded on racial and religious harmony. However, the last British colonial administrators did not depart our lands until 1963, when the Federation of Malaysia was declared, and Sabah, Sarawak, and Singapore joined the federation. And it would not be until 1965, when Singapore was separated from Malaysia, that the nation-state as we know it today would settle its borders[1] (the contemporary volatility of Asian and Pacific borders being due to the unresolved issues left behind by erstwhile colonial masters). In short, independence is something more easily declared than brought to life.

I do not give much credence to the labelling of the post-world war world as the 'postcolonial era'. Merely affixing the prefix 'post' to the word colonialism does not guarantee an end to colonialism. For example, post-industrial societies have not been able to effectively overcome the issues of poverty or reduce inequities, let alone assuage the plight of workers or alleviate catastrophic environmental impacts. And post-race societies, I find, are often the most racist. Postmodernity turned a blind eye to the conflicts that arose from modernity; plunging us into the same old ploys modernity has set as assumed destiny for human societies. Postmodernism may have given us some rich cultural offerings, interesting art and architecture, but it was not much more than a linguistic sleight of hand, as Wittgenstein would remind us. Meanwhile, elites in our postcolonial societies were dazzled by the mirage of the old colonial system and succumbed to its allure. The challenge lies in facing headlong the intellectual environment that could suck us into a cycle of history that closely resembles a hamster wheel.

So, to call myself a member of the Merdeka Generation still stands as potentially problematic. The Merdeka Generation of Malaysia, as immortalised in the films of one of Malaysia's greatest filmmakers, P. Ramlee,[2] could rightly be said to be a testament to the preservation of the Malay identity without having to trumpet the conviction of superiority. The prevailing theme of my generation was multiculturalism and inclusiveness, blended in a beautiful synthesis not often seen contemporaneously. Ours was also a generation of great socio-political awakening. It was a

2

time where the critical issues of national identity, poverty, and corruption were coming to the fore. These issues ignited the people, especially the students, in the 1960s and 1970s.

II

Under these circumstances, I found myself adrift in a sea of troubles. The struggle was no longer strictly academic. It was now one that required personal and direct commitment to the cause, if there was any hope of success in braving the challenges and risks associated with being an activist. Protests and demonstrations were staged to express our opposition to the US aggression committed against the Vietnamese, against apartheid in South Africa, and the insidious Israeli colonisation of Palestine. At home, we called out our government's failure for their incompetence and neglect of the poor. We expressed our discontent and indignation against the postcolonial elite who retained power in Malaysia for their disdainful attitude towards the people. This disrespect extended to our national language and our education system. While growing up in a traditional setting, grounded in Quranic lessons and religious teachings, I was very fortunate to have attended classes under the tutelage of great educators at the Malay College, Kuala Kangsar. But it was at the University of Malaya that I was exposed to the progressive and revolutionary ideas of the West. As a social science major, I delved deep into the writings of Western luminaries of political economy and philosophy. I learned to love the works of William Shakespeare and the Western canon of literature. And more importantly, I was instilled with a love for reading. I still remember the immortal words of the literary critic Harold Bloom, who noted the importance of reading the best of what has ever been written. He said, 'if we do not read deeply, we do not learn how to think. And if, as a nation, we do not learn how to think, someday we will yet cease to be a democracy'. And my love of reading had no limits. I rediscovered the Malay classics as well as the great works of classical Islam. The upshot was a convergence of culture and ideas, which would itself tend towards ossification. The ideas that stood out for me were freedom and justice and how these two would not see the light of day without democracy. Conversely, democracy would remain an empty slogan without freedom and justice. Attempts to bifurcate these concepts are to my mind, a Sisyphean task. These concepts also cannot be seen in isolation of the traditional values of society. As the philosopher and poet Muhammad Iqbal warned us in *The Reconstruction of Religious Thought in Islam*, we must set up guard rails against the philosophies of materialism, so that we do not fall head over heels for 'the enchanting idea of capitalism and socialism'.[3] This understanding was crucial to make sure we never lost sight of the enduring values of ethics, morality, compassion, and humanity.

The world before the world wars saw the rest bleed so that Europe could burn and, in those fires, advance beyond others. So, while Copernicus demonstrated that the Earth was not the centre of the universe,[4] it could hardly be assumed that Europe took this concept to heart until those very flames of progress began consuming themselves. Historians tend to simplify the world order that proceeded the world wars. They told us it was a bipolar world. Some say East versus West, but from our perspective, ascribing the United States and the Soviet Union the labels of capitalism and communism were too simplistic. Capitalism versus Communism, but it wasn't that simple either. Rather than addressing the problems of colonialism fully, those in power were more eager to sideline the less powerful with new 'rules' while bending them to give the perception that the playing field was fair. They achieved this by employing cunning semantics to suit their vested interest. Hence, 'colonies', which were no longer allowed in our more 'civilised' age, were renamed 'territories'.

Likewise, 'empires' became 'spheres of influence'. It is amazing how such a play of words could secure the erstwhile colonisers unlimited access to the rich resources, such as timber, tin, gold, diamond, and other valuable minerals, extracted from the lands they claimed to no longer lord over. They said the world was changing, that we were on the precipice of history. In reality, it was more of the same with different flags and a deceptive rhetoric that said one thing while meaning another.

The Cold War dichotomy of the world being bipolar held when the world was seen as split between two teams (the US and the USSR). Two US presidents solidified this worldview. First, it was Harry S. Truman who declared that the US and its military industrial complex would defend all 'free', 'democratic', and 'capitalist' states threatened by the viral idea known as 'communism'.[5] Second, Truman's successor, President Dwight D. Eisenhower, developed the Domino Theory to explain how one nation falling to communist forces would have a knock-on effect on its neighbouring 'developing' states—like a row of dominos collapsing upon each other.[6] Feeding such narratives was some master Soviet conspiracy, when in fact the Soviets had their own problems within the borders of the USSR itself, as if the Third World had no ability to think for itself. The US's fears in Cuba and Indochina (Viet Nam) gave life to a global spectre that became everyone's imperative to fear. Yet perhaps the two presidents should have taken heed of their predecessor Franklin D. Roosevelt's famous axiom—'we have nothing to fear but fear itself'.[7]

The rejection of colonialism and imperialism should have opened up new vistas of political ideologies. But the paradigm of the day insisted that we were now living in a 'Cold War' world. To appreciate the rich potential for new political paradigms hidden beneath this assumed duality, we need to debunk the idea that reinforced it. First, there were not ever simply two sides. We see this clearly in the First, Second, and Third World labels that were attached to various states—but even this is a gross simplification. The logic behind this dichotomy was faulty. To maintain two sides, you had to change your framing of the international community.

It was a tad far-fetched to think that 'communism' was a united force rippling through the 'East'. The trouble with this narrative was demonstrated early on when the People's Republic of China distanced itself from its neighbour, the USSR. Nor was this what Karl Marx and Friedrich Engels could have been discussing over a century prior.[8] Vladimir Lenin was certainly moved by Marx's writings as he assembled the Bolsheviks in Brussels (before they took off to Russia), as was Chen Duxiu in Shanghai, and, for that matter, Ho Chi Minh while he was studying in Paris. But while all three may have found inspiration in Marx, they all took different paths to the revolution called for in *The Communist Manifesto*. And beyond them Joseph Stalin, Mao Zedong, and Lê Duẩn further drove the 'communism' found in their respective movements in different directions. While Marx gives a detailed, multi-volume critique of capitalism in *Das Kapital*, and even lays the groundwork for the proletariat revolution that he argued was badly overdue, even in his own time, he did not live long enough to set down his ideas on what came next, particularly in terms of politics and governance.[9] We should take note of a strange phenomenon that left the 'communist' world in arrested development. The phenomenon is manifested when the spotlight shifts from intellectuals to the pragmatic strong men—each with their own packed agenda to be seen out. A similar phenomenon befell and damned many postcolonial states.

For us, the denizens of the 'Third World', on the one hand, communism held out the prospect, theoretically at least, of an egalitarian society. On the other hand, capitalism offered great promises for societal growth and prosperity, albeit also theoretically. For my generation, having been fed on the diet of Western education and political thought, these two contending ideologies seemed to be the only viable alternatives. Some of my colleagues were enamoured by the ideas of communism as espoused by Marx and Engels. The promise of a classless society where wealth would be distributed communally is hard to disagree with. They held on passionately to such academic expositions as Paul Baran's *Political Economy of Growth*. The concepts particularly resonated with those of us who had their sights set on resolving the plight of the farmers and labourers, and improving the conditions faced in the rubber estates of Malaysia. While there were indeed legitimate concerns, nevertheless there were many others, myself included, who felt there was greater urgency—and more sustainable solutions—in advocating and addressing issues concerning national identity, language, and education. Additionally, we observe a more fervent rejection of the prevailing influence of postcolonialism as manifested by an obsessive, almost obsequious, surrender to Western values, power, and the force of economic challenges.

While this was a period dominated by overarching discourse on the battle between capitalism and communism, there was at the same time, this underlying cauldron of concepts which formed the parallel discourse amongst us. As Europe grappled with its own identity crises, desperately clinging to their old empires, and their global domination, in all but name, the rest of us were ready to move forward. This was an age full of idealism. But realising what was at stake, the best of our 'postcolonial' thinkers could not sit by, waxing lyrical. They had to lead from the ground. This pressure forged the likes of Mahatma Gandhi, Frantz Fanon, Malek Bennabi, Ernesto Che Guevara, Malik el-Shabazz also known as Malcolm X, Ho Chi Minh, Nelson Mandela, and many others throughout Asia, Africa, and the Americas. Their personal philosophies and epistemological backgrounds, from local or tribal, indigenous outlooks to civilisational and modern worldviews were diverse and varied. However, they laid out the basic tenets of the postcolonial project: to tear down the notions of superiority and inferiority between the West and the rest and to strive for equality amongst all humans. In taking on the roots of much of the devastation of the twentieth century, these postcolonial thinkers also commonly stood for disarmament.[10] Once upon a time we were very concerned with the proliferation of nuclear arms. Some of us still are. The postcolonial project was to defeat racist and classist notions put in place through the age of empire. It was, in hindsight, rather simple, but brilliant enough to unite peoples across all continents.

Nevertheless, many of these great people of both thought and action did not survive their struggles, falling victim to the violence thrust upon them or other ailments. They did not get to see the home they fought for gain independence or enjoy that independence for very long. Societal anger and the indomitable spirit to challenge 'rampant corruption and moral decadence' had gone global, while others focussed on who would win the Cold War. Even here in Malaysia, a place not often thought of as an epicentre of the postcolonial struggle, the tension and the potential was palpable. I recall, from my days leading ABIM—the Muslim Youth Movement—in the late 1970s, being approached by a group of pre-university students, living on the outskirts of Kuala Lumpur—a group one would think cared little, if at all, about the thoughts of foreigners—who requested that I do a review of books by the French Afro-Caribbean psychologist and activist Frantz Fanon. Such was their zeal in the quest for further knowledge, and their thirst for enlightenment. In his two major works, *The Wretched of the Earth* and *Black Skin, White Mask*, Fanon posited the guileful effects of colonialism, and that racism ends up corrupting both the colonised and the coloniser.

According to Fanon, both the colonised and coloniser behave according to their neurotic orientation—the colonised enslaved by their sense of racial inferiority, the coloniser by his eugenic-based superiority complex.

The Algerian philosopher, Malik Bennabi, reinforced the ideas of Fanon in his seminal works *The Vocation of Islam* and *The Quranic Phenomenon*. Bennabi also asserted that colonialism was not merely an external imposition. It was an internal ailment as well, made possible by a weakness within colonised societies. To discuss this condition, he coined the term *colonisabilité* or 'colonisability'—the propensity to resign oneself to be colonised. This is partly attributed to an inaccessibility to knowledge or defeatism on account of being subjected to protracted psychological assault. Domination, he argued, was not sustained by brute force alone, it was nourished by intellectual inertia, political stagnation, and social fragmentation. True liberation then, was not simply about casting off foreign rule—it was about renewing or seeking the rebirth of the very foundations of society, without which moral and ethical stagnation would set in. These ideas were truly impactful and resonated strongly with activists and students alike. The clarion call that resonated was 'colonisability', 'guiding ideas', and 'inner struggle of conscience'. The internal process of decolonising that Fanon and Bennabi advocated compels us to redouble our efforts; prompting us to act with even greater urgency and resolve.

Mohandas Gandhi, the great proponent of non-violence, not only reminded us of how colonialism used oppressive instruments to plunder the wealth of the colonised—especially, if all else failed, through the imposition of high taxes—but he also showed us how to stand up to these often-titanic forces. Colonialism, through its various nefarious methods and institutions dispossessed the colonised populations of their material wealth and of their moral and spiritual selves. As a result, the masses became poorer, leaving the people particularly vulnerable to pandemics and famines. Regardless of how well we came to terms with our internal conflicts, the external ones appeared insurmountable. Nevertheless, Gandhi's nonviolence methods—predicated on resistance through the principled values of *ahimsa*, one of the highest dharma pledging nonviolence in action, thought, and words, and *satyagraha*, a complete dedication to truth in all matters—were proof-positive that the old, unjust oppressive ways of colonialism could not hold.[11] Gandhi produced results and gave us all an example to look up to. I fondly remember my encounters with the living embodiments of the Gandhi spirit, namely his grandson, Rajmohan Gandhi, whom I first met in Poona in 1967. I was still at the university then, but having read widely on Gandhi, he was fascinated by my keen interest in the life and struggle of his late grandfather. This encounter with Rajmohan was the beginning of many more engaging conversations and exchanges.

Outside of the internal and external trials of colonialism, a parallel approach was put forward by such thinkers as the Japanese polyglot philosopher Toshihiko Izutsu. Alongside the direct conflict between the colonised and the coloniser, there is a need to seek new ways of building our epistemological knowledge bases beyond those dominated by our former overlords. Instead, these new approaches ought to lean into the intersectionality between our languages, ethics, and faiths. Izutsu is most well-known for first translating the Qur'an into the Japanese language, a feast of unparalleled distinction and a testament to his profound linguistic skills. Izutsu was able to capture the essence and semantic nuances of the original text, leaning on an intimate understanding of both the Arabic language, the Islamic tradition as well as other Semitic and cognate linguistic cousins. This work exemplifies his commitment to bridging cultural and linguistic divides. Izutsu developed a deep respect for Islamic thought and philosophy throughout his work. By advocating for an empathetic perspective and urging scholars to understand religious texts from within their own conceptual frameworks, Izutsu paved the way for a more nuanced and respectful approach to cross-cultural dialogue.[12] His magnum opus, *Sufism and Taoism*, stands as a leading study of the metaphysical and mystical thought system of both. Something that is urgently needed not only in sloughing off our postcolonial angst, but in the wake of a return and rise of obscurantism bigotry and intolerance that threatens to divide societies and undermine global peace. By promoting empathy, understanding and respect, we can counter the force of division and build bridges across culture, religions, and nations.

While these anti-colonial luminaries were indeed fundamentally profound, articulate, and sharp in their critique, the broader postcolonial influence persisted. Nevertheless, there was one glimmer of hope for those undermined by the postcolonial project when the Non-Alignment Movement (NAM) was assembled in Belgrade, Yugoslavia in 1961. This was a *bona fide* third way for the bipolar, post-world-war world. Formed in response to the first proxy war of the Cold War and the Korean War, a formidable grouping of neo-nationalists, including Yugoslav President Josip Broz Tito, Indian Prime Minister Jawaharlal Nehru, Egyptian President Gamal Abdel Nasser, Ghanaian President Kwame Nkrumah, and Indonesian President Sukarno, converged with a well-crafted plan. They, including China's Zhou Enlai, had gathered earlier in Bandung, Indonesia in 1955. This was the first ever Asia–Africa Conference touted as a point of genesis for what we today refer to as the Global South.[13] Regardless of the inability to achieve its objectives, largely because of the geopolitical dominance of the superpowers from the Western and Eastern Blocs of the time, this movement had noble intentions and cannot be castigated into the dustbin of history. The upshot was a bipolar world necessitated by the dictates of *realpolitik* and pragmatism.

III

Once independent, the postcolonial states found themselves in a very precarious situation. Almost every day was an existential crisis. And the radical change many desired was a risky move that threatened everything and everyone. Indeed, one can declare independence, but states do not exist in vacuums. They exist in a world in motion. And society needed continuity. Unfortunately, many postcolonial state governments opted for convenience and adopted familiar oppressive laws to stifle dissent and maintain order. If it had worked for the colonial overlords, why wouldn't it work for the new elites when they assumed their new positions of power? Perhaps, in the chaos that accompanies the birth of a nation, we can understand why such a move might be taken. But it is imperative that the restoration of stability must be in tandem with the pursuit of reform. Failing to do so, the new elites of these postcolonial states run the risk of becoming neocolonisers themselves.

In the newly independent Malaya, like many of its postcolonial peers, the ruling elite governed the country with Western-oriented prescriptions. It should not be glossed over that this style of governance had its benefits. Most readily, this was seen in a smooth and efficient administration and civil service copied almost directly from the British. This style of governance also gave way to Malaysia. Eventually, it fostered Malaysia's socio-political development. The flaws of this system were revealed by the paramount prioritisation of the maintenance of law and order, as well as peace and security. But our fledgling nation was threatened from multiple sides. The threat of insurgent communist guerilla troops was real and present. Likewise, tensions and fears amongst our neighbours and the threat of internal, ethnic conflict placed us on the precipice of complete disorder. We did not have one, but multiple swords of Damocles hanging over us. Under these circumstances, a mechanism for declaring state emergencies was purported to be essential. So followed the all-encompassing, notorious Internal Security Act (ISA) in 1960. This draconian law was one dark legacy of British colonisation. Other postcolonial states had their own versions. In India, for example, it came in the form of 'Bengal Regulation III', sanctioned by the East India Company in 1818. It later became the infamous Rowlatt Act of 1919. The purpose of the legislation was preventive detention to counter and suppress organised violence. The intention was no doubt laudable but, as they say, the path to hell is paved with good intentions. Ostensibly this act enabled the power to arrest and hold individuals indefinitely without charge or trial, all in the name of maintaining 'public order'. Initially the rationale of this law was to counter the communist insurgency, but eventually it was exploited as a tool for the elite to stifle dissent and perpetuate their hold on power. Additionally, it became a means to consolidate their links with the erstwhile colonial power. For the British Empire, the Malaya economy—largely dependent on tin and rubber—was a crown jewel. As it turned out, this piece of legislation was transformed into a weapon of mass oppression. Political dissidents, trade union leaders, and civil society activists were rounded up and incarcerated without trial.

When I found myself caught in the dragnet, I could relate to how farcical and ludicrous the reasons for arrest could be. In 1974, I joined the ranks of those held under the dreaded ISA, following months of nationwide demonstration over the plight of poor farmers and labourers, culminating in student demonstrations in downtown Kuala Lumpur in December. First held at the Jalan Bandar lock-up, I was given a cell without so much as a few words in justification. Though it was not legally required, after a few days, I was given the grace of rationale. The first recorded documentation of my detention stated, underneath 'Reason for Arrest', two words: 'student agitator'. Though it did not look like much, it did technically fall under the Universities and University Colleges Act 1971, which limited student political involvement, free expression, and assembly. This document followed a letter requesting that my detention be extended while further investigations were carried out. A day or so later, a short charge sheet followed, claiming I was a 'pro-pro-Communist' who was advocating for the creation of an Islamic University and distributing Dr Mahathir Mohamad's book *The Malay Dilemma*. To this day I am still unsure what exactly a 'pro-pro-communist' is, or how could I be supporting a movement and a party that was manifestly atheist while also being a radical Islamist demanding an Islamic university. Interestingly, at this point, Dr Mahathir was the government's minister of education, yet the home affairs ministry had not got around to taking *The Malay Dilemma* off the banned books list. So, indeed, in the eyes of the powers that be, I was guilty of distributing this book.

Two months later, by which point I had been moved to Kamunting Detention Centre, a maximum-security prison approximately 280 kilometres north of Kuala Lumpur, a more elaborate document detailed my crimes. It began with the 'grounds on which the order of detention is made':

> Since MAR 69, you, ANWAR IBRAHIM have consistently acted in a manner prejudicial to the security of Malaysia, in that you have actively, knowingly and willingly become the main agitator of several undesirable activities, acts of lawlessness and illegal demonstrations amongst students of the University of Malaya and other institutes of higher learning agitating against the Government policies, on various issues in the country, with the ultimate aim of overthrowing the legally constituted Government of Malaysia by unconstitutional and revolutionary means.

What followed this purple prose preamble, was a laundry list of all my 'nefarious' moves against the government. Importantly, the list begins before the 13 May tragedy, so that I could be tied to stirring tempers during those turbulent times and in violation of the state of emergency that followed. I 'unrelentlessly' called for the Malay language to be the official language of Malaysia. A protest organised during the Thai premier's visit to Kuala Lumpur, noting his unfair treatment of the southern Thai Muslims of Patani, were a 'clear indication' of my 'militant outlook' and the 'infinite extent' of my 'disregard for the constitutional rule of law'. My rhetoric also had a tendency to provoke 'whispering campaigns' which stood as 'another manifestation' of my 'advocacy for violence'. A 'planned' demonstration 'urged the students to be armed with offensive weapons in order to safeguard from Police intervention. Though the demonstration did not materialise, it is sufficient evidence of the extent of militancy implanted in you'. My calling out of the government for prioritising the creation of the Tunku Abdul Rahman college over an Islamic University represented my 'calculated efforts to cast doubts and thereby creating disaffection towards the Government'. My public declaration of support for the Palestinian liberation struggle in 1973 'had generated antagonism' against the Soviet Union and the US and 'created doubts on the Malaysian Government's non-alignment posture thereby affecting public confidence in the Government foreign policy and its cordial relations'. The charges were capped off with the 3 December 1974 demonstration at the Selangor Club *padang* and Masjid Negara. The 'illegal mass demonstration' protested against 'inflation' and the newly created concept 'stagflation'. It was noted that 'students became unruly and violent necessitating immediate Police dispersal action'. It further highlighted that 'there was pandemonium and destruction'. And although I was not present, 'Anwar Ibrahim, in his yet another manifestation of militancy, was engaged in manipulating from behind the scenes the altruistic motives of many students who thought they were championing the cause of the poor peasants in Baling'. By formulating these charges they inadvertently acknowledged the reality of abject poverty in Baling, a fact which they had persistently denied. The significance of the poverty crisis in Baling cannot be overstated as it constituted the first ever peasant upheaval against the ruling elite since independence. Ironically, just three years before the farmer demonstrations, the government launched the New Economic Policy (NEP) signifying their realisation of the poverty and inequities affecting the people. Clearly, the three year interval was insufficient to rectify the problem.

The dark side of the ISA was that they could be used arbitrarily and capriciously against anyone who was in the crosshairs of the powers that be. And this would continue until 2012, when political opposition and civil society clamoured for its abolition. Nevertheless, the repeal of the ISA was followed by the problematic Special Offences (Special Measures) Act 2012, also known as SOSMA, an ISA updated for the post-9/11 age, borrowing from the language used to advance the US's Patriot Act. In lockstep with the legacy of the colonial era, and under these pretexts, this draconian law was employed to incarcerate such activist luminaries as Ahmad Boestamam, Burhanuddin al-Helmy, Aziz Ishak, Lim Kit Siang, and Syed Husin Ali.

Looking back, as has been seen in their other colonies, the British implemented the strategy of 'divide and conquer'[14] in Malaya. The strategy was simple: find the opportunities that already exist for division within a colonial territory, then exploit them so that different social groups under colonial control, who might otherwise exist in harmony, will be too busy fighting or being suspicious of one another. The Malay Archipelago had been a central hub of trading between the East and West, notably during the Malacca Sultanate. Naturally the empires that controlled the lands of modern-day China and India had their peoples travelling through the area and some of them setting up shop in the archipelago. Even the occasional Western explorer and trader would find a home here. Once the archipelago was divided up by Portuguese, Spanish, Dutch, and eventually British colonialism the ebb and flow of immigration was exploited. This was part of the colonial agenda to perpetuate the policy of divide and rule. Contrary to J. S. Furnivall's account of a plural society,[15] the colonial masters devised a campaign of racial segregation. In British Malaya, while the Malays were assigned to purported privileged positions in the lowest rung of the civil service, the majority were consigned to the occupations of farmers and fishermen. This was clearly intended to keep them in an economically disadvantaged position and perpetually trapped in poverty beneath the British. An influx of Indians was largely brought in by the British as labourers or 'coolies' in European-owned rubber estates to languish in deplorable conditions. Following the Indian Rebellion of 1857, the Indians were classified by the British as a martial race, so they were also given positions in the military and policing authorities. Pre-existing concepts of caste from British India created social divisions within the Indian community in Malaya. The British brought in Chinese labourers to work in the tin mines. But the existence and growth of a Chinese merchant class created a stratification within that community. The perpetuation of these racial divisions spurred further social stratification within and between the racial communities of British Malaya. Disgusting stereotypes, xenophobia, and the myth of 'lazy natives'[16] metastasised. This fuelled distrust and are the roots of today's deep wealth inequalities. And once Malay elites were allowed to take over the civil service as the British transitioned out, the divisions within even the majority community were allowed to germinate further. It would be naïve to imagine that centuries of societal division can be undone overnight. A system designed to pit one ethnic group against the other by special segregation and economic fragmentation certainly worked well to ensure that the colonised remained disunited. The system did work well for the British. The challenge for the new elite was whether to maintain the status quo and perpetuate their hold on power, or to start fresh on a more progressive agenda.

The 'what ifs' of history can be a dubious task, but one cannot help but wonder how things might have been different had Malaysia been allowed to come about more organically—even via an allowance of self-determination. I often refer to the national Hero of the Philippines, José Rizal, as also being a *Malayan* Hero. Rizal was executed by the Spanish colonists at the tender age of thirty-five in 1896. In those days, the Malay Archipelago was also known by the old Javanese term Nusantara, which included modern-day Malaysia, Indonesia, Brunei, Timor-Leste, Taiwan, and the Philippines. And there was some unity in this diversity. Take as example the Radcliffe Line[17] between India and Pakistan, or the Sykes–Picot Agreement[18] concerning the divvying up of the Ottoman Empire after World War I. Thus, Peninsular Malaya, which bore a majority Malay Muslim population with both colonial structures of governance and sultans, was smashed together with Singapore. This brought in a large population of ethnic Chinese, as well as Sarawak and Sabah, who both brought large indigenous populations and a large Christian presence into the fold—all of which disturbed the ethnic and cultural balance in the country. The ethnic diversity was far broader than the original elites had believed and that the British colonial agents had anticipated. From one angle, one could say this new nation lacked an identity. From another, one could say we had too many identities. Even geographically the landmass was split by the South China Sea. Race was the problem before the project even started and hubris dictated that the elites would attempt to use race as the solution. The government attempted to sugar-coat the problem by giving it the new name: 'communalism'.[19] The consequence was twofold. First, it attempted to show the government had a plan to address the issue. Second, this did help in giving a greater appreciation of the complexity of race in Malaysia which conventional racist rhetoric tends to simplify. And then, not even a decade into existence, Malaysia experienced its tragedy: the 13 May Incident of 1969. Ethnic clashes largely between the Chinese and Malay communities, resulted in the deaths of 196 individuals and the injury of 439, and the damage and destruction of hundreds of buildings and vehicles. But beyond this it was easy for the ruling elite to associate the ethnic Chinese with communism as well. So, there was another reason to divide further the Chinese from the other ethnic groups in Malaysia.[20] Our elites took on the narrative fear of the communists as they became the bogeymen waiting in our own jungles.

In 1952, Frantz Fanon made a keen observation about colonialism in his seminal book *Black Skin, White Masks*.[21] Colonialism not only depended on establishing a relationship of superiority and inferiority between coloniser and colonised, or even the simple dehumanisation of the colonised into a lesser being. Crucial to colonialism was the ability to make the colonised think that they really were inferior and that they needed the coloniser in order to exist or survive. The postcolonial project then is not simply re-education or even the rekindling of indigenous notions, it requires both social and psychological heavy lifting. Not only that, but now that colonialism has existed, it needs to be dealt with. We cannot simply move on and decolonise until kingdom come, lest that be the only thing we accomplish with our limited time on this earth. We have to face the reality that the experience of colonialism has fractured the minds of the colonised. In Fanon's reckoning, we perpetually carry the postcolonial angst with us. But it does us, the people of the postcolonial states, no good.

Despite how much the elites needed to hold onto the power they were given by the British, predictably, they had noble intentions. There was a general will to improve the livelihood of all of

Malaysia's diverse citizenry and drive the nation, at least as much as was possible, towards the trajectory of some of our more developed neighbours. But a real inequality existed and required immediate action for the stability of the nation. At the end of British rule, much of the nation's wealth had become consolidated largely in the hands of foreign entities and non-indigenous communities. Certainly by any measure, it would be untenable for any nation to have its majority population languishing in poverty. Hence, certain provisions were incorporated into Malaysia's constitution to provide for socio-economic safeguards for the Malays and the indigenous peoples of Sarawak and Sabah.[22] Fundamentally, this constitutional scheme could be considered a sound strategy to rectify racial economic diversity with affirmative action policies. This approach could also be regarded as a deliberate design to effectuate a societal remedy for the ills and flaws caused by colonial exploitation. The legacy inherited from the colonial powers was regretably one built upon a culture of racism. So, the negative upshot of such an influence is the tendency to conceive policy through ethnic lenses as if such an approach would be the be-all and end-all cure. With the passage of time, it is abundantly clear, while there is merit in a race-based policy—that is to ensure that certain marginalised ethnic groups are not left behind—the reality is that a more effective and sustainable socio-economic paradigm for the retification of wealth inequities has to be needs-based.[23] Logically, such an approach nececessarily ensures that the objectives of the race-based strategy would also be achieved. That said, it pays to be mindful that between equality and equity lies the grey shadow of ambiguity. Such a realisation should, therefore, jolt us to the fact that even within our ethnic groups, gross inequities continue to persist.

Again, the earliest proponents of postcolonial movements held to three overarching objectives: decolonisation through removal of the mechanisms of oppression, opposition to racism through the promotion of human equality, and disarmament and peace, seemingly by any means necessary. Pursuing this course, Malaysia was able to circumvent the extreme and unreflective style of decolonisation that took place in other postcolonial states. Consequently, the possibility of the Sukarno style 'guided democracy'[24] did not arise, let alone an outright dictatorship which, unfortunately, was the fate of many former colonial states. Indeed while these concerns were considered crucial, nevertheless, the preoccupation of the elites was so centred on keeping themselves in power that it seems other considerations were relegated to a lower priority. The recourse then was to ensure the process of a parliamentary democracy and constitutional monarchy should continue inviolate.

IV

Then came the tipping point of the 13 May 1969 tragedy. Tunku's administration could not make the Malays feel secure or solve the widening economic gaps. His successor, Abdul Razak bin Hussein, stepped in to navigate. Since Razak was the Number Two Man of Tunku's premiership, it was a quick and smooth transition. But this 'new' leadership[25] had failed to sufficiently address two crucial issues which had significant long-term implications. First, since race had superseded other national concerns, the problems of poverty and economic inequality were conflated as a race problem. Second, few at the time realised the fundamental connection between politics and economics: the two are intimately related. Political stability and progress cannot be advanced when economic inequities continue to be propagated. Likewise, economic growth and prosperity cannot come to fruition in the absence of political stability.

Abdul Razak, wasted no time in being seen getting down to the ground and listening to the problems of the common man.

Being an effective communicator, he quickly gained the lost confidence. One of his top apparatchiks was Ghazali Shafie, whom we knew as 'King Ghaz'. King Ghaz was crucial to finding just the right piece to fill the whole Malaysia in terms of a national identity with the *Rukunegara*, or the Pillars of the Nation, which acted as an ideology to bring together all Malaysians—notions of race need not apply. The tragedy which left deep scars, exacerbated interethnic distrust and compelled the Razak Administration to propound a paradigm shift in the socio-economic policies of the nation. A primary concern was the gross disparity between the ethnic groups that had generated a deep underlying sense of insecurity among the Malays and other indigenous peoples of Malaysia. King Ghaz pushed for *bumiputeraism* to be the new guiding principle for policymaking in Malaysia.[26] At the centre of the idea is the *bumiputera*, which literally translates as 'sons of the soil', meaning they who inherit the land. The key policy move that would see bumiputeraism put into practice was the NEP in 1971. It would be apparent at the outset to see what might appear to be a contradiction between the aspiration of the *Rukunegara* and the doctrine of *bumiputeraism*. The NEP was driven by a lofty dream; and not intended to be ethnic centric. The thrust of the policy was to develop the country, eliminate poverty, and end race as a determining factor for anything in Malaysia. Admittedly utopian and vague, but this does not make the NEP a bad idea. Its aim was eradicating poverty and restructuring society so as to generate economic wealth for equitable distribution among the people. Admittedly, affirmative action was leaned on to assist the bumiputeras, particularly in advancing social mobility through training and education. Too many contradictions and its immeasurability prevented the NEP from attaining its fullest potential. For example, the plan intended to use the language, and therefore the historical weight, of race to end racism. However, the unfortunate truth was that racial language perpetuates racial structures. There was a hope that this might be curbed by making Malay the national language, which was done at Independence in 1957, and was reinforced through the National Language Act of 1967, which made Malay the official language of government affairs. Linguistic affinity for Malay had already made it the lingua franca regardless of ethnic or cultural background. The true root of distrust and ethnic enmity was generally believed to be the perpetuation of economic imbalances and social inequalities, which were inherited from colonial rule. The strength of the NEP was found in its quick and effective implementation. The message was clear, this new generation of leaders stood with and understood the plight of the people. The plan truly captured the imagination of the bumiputera, putting in place strong institutions such as bumiputera banks and other agencies to train and aid the maturation of bumiputera. Other boards and agencies were closely managed so that they could strengthen and increase allocations for land development as well as agricultural and technological advancement. A solid civil service was built under the direction of some of the most respected civil servants in our nation's history, whom Razak could trust to get the job done. Rural as well as urban development was spearheaded through well managed infrastructure projects with an emphasis placed on basic educational and healthcare facilities.[27] Ultimately, the NEP did reduce poverty. But poverty is a very relative concept.

Recognising the discourse on the wealth of nations and how societies can prosper aided by unbridled capitalism in the pursuit of free enterprise, the same enthusiasm cannot be said with regard to the poverty of nations. While setting a Poverty Line Index (PLI) has proven to be effective as a measure of success in poverty reduction, nevertheless this process is liable to be skewed by governments in order to present an arbitrary picture of reality. All one needs to do is set a Poverty Line Index (PLI). Granted, most PLIs are set using rigid standards to determine indicators that actually try to get at finding the actual household income that differentiates 'the poor' from 'the not poor'. But no nation, particularly a developing one, wants to be seen as having a high poverty rate, and cooking the books on poverty is not an unheard-of phenomenon. In their 2013 book *An Uncertain Glory: India and Its Contradictions*, Indian economists Jean Drèze and Amartya Sen reflect on their experience in helping to set the PLI in India, debating if there was a difference between the level of poverty and the level of destitution.[28] It's a tricky calculation inundated in complexity and to this day it confounds financial policymakers the world over. Household income needs to be thoroughly considered. So too does the Consumer Price Index, the measure of the average change of the price of goods and services over a period of time. And cost of living expands beyond that, requiring considerations of nutrition, life expectancy, general wellbeing, and disaster—be that floods or a global pandemic. In the formulation of the NEP, particularly the measurement of poverty, this factor was not considered.

Critics have voiced concerns about the excesses seen in the implementation of the NEP. Chief among the flaws included the powers that be abusing the system in order to benefit a small coterie of well-connected individuals. Contracts and privatisation were awarded without a transparent tender process. It would be fallacious to assume that such cronyistic practices were the sole prerogative of the Malays. The reality is that these excesses were also perpetrated by and for other ethnic groups. This was the crux of the criticism levelled against the NEP by Malaysian economists such as Jomo Kwame Sundaram.[29] To the Malay farmers, land is not seen purely in terms of material wealth, but rather as a possession—as part of their economic ethos—of planting and harvesting and enjoying the fruits of their labour. This ethos was encaptured in the rationale of the Federal Land

and Development Authority (FELDA) and other related indus-tries. However, inadvertantly, what was sorely missing was the insights of traditional farming and fishing villagers. Such an oversight was consequential as can be seen from the fall of pro-ductivity and the decline of income in this sector. The gestation period of the NEP could have represented a major victory against the plight of poverty. Yet the prescribed solution did not seem to be as effective in alleviating poverty. For instance, the prolifera-tion of agencies to deal with the issues of capital, the growing pains becoming a manufacturing-based economy, and further research and development did achieve some measure of success, but many of these agencies added more layers of bureaucracy and opened up more avenues of corruption. As a result, the many of bumiputeras the government intended to help are now entombed in an inescapable debt.[30]

In attempting to analyse the socio-cultural antecedents of Malay society, particularly with regard to the question of rural poverty, it is crucial to examine its historical ethos. In this regard, the phenomenon of slavery in the Malay Archipelago warrants analysis. There is a false notion that slavery was only a Western machination, but in fact it existed even here in the Malay Archipelago in the not-too-distant past. While the chattel slavery of the Atlantic Slave Trade was indeed a grotesque extreme of the dehumanising nature slavery can take on, at the same time we need to subject ourselves to the same yardstick. The Southeast Asian historian, Anthony Reid, described the slavery that took place in what is today Malaysia and Indonesia in his 1983 book *Slavery, Bondage and Dependency in Southeast Asia*. Most of the slavery was due to bondage debts resulting from the pressures of life where a marriage dowry could not be paid off, or a deal gone wrong threatened life and limb. These debtors would be sold into slavery in service to both sultans and tycoons in the markets of Betawi, located in contemporary

Jakarta.[31] In 1791, an alliance between the Sultan of Kedah and the Governor of Penang was contingent on all runaway slaves who had made it to Penang being returned to their owners in Kedah.[32] The great nineteenth-century Malaysian writer, Abdullah bin Abdul Kadir Munshi (also known as Munshi Abdullah), made account of the slave trade in Terengganu and Kelantan in the 1830s, where hardened criminals and murderers would sell themselves into the service of the sultan in order to obtain mercy.[33] Early British colonial administrators noted a hesitancy amongst the locals for accumulating property because the sultan could confiscate the land at any excuse; and without assets, one would be forced to sell themselves into slavery. Tunku Abdul Rahman, in his own account as a child in the royal palace in Kedah, talks about the presence of two slaves in addition to being served by a retinue of debt-bonded slaves. They were victims of extreme poverty, made into bonded slaves due to their inability to discharge their financial or land obligations.

Even popular consciousness was influenced by this practice. The Indonesian writer Goenawan Mohamad, founder of the notable magazine *Tempo*, has written about a class of missionary colonists who by day preached liberation, civilisation, and trade in the name of Jesus Christ, but by night profited from those they colonised and traded into slavery.[34] The hypocrisy could not be starker when we realise that while ruling as colonial masters, plundering and looting the wealth of the country, and effectively treating the people as slaves, they purported to make the local laws more humane by outlawing slavery. The British indeed outlawed slavery once they took over Malaya, but that did not necessarily see an end to the practice.

We can safely say that things given a new name do not magically become different and certainly do not, all of a sudden, earn justification. While the British outlawed slavery, new forms of oppression remained at large through the power of debt, from the landowners to pawnshop, the Indian Chettiars and the Chinese rice millers.[35] As late as 1909, slavery still existed in Malaya, but the individuals were no longer called slaves, but debtors. Families who could not feed their children could bring them to the palace and receive a worthy sum of money for the handing over of their offspring to the service of the sultan. Even Frank Swettenham, the first Resident General of the Federated Malay States under the British Administration, reported how the sultans would give out loans with exorbitantly high interest rates that many of them could not pay off. In desperation they were made 'debtors'—slaves—working for low wages, only being released from their servitude once the debt had been paid off. And those who managed to pay off their debts would become complacent to the system, comfortable with their dependence on their master's kindness. While the success of our postcolonial project can be seen in the advances of education and development, the underlying ills of racism, power abuse, and abject poverty continues to plague us.

Another consequence of colonialism is the unfolding of a dependency syndrome where less developed countries are caught in the economic shackles of capitalist economies. This phenomenon was aptly theorised by the Egyptian-French economist Samir Amin. While at the time, Malaysia was considered by many as part of the Third, or developing, World, we were excelling at playing the perfect role in a larger game. Amin astutely coined this as a state of dependency, where rich economies feed off the wealth of the natural resources obtained from poorer countries. Amin also kept a keen eye on the crooked garden global capitalism was becoming during the Cold War.[36] While politically there was the obvious cleave between the Western and Eastern Blocs, Amin noted another dichotomy within the 'capitalist' states that separated the world further into the core and periphery economies. This was central to his Dependency

Theory which declared that the core states become wealthy from the exploitation of the periphery states. Due to the poverty of the periphery states they become dependent—debtors, if I dare say so—to this 'world' system which enriches the core states at the expense of the periphery states. This is the trap of free trade and explains why much of Latin America and Africa have seen little to no development, except for in what Amin refers to as 'the development of underdevelopment', where oppressive governments are propped up in order to keep wages low in periphery states, so all of that labour value rises up to the core states, lining their pockets. The exploitation of the periphery becomes super exploitation through the upholding of Amin's 'global law of value', whereby the core states hold a strict monopoly over technology, financial flow, military power, ideological and media content, and over who has access to natural resources.[37] While the age of empires may have been over, the cycles of exploitation were allowed to continue across the globe under the disguise of a new vocabulary. New dispensations in the aftermath of the world wars.

There are alternatives; and the Malaysian administration of hajj, the Muslim pilgrimage to Mecca, provides a good example. The practice of hajj was prohibitively expensive and exemption was made to the common peoples of Southeast Asia. But once the hajj journey became more commercially viable, a new practice arose where older Malays, towards the end of their lives, would sell all their worldly possessions before embarking on what was, until much more recently, a rather arduous journey. The assumption for many of these individuals was that they would die somewhere along the way, so there was no point in leaving anything behind. But once the journey became more streamlined, the practice continued, and those who survived their hajj could find themselves in financial difficulties. The late celebrated Malaysian economic scholar, Ungku Abdul Aziz, observed this practice.

After cranking through the numbers, he realised that earlier Islamic economic structures, such as *zakat* (almsgiving) and *sadaqah* (charity), could be channelled to help create a hajj fund for the Malays. The pilgrimage could then be paid from the fund. So, potential pilgrims would have no need to sell everything they had, plunging themselves into poverty.[38] From this simple observation Tabung Haji was born and today the fund manages over 30,000 pilgrims annually.[39]

V

For us, the formative pupils of the 1970s, the supposed inheritors of the future (which unbeknownst to us was already pretty colonised by the then postcolonial present), it was a confusing time. Ideas were buzzing in every direction, and thousands of words written lay in wait for us to read them.

One of my more treasured reads from my student days was Leo Tolstoy's *The Death of Ivan Ilyich*. Rich in themes, it is a beautiful story that leaves the reader with a feast of takeaways to choose from. In reflecting on the colonialism of Malaysia, I cannot help but see our nation as the family gathered around the titular character Ivan Ilyich's deathbed in his final moments. The story largely focusses on Ivan's regrets as, after learning of a terminal illness, he begins to realise that every choice he has made in life was made in order to fulfil some standards placed on his shoulders by the world around him. He believes that he never lived an authentic life and struggles to accept his fate—the fate that befalls us all. In realising the fault in his ways, he pleads with his children that they do not live for the selfishness they desire; their desires are actually the desires of others hidden in the mask of a rugged individualism. He points out that they have the power to make their own choices and not to yield to what are considered the norms of society.

Cycles of colonisation need not be our fate. In 1961, months before he succumbed to leukaemia, Fanon published his last work, *The Wretched of the Earth*. Fanon built on the deep psychological impacts of colonialism to lay the groundwork for a movement of decolonisation. My reservations on violence aside, I appreciate the pragmatic reality of taking on colonialism, an ideology that is tenacious, even on its decline, and will certainly not go down without a fight. The critical takeaway from Fanon is that decolonisation needs to be a sophisticated, critical exercise that is launched on multiple fronts. It is not enough to simply throw out all that the coloniser brought to your land and pretend the whole thing never happened. Because the impacts were real. The impacts *are* real. And all that is out there can be a source for us to construct the knowledge we need to advance our aims as a collective human society.[40] Again, no need to throw the proverbial baby out with the bathwater. Decolonisation cannot be done with a microscope or a spyglass, it must be done from an open balcony that allows us to see all that lies before us. It is a struggle that involves the whole of society, and that requires personal reflection.

Colonialism, however, is not just a historic and contemporary scourge; it is also a future trepidation. For the future, too, is being colonised. By technological determinism. By denial of truth and objectivity. By the malicious refusal to see other humans as humans, and belligerent rejections of their human rights. By the determination, at all costs, of a single culture and so-called civilisation to continue its domination and reduce all diversity into monolithic sameness. I take the colonisation of the future seriously for there is a real and present danger that the future would be a continuation of the paralysed pasts of non-Western states and contemporary impasses in the global world order. Moreover, colonialism is not just about the colonised societies. As the renowned Indian psychologist and public intellectual, Ashis Nandy, points out, it has also seriously damaged the colonisers and their societies as well, particularly with the Western notions of masculinity and adulthood.[41] The tools of conquest also conquered those who wielded these tools. In our blindness we are wilfully colonising ourselves. We thus have a very fractured, marred, and myopic 'West' to deal with.

In the light of colonialism and postcolonial history, we must be constantly wary of the hazards and challenges that confront us as we attempt to uplift ourselves for the future we desire. It was certainly a future fraught with threats and hazards. We will continue to participate in the flow and tide of global events. But we must do so with our eyes wide open. At this juncture in human history, we—East and West—are all colonised. It matters little whether you come from a country that in its history experienced colonialism from one that colonised others, we are all largely subjugated. And our future is threatened too. To resist this, we must move on two fronts. Personally, as well as in our communities, we must strive to undo the systems of oppression we are entangled within, while seeking the true equality amongst all people. Simultaneously we must create a system that will free our future generations to continue this struggle, that must remain ongoing if we are to have a hope of breaking out of the hamster wheel of historical pitfalls. We have the ability to change and seeing as the world shows no signs of slowing in regard to change, we would do well to change ourselves. Then, just maybe, we will no longer have to fear others and can live by our own definitions of authenticity.

In order to move forward and move up the trajectory of progress, we must join the fraternity of free trade nations, without losing sight of our values and our culture. As we pursue material wealth, we must never turn a blind eye to the injustices. We have to call out those who persist in violating international norms and humanitarian principles. This is crucial if we are to live our true authentic selves, perhaps we can begin this new journey by using justice to reorient ourselves in these choppy waters.

Two

JUSTICE FOR OUR TIME

I

In prison, apart from the Qur'an, I only had one other book at my disposal before my library access was expanded. This book was a gift of sorts. Accompanying the book was a note stating that this ought to be where I focus my intellectual energies while in prison. Perhaps, I would learn the error of my ways.

It was a book of prayer.

I was not one to look a gift book in the mouth. Something to read was, after all, something to do when there was no excess of that particular commodity. But this was not just another prayer book readily found at your nearest bookshop. This book of prayer was *Munyatul Musalli*, written by the nineteenth-century Malay scholar Shaykh Daud bin Abdullah Al-Fatani. *Munyatul Musalli* translates from Arabic as 'the dream of a praying person'.[1] Al-Fatani is perhaps only familiar to Muslim students in the Middle East and Southeast Asia. He was born in Pattani, a region that once covered the area where the south border of Thailand meets the northern border of Malaysia. The fall of the Sultanate of Pattani to the Kingdom of Siam, taking place during

Al-Fatani's own lifetime, had a profound effect on his political commentary in his later works. He was an Islamic scholar who travelled around the Malay Archipelago, spending time learning from the great sheikhs of Aceh. At the height of his career he journeyed to the Holy Land, studying between Mecca and Medina for approximately thirty years. Apart from his own studies he also taught and even served as a hajj sheikh. After a long and storied life, he died in Mecca where his burial site can be seen to this day. He is considered by many the greatest Islamic scholar born in the Malay Archipelago. His book, *Munyatul Musalli*, is a detailed instruction guide that notes the various prayers a Muslim performs along with the rituals associated with them. At first glance it is a rather elementary text, although authoritative as this was the culmination of many of his travels and studies. Also, beggars are rarely granted the freedom to be choosers. So I took to Al-Fatani, in search of the motion, denied to me in prison, now guaranteed in recounting all the prayers, their etiquette, and even a step-by-step playbook for the hajj, the Muslim pilgrimage to Mecca. Reading through the disciplined articulations, I was suddenly struck when I happened upon the final chapter. Seeming a bit out of place, it was a discussion of justice, and it definitely had my attention. What did a philosophical discussion of justice have to do with a practical manual on prayer?

However, this sudden change of tone was not all that out of the ordinary. Rather, it adhered to a fairly common practice in the Muslim scholarship of yesteryear. It was once conventional for a scholarly discussion to be capped with a *tatmimul faedah*, or concluding benefit. It is something like an epilogue, but more similar to an author's note. The last words are intended to amplify the text beyond the page. This practice, in accordance with the shariah, would apply the discussion at hand to the day-to-day business of the intended audience. The original audience intended for *Munyatul Musalli* was the Sultan (which one remains a topic of debate) who commissioned the work. Al-Fatani saw fit that his additional benefit be a chapter of anecdotes on how a ruler might improve the overall well-being of his society by practising just governance. It is necessary for the proper form of prayer to follow through into the ethical life. This anecdotal style of presentation of justice was commonly used throughout the Malay Archipelago.

One such anecdotal vignette narrates how ancient rulers used to give their ministers three pages which contained messages that were to be given to the rulers when their reign tipped towards tyranny or wrath. The pages remind the rulers, first, that they are not God and shall return to the dust; second, that demonstrating mercy on Earth will ensure its reflection in the Hereafter; and third, that the rulers' duty to uphold justice in accordance with Allah's law has no compensation. Another series of anecdotes features a farm animal or agricultural product that yields surplus, but when stolen by the ruler only yields deficit, as the maintenance of justice was the cause of the originally yielded surplus. Thus, it is only when the magical source of wealth is returned to the people that justice is reinstated and surplus allowed to flow forth. Other anecdotes speak to the quality of the rulers' advisers. It compares viziers to the gates of a city or as mirrors of the rulers themselves. If they do not reflect the values of the rulers, then the blemishes are also present on the rulers. The general idea of justice crafted by these stories is one in which respect is paid to a proper order in society, especially concerning distribution of wealth and goods. The justice spoken of here was installed by God, but requires practical and ongoing refinement by all humanity, the rulers and the ruled. Subtly, the responsibility incumbent on participants in a just society is alluded to along with justice being an ongoing process, as opposed to the classical Western notion of it being a heavenly ideal to be aspired to.

One could read Al-Fatani's final thought as his chance to take advantage of his position. Perhaps, in preparing a guide for the Sultan to perform hajj, with a local's fluidity, he could sneak in a few of his own political opinions in that clever way intellectuals like to do with their words. I disagree with this assessment. I feel that Al-Fatani was aiming at a much more profound end. For instance, he spends a part of this final chapter discussing Caliph Umar's treatment of Jews and Christians, affording them *Eman*, assurance of safety, to live and practise their religion freely in return for payment of taxes and some restrictions on public displays. Indeed, it was a gracious and just action that would not likely be reciprocated by non-Muslim rulers, yet is essential for peace in multicultural societies. This may have also reflected on an important historical fact to bear in mind, particularly in the light of what was happening in Pattani during Al-Fatani's time.

As I pored over the book of prayer I fell into deep reflection. Prayer is an institution that is fundamentally central to being a Malay. One could make this claim about any community in touch with its religious identity, but for Malays and the rest of Muslim societies where Arabic is not our first language, and our cultures diverge greatly from those of our brothers and sisters in the Middle East, our adherence and respect for prayer make for a point of strong connection between Malays and the *ummah*, the worldwide network of Muslim societies. Steeped in this tradition of prayer, we also find a deep commitment to justice. Al-Fatani not only teases at the entangled relationship between prayer and justice, but he highlights the direct role each of them plays within our hearts and our acts, being an integral, deeply embedded part of our tradition. In other words, I think of the American philosopher Cornel West, who famously noted in his book *Race Matters* that 'justice is what love looks like in public'.[2] In Islam, we continue this sentiment; justice is what prayer looks like in public. In exploring this idea, we must elevate justice beyond its current buzzword status so that it may live and breathe again in a world that has allowed it to go too long neglected into atrophy.

II

When we suffer confinement, as I did during my imprisonment, and as we all experienced in varying degrees during the global Covid-19 pandemic, we suddenly become aware of an obvious fact. It is a bit like breathing; one only becomes aware of it when something goes wrong. Human beings require movement. Just as we reach the end of one motion, we have already started planning the next. If we are stopped, we figure out a way to go again. If we truly must be still, then we must socialise, which is, in and of itself, movement of another type. And even when we are at our most powerless in provoking ourselves onward, that most beautiful organ, the human brain, picks up the pace for the sake of progress. Immovability is an existential crisis. Our ontologies are quickly made inadequate before reality and the uncomfortable chill of panic looms heavy. The reality of humanity's need for progress and perseverance comes as a lesson we would do well to heed from the last pandemic, perhaps so that we might be ready for the next one, which experts agree may be closer than we think. We repeated the line that 'we are all in this together', but are we capable of looking away from the mirror? That discomfort we all felt coupled with the various headlines and platitudes from that period pointed to, and rather verbosely, the fact that things are not right. But we paid only slight attention to them and allowed them to be normalised, blended into the unseen and less-reflected-upon background of our lives. The grinding halt of the world as a consequence of the virus gave us the whiplash that primes an individual for learning, but our inability to put a face on the problem gave power to our devices of normalisation.

The clock keeps ticking and the present carries on. The virus shone a light on many trends established prior to the pandemic—racism endemic to societies all around the world, existential fears that drive dehumanising identity politics or hateful xenophobia, and the horrific inequalities our global economic systems readily perpetuate. Anyone who was different or foreign was libelled as the ones who brought this disease into our homes. Chinese and peoples of Asian descent around the world found themselves again on the receiving end of a familiar tune.[3] Muslims around the world were targeted by wayward conspiracy theories, which, of course, was not a new phenomenon. But because a mosque gathering turned into a super-spreader event, it had to be rationalised that all mosques everywhere were hives of infectivity.[4] There are no clear statistics for the number of migrant workers who were victims, both directly and indirectly, of the disease, since most countries don't count them as actual people. Therefore it is deemed acceptable to pay them less and stick them in accommodation we barely deem tolerable for prisoners (even twenty-five years ago!). Close confinement and poor sanitation without the PPE to spare beyond those who could afford it.[5] And suffering with the migrant worker, abandoned to die far from home, are the poor, who never had a chance from the start, abandoned to die without a home in their homelands. While millions joined the ranks of the unemployed and impoverished, those already below our dramatically underestimated poverty lines, sank deeper into pre-existing inequalities without anything to grab onto and maybe pull themselves back up with. The circumstances left available to the global poor only made them prime targets on the pandemic's warpath.

By the end of the pandemic, much as was the situation before and during the crisis, justice remained conspicuously absent.

III

Sure, justice has occasionally been allowed to shine when convenient, for the privileged few, but 'justice for all',[6] well, this is a fantastic delusion. And in light of the West's track record in pursuit of justice, it is fair to ask, why should we run the gambit from Hobbes to Rawls? The answer to this question is multifaceted. Some elements of Western control, due to its dominance over the last couple of centuries, go deeper than formal rule. The power to define has not only kept the West in its dominance through the supremacy of language and thought, but it has also established a set of norms which cannot simply be cast away. They need to be transcended. For true transformative change to take place, a change that could even overturn the era of Western dominance, the successes and failures of the West ought to be taken note of, built upon, and criticised. The alternative would be a foolish pursuit of a new way that ignores history, the complexity of the modern world, and rides dangerously close to narcissism. So, we learn Western political theory and analyse Shakespeare not only because it is enjoyable, or even because it is the be all and end all of enlightened thinking, but because it is there, and we can learn from it, and derive immense pleasure as well as emotional and mental solace from it in the process. And in the postnormal times, this in-between moment defined by the overlapping of complexity, chaos, and contradictions is about polylogue, which requires many different voices and viewpoints, even if they have a history of violence against us and even if they are blatantly wrong. If we can see what's wrong, perhaps we might be persuaded to do right. And from within, using the voices of those who have held power in the past, we can bring in our own voices and the voices of others. This is the strength of an integrated approach. It is slow, it is an exhausting struggle, but short of brutality or the risk of greater injustice, it is the only way to go about lasting change. Granted, a lot of barricades require tearing down first, including those in Muslim countries and for Muslim thought.

The notion of justice has been mythologised through many historical impediments. Casting it as some higher form, forgetting that it is lived tradition, it becomes a peak we can no longer summit. Despite justice being embedded in Islamic tradition and scholarship, and being a fundamental objective of its adherents, injustice is taken as given and we have almost surrendered our agency over justice in the real world. Modernity consigned justice to a nebulous notion of egalitarianism. Its basic aim was to keep the wheels of production turning to ensure constant growth, perpetual progress, and assume that some benefits would trickle down to the downtrodden. Postmodernism did us no better. The discussion devolved into 'justice for whom' or 'justice with respect to what': the holistic totality of justice thrown to the wind. Objective justice has been assassinated. In this subjectivity, we reduce justice to a notion of exchange. As if it could be a commodity anyone would want to trade on the floor of the stock exchange. Left unspoken it becomes quieter than a whisper, a noise at the mercy of a cacophony of background sounds. A war in Ukraine is just allowed to go about its business, as if a land war in Europe was normal, let alone acceptable.[7] And the systematic extermination of Palestinians carries on with impunity.[8] Maps redrawn; a people erased. And then, of course, there are the countless other conflicts and wars that we ignore by leaving them out of the repetitive and news-lacking headlines and clickbait-ridden social media feeds, or by labelling them as 'civil strife', as if that reduces the suffering and pain felt by those within the storm. Not only is there no justice, but there is also not even a concern for justice.

I have learned that there is a certain naivety among revolutionaries. You discover that injustice goes beyond wrongful imprisonment or tyrannical despots. Injustice also seeps through the nooks and crannies of economic, commercial, or social exploitation. Look at the refugees, those being ground down by the zero-hours contract, the workers in sweatshop factories making garments for the luxury fashion houses in the West, sold back to the elites in the East within air-conditioned monuments to the ouroboros that is global capitalism. On the faces of these labourers is written the contemporary problem of justice. And the problem at hand goes much deeper than what is often credited. The faces behind injustice, or more appropriately the absence of justice, invoke the reality, which we would rather ignore, behind poverty and those pushed away as outliers of society. And in our ignorance, we deny them the dignity we thought was inalienable to human beings. The fragility of our comfort and security in these uncertain, postnormal times echoes a turning of the screw on injustices around the world.

I now shared in a history common to many prisoners of conscience. Those who refuse to bow to the tyranny of autocratic dictatorial power on the grounds of principle. Those who take a critical look at governance, power abuse, or outright corruption. I learned all too well the truth behind the American writer Mark Twain's words, 'if you want to see the dregs of society, go down to the jail and watch the changing of the guard'.[9]

As a mode of escape, Shakespeare's tales rang all too real. 'For as thou urgest justice, be assured thou shall have justice, more than thou desir'st.' I had desired perhaps Portia's monologue appeal to mercy, yet this line from *The Merchant of Venice* is indicative of the togetherness we all too often forget pertains to justice. The seventeenth-century English poet John Donne penned a similar meditation which would go on to inspire Ernest Hemingway's novel *For Whom the Bell Tolls*:

No man is an island,
Entire of itself;

Every man is a piece of the continent,
A part of the main.

If a clod be washed away by the sea,
Europe is the less,
As well as if a promontory were:
As well as if a manor of thy friend's
Or of thine own were.

Any man's death diminishes me,
because I am involved in mankind.
And therefore never send to know for whom the bell tolls;
It tolls for thee.[10]

Donne's bells are those of the churches in England which rang
either to signal a wedding or a funeral. These tolls specifically
were for the latter. Yet, he might well have spoken of the popular
retributive characteristic of modern justice. But let us not forget
Mahatma Gandhi's quote about an eye for an eye. As humans we
are all united in various commonalities, especially our own mor-
tality. One individual's death, then, is not just a loss for the
individual or those close to them, but a loss for us all. A loss for
our community. A loss for the great human stories. Or, to put it
in the terms of the Qur'an, 'if anyone kills a person ... it is as he
kills all mankind' (5:32). This lesson bears great weight in these
unprecedented times when all of us are at the mercy of a seemingly permanent state of simultaneous crises. Hemingway provides us with an interesting example. In his novel, he notes that
Spain's trading of democracy for fascism and dictatorship which
followed the Spanish Civil War was not just a loss for Spain, but
for the international community and the beautiful idea of democracy. It was a stain on the progress promised after the atrocities
of the twentieth century.[11] Then again, the climate catastrophe
might just see to the end of us all. Somewhere along the line,
justice lost its living, breathing quality, doomed to fossilisation.

This resultant ossification is a problem of mentality. The corresponding manufactured pause on the discourse of justice is not just a fault of culture, but of the very structural pedestal upon which the West confined justice. It has been made into a sort of perfection, an ideal state, that can never be achieved. And who wants to be Sisyphus? This is the origin of academia taking the concept of justice for granted. Students learn of Plato's ideal city[12] or Aristotle's virtuous man.[13] Yet, in Gore Vidal's *Creation*, we are told to take Greek accounts of history with a ton of salt.[14] But their expositions on philosophy are indispensable to scholarship. In attempting to define justice, for example, Plato in the *Republic* ends up telling us what in effect is social justice, though such a phrase is not used. Through Thrasymachus, one of the dialogue's participants, we are told that a just man always gets less than an unjust one. In contractual dealings, you'll never find that a just partner will obtain more than an unjust one. In municipal matters, a just man pays more taxes on the same property than an unjust one. When the city is giving out refunds, a just man gets nothing, while an unjust one makes a large profit. Finally, in public office, a just person finds that his private affairs deteriorate because he has to neglect them and he gains no financial advantage because of his justice, and that he's hated by his friends and relatives when he fails to do them favours. In other words, 'this is tyranny, which through stealth or force appropriates the property of others, whether sacred or profane, public or private, not little by little, but all at once'.[15] This negative definition of justice may be contrasted with Aristotle's conception in the *Nicomachean Ethics*: justice as the fairness of a good ruler in a good community, while universal justice exists only in a perfect society.[16] Ethics and just actions are then confined to the inaccurate calculus of the middle way. It is a tragic interpretation of the famous line from American author John Steinbeck's *East of Eden*: 'And now that you don't have to be perfect, you can be good.'[17] Originally this line was meant to combat the modernist craving to be perfect at the expense of morality, but when taken in consideration of the history of Western discourse on justice, it appears to be the rejection of perfection so as to deny the responsibility demanded by morality. If you cannot be good, at least you tried. This mentality carried on in the development of Christendom and the nation-state in the West. Today it infects the academic-industrial complex of Western disciplines from Perth to Paris and Timbuktu to Kuala Lumpur and beyond. We need to be more critical in our thinking or provoke greater creativity and imagination. And perhaps for too long we have waited for this sort of revelation to be delivered from on high, instead of seeking it out.

IV

There was a moment of hope in the West with the arrival of the Enlightenment. Such a storm of turmoil ought to have shaken a few things up. The state, the church, the arts, and humanity's place among it all were brought into question. Following the classical period, most conceptual discussions were restricted to looking for biblical justifications for the truth claims made by the pagans of yesteryear, or to letting them be damned to eternal hellfire. Their diligent work provided the framework by which Latin America has been burning since the colonial period and such abominations as Just War theory were crafted.[18] The Enlightenment called for new ideas, needed to fill in the gaps left by Christianity and feudal society. This also kicked off the great secularisation of Europe which claims to be riding strong in the sophistication of *laïcité*[19] of the great European Union today. The EU too is confronting the challenges of a new-fangled fascism from the extreme far right. As an organisation created to ensure that fascism would 'never again' return to the continent, it is faced with a real existential threat.[20] It is most ironic that despite the values crafted by the Enlightenment, justice itself is put on trial.

But one does not simply remove justice from the pedestal the ancient Greeks put it upon. To do so would tarnish the concept, making it somewhat less. So, a vessel must be created to keep intact the perfect nature of justice. The Enlightenment thinkers devised the social contract to do just that and to build up to what we must go back to, the state of nature.[21] An obvious allusion to the Garden of Eden, it is the port of call for the journey to be taken towards an ideal justice—anchored on freedom, equity, and good conscience.

For thinkers of the Enlightenment, freedom is unbridled. Freedom at the cost of all else, including responsibility, or the survival concerns of society. This was freedom from structure, shame, order, and, where natural law dictated, the way of the world. Humans, endowed with reason, would exist in the state of nature by way of the social contract, conquering everything—and apparently everyone—along the way. The total freedom of the state of nature had to be sacrificed to or negotiated with an ordering entity dubbed the sovereign. Thoughts range on a spectrum from absolute rulers to true rule by all. Monarchy, dictatorship, oligarchy, republic, and democracy were given a long overdue critical analysis. For Thomas Hobbes, the state of nature was a dangerous dog-eat-dog world, and a citizen must surrender all their freedoms to their sovereign, a powerful absolute tyrant, the titular character of his 1651 opus, *Leviathan*.[22] John Locke took more stock of these freedoms or rights, seeing them as sacred and inalienable. The point of the social contract was to check the sovereign, who he thought ought to be rather a body composed of the people, whose purpose was to defend the rights which pertain to a citizen's preservation of 'life, liberty, and property'.[23] Across the English Channel, Jean-Jacques Rousseau was more eager to suss out democracy in its pristine form. His idea of the state of nature was more puritanical than Hobbes's and he thought that the structures of society had robbed humanity of its ability to be truly free. The social contract thus was instituted to emulate the freedom of the state of nature without disrupting the practicality of history. Equality, liberty, and fraternity were the greatest rights that small, localised democracies must actively engage with to perfect.[24] These men stand out in an age of rigorous debate and ripe ideas on how to build a better world, at least for some. The context of their words should also not be neglected, as they often are when taught in contemporary political science classrooms. When they spoke of freedom, rights, and justice for all, that *all* was rather exclusive. This *all* often referred to all men, but also men of a particular complex and national identity. Women and minorities did not have access to these rights and these Enlightenment structures often abided structures of slavery and imperial exploitation of others.

While the Enlightenment was an age of new ideas, the idealist sentiment of justice continued to look at society in a vacuum, as a subject in the laboratory. Society rarely ever survives under such conditions. A theory was needed to allow for practical progress that did not diminish the perfection of justice. According to the Englishman Jeremy Bentham, given such an imperfect world, there must be a simple categorisation which could be used to ascertain the moral value of an action. He referred to this method as the felicific calculus, which welcomed utilitarianism to the world. The world was thus simplified into pains and pleasures, and the objective of society was to bring about the most pleasure for the greatest amount.[25] Building on this, Bentham's protégé John Stuart Mill would advance the doctrine of utilitarianism. This philosophy has gained a troubling currency in our contemporary world through the problematic simplicity of 'effective altruism'. The young Scottish philosopher William David

MacAskill and his merry band of Silicon Valley-minded educational rejectionist entrepreneurs have given rise to effective altruism, 'branding' it as 'Not Just Utilitarianism'.[26] Indeed, it's far worse. Not only do the ends justify the means, but the means do not matter at all. Undermine truth. Commit genocide. Destroy the planet. It doesn't matter as long as the money you make along the way is given to a good cause: a good cause, something increasingly hard to judge in our confusing, postnormal times. Obviously, in our imperfect world, we cannot please everyone, but we will try. Never mind the costs! The effective altruists see their Enlightenment predecessors as unappreciated geniuses, or just simply choose to ignore the implications of their problematic thought. Bentham, for instance, argued for severe punishment as a good deterrence, never mind its commensurability with regard to the crime. He also advocated for an authoritarian surveillance state, to make sure utility was maximised of course! Bentham also was not very receptive to criticism, not a hallmark of the wise scholar! And we must see the flaws of his top pupil, John Stuart Mill, too. Mill defended his mentor's utilitarianism to disappointing ends. He often argued that the status quo was more important than a just society. This is seen in his argument for 'necessary evils', such as slavery or horribly bloody civil wars. Today, Mill might see the horrors taking place across Africa or in Syria and Myanmar as necessary, of course only if the outcome is positive, whatever a positive outcome may look like, or if it is even possible at this point in time. Only in the true depth of our real societal disenchantment can I see the appeal of this philosophy. Our world is far too complex, and we need to give this reality its due. Or else we plunge head first into the manufactured justice discourse lapse that was revved up for a repeat of the transgressions and mockery of the nineteenth and twentieth centuries. In our futile attempt to feed the pleasure of utilitarianism, we hear the echoes of former British Prime Minister Winston Churchill's words spoken on Armistice Day of 1947, which sum up the accomplishment of a history of Western notions of justice:

> Many forms of Government have been tried, and will be tried in this world of sin and woe. No one pretends that democracy is perfect or all-wise. Indeed, it has been said that democracy is the worst form of Government except for all those other forms that have been tried from time to time.[27]

This mantra, which is sacrosanct to most democrats, stands in stark contrast to the cherished ideals of the Enlightenment. Such cynicism takes us nowhere. What motivation is there for innovation and progress where perfection is impossible and yet the goal? This great contradiction in Western thought ushered in an era of catastrophic failures and lessons left unlearned, not just for the West, but for the world. Its colonial power was strongest not only in the land it controlled via labyrinthine administrations or 'divide-and-conquer' policies, but also in the Eurocentric education of dominance they considered their burden to impart upon those they called 'savages'. We, the people of what was once called the 'Third World', had to fight for simple recognition as humans with the capacity for reason and thus worthy of citizenship. It is no wonder the postmodern thinkers thrived so much on the husks of hollow morality and brittle ethics. Not dissimilar to Dante's descent into hell, perhaps a fitting disclaimer should be placed upon the history of justice in Western thought: 'Abandon all hope, ye who enter here.'

For almost two hundred years, many had written off the Western conception of justice as theoretically resolved, for lack of a better term. A toxic marriage of utilitarianism mathematics and the paramount freedom of the social contract doctrine of John Locke, who became the name and victorious face of the Enlightenment justice debate. The malaise of Western justice was that, in summation, individuals are free to do whatever does not harm another. Justice was given the simplistic definition of the condition in which such freedom was permitted. I am giving Locke short shrift here, simply because he is just too well known and accepted without much critical analysis. Even today, he remains the convenient sticking point for others to launch their own prescriptions from, even if so-called 'freedom' and 'justice' come at the expense of all else.

American philosopher John Rawls aimed to provide some hope when, in 1971, he published *A Theory of Justice*,[28] effectively reopening the book on justice discourse that had been left idle on the bookshelf for far too long. Rawls primarily wanted to give a contemporary defence of social contract theory using the hot new method of the time, analytic philosophy. He needed to put to rest the popularity and ease with which utilitarianism and right-wing libertarianism were sweeping across much of Western political thought, once and for all.

Rawls transformed the discourse on justice from looking for the ideal world to something more practical. He decided that what we need to do first was to derive the important principles that make a just society. It was to be the veil of ignorance, which would ensure fairness above all and also break down social inequalities and tyrannical structures. To determine the principles of a just society, each member would enter the original position, which sounds like the state of nature, but is more like a very plain conference room used for a market research study. Wealth, class, family, birthplace, citizenship status, employment, and so on, would all be left to the realm of the unknown for participants in the original position under the veil of ignorance. In the parlance of postnormal times, this would be second order, or 'vincible', ignorance. You are aware that these categories exist, but you do not know which one the lottery of life will draw for you. In this position, the participants are forced to find principles that benefit the worst off in a given society, lest it be you for whom the bell tolls! This set-up allows for two major tenets of justice as fairness to arise. First, each person in a given society will have equal rights and access to the most basic fundamental liberties. Second, if there must be inequalities, then the only allowable ones are those that benefit the worst off in society. In accordance with the first principle, the benefits of these inequalities must be open and equally available to all members of society.

The publication of *A Theory of Justice* stirred the sleeping giant of Western political philosophy. Fifty years on, Rawls keeps making a comeback with each contentious and fractious presidential election in the US and the debates around them, forcing all to confront the issues of injustice, inequality, and social division each time.

Ironically, Rawls and his greatest academic nemesis, Robert Nozick, held offices in the same department at Harvard University.[29] Nozick leaned towards a rights-based approach that would rally the libertarians who stood against Rawls's liberal dreamland. How does justice as fairness account for the dynamics of the family unit, for women's rights, or the inherent injustice in the capitalist system? Others questioned his reliance on structures. He believed that institutions devised under the veil of ignorance could do no wrong. This, of course, was a major point of attack for Nozick who held to a minimalist state, which is limited to protection against force, theft, fraud, and the enforcement of contracts. The minimal state is the most excessive state that can be justified. Any state more extensive violates people's rights. As Nozick says, 'The state may not use its coercive apparatus for the purpose of setting some citizens to aid others, that is, there should be no compulsory charity. In short, justice is no business of the state.'[30] Against Rawls's claim that a more extensive state is justified in order to achieve distributive justice among its citizens, Nozick propounds the entitlement theory. Here, Nozick argues for a model of distribution that is not *a priori* fair, but one that is practical and accounts for how justly resources were acquired and the rectification of past injustices within society. Like Locke, Nozick assumes that people have natural rights, that is moral rights, which positive law ought to neglect. But unlike Locke, he does not postulate a general meeting of reasonable people concerned about the inconveniences of the state of nature. To my mind, even though he does not mention it specifically, Nozick is essentially advancing the doctrine of spontaneous order of the Austrian School of Economics championed by Carl Menger and Friedrich Hayek. Hayek himself argues that one cannot know enough about each person's situation to distribute to each according to his moral merit, and objects against all attempts to impress upon society a deliberately chosen pattern of distribution, whether it be an order of equality or inequality.[31]

But Nozick goes two steps further by dispensing with the theory of consent altogether, tacit or otherwise. There is, therefore, no moral duty to obey the state. After all, the rights protected are minimal. To tax someone to provide welfare is equivalent to wrongfully taking his property, theft, and partially enslaving him. Taxation of earnings from labour is on a par with forced labour. The fact that others intentionally intervene, in violation of a 'side constraint' against aggression, to threaten force to limit the alternative to paying taxes or bare subsistence, makes the taxation system one of forced labour and distinguishes it from other cases of limited choices. Nozick postulates absolute rights, expressed as 'side constraints', which must not be violated and the procedures to guarantee them must be accepted, no matter what consequences may ensue. Citizens have complete freedom over the pursuit of social goods including removal of deprivation and destitution, which as we know are the mainstays of social justice. In short, they are of absolute priority. The sheer absurdity of this aspect of the theory can be explained by considering the consequences of applying such a prescription to emerging economies—especially those of Nozick's time of writing in the 1970s. Yet, even in the so-called armchair democracies of the West, it is unrealistic to assume that this would be endorsed as some guiding philosophy in statecraft.

Rawls, in *Political Liberalism*, the celebrated sequel to *A Theory of Justice*, fine-tunes his doctrine of justice as fairness by declaring the two principles of justice as follows. Firstly, 'each person has an equal right to a fully adequate scheme of equal basic liberties', which is compatible with a similar scheme for all. Secondly, 'social and economic inequalities are to satisfy two conditions; first, they are attached to positions and offices open to all under conditions of fair equality of opportunity; and second, they are to be to the greatest benefit of the least advantaged members of society'. These basic liberties are specified as freedom of thought and liberty of conscience; the political liberties and freedom of association, as well as the freedoms specified by the liberty and integrity of the person; and, finally, the rights and liberties covered by the rule of law. Significantly, Rawls maintains that the exercise of liberty has a pre-eminent value and is the main, if not the sole, end of political and social justice.[32] Specifying these liberties is consistent with the tradition of democratic thought where the focus has been on achieving certain specific liberties and constitutional guarantees, such as those set down in the 1948 Universal Declaration of Human Rights.

The Rawls–Nozick divide is a major segment of the line upon which Republicans and Democrats in the US today debate. Both men agreed that justice must be derived from principles. Yet both fell into familiar pitfalls. They had each developed a utopian system, and people needed practical, real-world solutions to the impending doom of inequality that kept on creeping as we approached the last chapter of the twentieth century. The prob-

them into the contemporary context.[36] This dual-natured stalemate is not only ridiculous; it reveals why the discussion itself cannot gain any traction in the contemporary world. The status quo is allowed to flourish and run amok.

In contrast to Western scholars, Muslim thinkers of the classical period had two major advantages. First, it was not of great importance to these thinkers whether their sources were Muslim or not. Islam does not see itself as separate from history. Perhaps the biblical language of 'God's chosen people' established a major hurdle in separating the praiseworthy from the heretical. The Qur'an clearly states that God's revelation to the Prophet Muhammad is for all humankind, believer or not, Arab or otherwise. This revelation is also the last in a series, thus prior scriptures or writings are available to be studied and for constructing knowledge and developing wisdom. After all, who can discredit the great advancements in thinking that came before the Qur'anic revelation? What an opportunity it proved for Muslim scholars to build upon the past as they did in numerous fields of inquiry. Second, classical Muslim thinkers were not trapped in dualities and categories. This obsession of Western thinkers has bedevilled the minds of generations. The dichotomies of mind, body, soul, or what have you, were not as rigidly accepted in the Islamic thinking of the time as they were in the West. Islamic thought was more open to blending and working with synthesis, less concerned with the precise dissections and clear-cut demarcations of their Western contemporaries. The tenth-century celebrated philosopher Abu Nasr Al-Farabi had no problem building on the Philosopher King and the state discussed in Plato's *Republic* when developing *The Virtuous City*, whose leaders and citizenry should hold justice as their highest attribute.[37] The ideas of Aristotle, who considered justice as the 'principal order in a political community', through to those of the nineteenth-century French philosopher and political scientist Alexis de Tocqueville, who said 'justice forms the cornerstone of each nation's law',[38] resonate across history in the words of classical Islamic thinkers. This reverberates from the heart of the Qur'an, which reads, 'whenever you judge between people, judge with justice' (2:58).

The early Christian church rose to a position of power largely based on its liturgical structuring. The very relationship between believer and Creator, God, required the intermediary of the clergy, from a common priest to the highest intermediary, the pope. This may have begun out of the need for a literate member of the community to read the message of the Bible, but this role quickly evolved into a lucrative source of power, reaching its apex with the selling of indulgences. The church not only rose to hold power over who would or would not receive salvation, but political and territorial power also. Islam did not have this history as it did not have a clergy, even though some ulama—religious scholars— did hold a prestigious position in society. Maturing in a culture more attuned to the oral tradition, and the Prophet himself being unlettered, the relationship between believer and God was more personal. This personal relationship required that humanity had a responsibility and stake in the world they lived in with the perks of freedom and the Hereafter. The competing or cooperating interests of church and state were thus not as contentious. As both the Western and Islamic civilisations continued to do as humans do and spread across the map, they were bound to meet, or in the words of Samuel P. Huntington, clash.[39]

As the West rose to dominance, so did its views, histories, and internal problems for everyone under its influence. By way of analogy, the failures of the early Christian church were thrust upon Islam. From my personal experience in school, the likes of Bertrand Russell's 'Why I am Not a Christian' became a convenient pretext to some of my colleauges bent on dismissing Islam as a route to democracy. And now a common belief holds that Islam cannot get to where the West is unless it first undergoes its own Enlightenment or an equivalent. But I call the West's bluff. I look at their constitutions, and more importantly the debates that forged these great documents; what is not directly copied and pasted from scripture is hardly distinguishable from moral ethics derived from a worldview informed by the Christian faith and ethical framing. And that doesn't have to be a problem. Many different framings can lead one to a logical conclusion of right from wrong. So why not Islam? Is it not at least intriguing how much alike all these modern-day, secular constitutions are to that Constitution of Medina, drafted by the Prophet Muhammad in 622? And is it not best to get as many reasons for what is right or what is wrong as possible? Is this not the scholar's errand and must it not be undertaken meticulously and with a critical lens? And what did the Enlightenment get Europe? Two world wars and a century of destruction and atrocity, genocide, upwards of 100 million casualties, and the destruction of Other cultures and traditions on a mass scale. 'The Enlightenment legacy', writes Ziauddin Sardar,

> that Islam and Europe have nothing in common, that Islam is only a darker shadow of the West, that liberal secularism is the destiny of all human cultures, is much in evidence in our newspapers and television, literature and scholarship, as well as in our politics and foreign policies. It is the bedrock of Francis Fukuyama's 'End of History' hypothesis, Samuel Huntington's 'Clash of Civilization' thesis, and the neo-conservative 'Project for the New American Century'. *Voltaire's Bastards*, to use the title of John Ralston Saul's brilliant 1992 book, are busy rationalising torture, military interventions, western supremacy and demonising Islam and Muslims. The Enlightenment may have been big on reason but it was, as Saul shows so convincingly, bereft of both meaning and morality. Forgive me if I don't stand up and salute the Enlightenment.[40]

We need to get over the notion that the West has won history and, therefore, the right to tell the story of the past for all and set the terms for the future of everyone. The rule that anything and everything must be done for the maintenance of the supremacy of the West needs to end. And despite the reams of evidence to support this, perhaps the global cataclysm of Covid-19 and our precocious state of subsequent permacrisis ought to have opened our eyes. There are other stories out there and other paths to reach the things we as humans stand united in desiring.

The Islamic discourse of the classical period was a global discourse. The history of Islam, as the twentieth-century American historian Marshall Hodgson shows in his multi-volume *The Venture of Islam*, was world history.[41] In the tenth century, Al-Farabi held Aristotle as the 'first teacher', and in accordance with this adoration was known as the 'second teacher'. He delighted in as much Plato as he could get his hands on. He even wrote of how the Prophet Muhammad was the philosopher king Plato longed for in the *Republic*. In fact, we should not see the ancient Greeks as just belonging to the foundation of the Western or European tradition; this would only feed into their narrative. In fact, had the classical Muslim scholars not adopted and transcribed the works of ancient Greece, they would never have survived to be claimed by medieval Europeans. From the Constitution of Medina to the construction of the State, the Prophet's examples demonstrate that a just society, as Plato and Al-Farabi longed for, can be realised. Al-Farabi laid this out in his two major works, *Al-Medina al-Fadilah* (*The Virtuous City*), and *Al-Siyasah al-Madaniyah* (*Political Governance*). Through both works, Al-Farabi examined the science of government to gauge how political leadership should be judged, ultimately to make the ideal city, or even state, using Islamic virtues and principles. His inquiry bridged Aristotelian and Platonic thought in arguing for a philosophical ruler with a keen intellect. The template left by Al-Farabi established a guide to the art and science of government, bearing in mind that no one but the Prophet could ever attain the status of being the ideal leader. This was not a lofty aspiration but a realistic goal that could be achieved. In the twelfth century, Ibn Rushd aligned with Al-Farabi's thinking, emphasising the critical role philosophy plays in political order and justice. The Qur'an asks us to be just; for Ibn Rushd, this is a call to philosophise.[42] For critical thought and contemplation must take place for all politicians and law practitioners. Otherwise, we are just applying the law and this is insufficient for the fulfilment of the definition of justice. This is only a sample of the global discourse that extended from Baghdad to Andalusia with Ibn Bajja and Ibn Tufayl across the twelfth century, the height of the 'Golden Age' of Islam.

The postcolonial spirit and revived Muslim nationalism between the 1970s and 1990s showed that certain aspects of the Muslim intellectual exploration of justice tended towards a similar trajectory to the West. Many of their calls and intellectual efforts took the Western scaffolding as given and tried to 'Islamize' it.[43] Opponents of this approach point to how this makes the Islamised idea subservient to and subject to the same flaws as the Western paradigms. The lack of attention to the principle of adl wal ihsan continues to be a point of contention on account of an overly strict, legalistic interpretation of Islamic rules in the practice of Islamic banking. Consequently, the paramount issues of redressing inequities of wealth and resources are ignored. This is contrary to the dictates of the maqasid al-shariah—the higher objectives of the shariah.[44]

To help in refuting the mischaracterisations of shariah, Khaled Abou El Fadl boils it down to its original definition, so that you are not tempted to immediately make the jump to Islamic jurisprudence. Shariah, simply put, is a path to water. Water, being a pretty useful find in a desert climate, extrapolated as a pathway to nourishment or the 'good'. The brilliance of El Fadl comes in his positioning of openness as fundamental to Islam. Islam is

God's final message, but not his only message.[45] Shariah could readily refer to the laws of Moses, the path of Jesus, or the tradition or life of the Prophet Muhammad. It is this openness that stood as the bedrock to *La Convivencia* of Umayyad Spain.[46] The history of Andalusia would readily attest to the openness and inclusiveness of Islam. This was a classic example of multicultural, multi-ethnic, and multi-religious convergence and coexistence of Muslims, Christians, and Jews way before the terms became fashionable. This is religion and enlightened leadership at its highest level, religion that expounds a universal perspective, religion that heals bigotry and fanaticism. This is not a call for uniformity, as if such a dream could practically be imposed. Look at the difficulty we have all seen in getting the public to follow the safety protocols for the pandemic when their lives truly depended on it. We need a global togetherness where we can simultaneously cherish difference and cherish our own identities. This is the beautiful unity we need for our contemporary times, and stands at the heart of *tawhid*, the oneness of God that is foundational to Muslim faith.

This harkens back to Al-Fatani's notion of justice as the ultimate lived practice of prayer. The openness seen in El Fadl should both be examined beside other non-Muslim sources, but located in the contemporary world. Justice after all, as described in the Qur'an, is fundamentally a balance. And even this notion was not the advent of Islam, for Islam did not appear out of nothingness, it came to a world where the clock had already been ticking in a region that was a crossroads to trade and cultures. The notion of justice as balance is also seen in the Vedic tradition of India and is played out in the *Bhagavad Gita*, where Arjuna's major arc is to balance his duties and his actions.[47] Although Arjuna projects his struggles through his conversation with Krishna, the struggle is deeply internal and brings to mind, according to some interpretations, the inner *jihad* of Muslims.

The balance of justice also recalls the balance of the *Dao* (道) of ancient Chinese philosophy.[48] Islam demonstrates a special elegance not only in its ability to derive similar conclusions as other schools of thought, but also to build on them in a way that leads towards a greater harmony and collaboration.

'Justice is a state of being, a condition of things being in their proper places. It is also the quality of human act', said the Malaysian scholar, Syed Muhammad Naquib Al-Attas.[49] Justice is both a completion and a project in development at the same time. A mutual understanding echoes in the teachings of Confucius. Despite being an intellectual adversary of Daoism, Confucius appeals to the metaphysical conundrum that arises in attempting to understand the Dao and uses this understanding as a mode by which we seek truth, a metaphor for being a good person. *Junzi* (君子) can be translated as 'gentleman' or 'exemplary person' but is often mistranslated as 'sage'. To Confucius, to be a sage is a lifelong vocation—and a utopian ideal—that can never be attained in a human's lifetime (lest one lose the motivation to continue being good), but the exemplary person is one who tries to do what is right and works to correct past wrongs, and is always constantly working to better him or herself.[50] In keeping with this, with regard to the knowledge required to uphold justice, Al-Attas appeals to the term *wusul*, or arriving. The arrival intended here is not a final destination. Rather, it is an active, always ongoing process. The pursuit of justice never ends. An apt metaphor for *wusul* is found in the Mike Oldfield composition 'Tubular Bells',[51] originally recorded in 1972 using a 16-track tape recorder. Once a decade, Oldfield would re-record the tune as new instruments and new technology allowed him to meticulously continue perfecting the tune. As more techniques become available, presumably Oldfield will continue to tweak the song until it matches what he hears in his head.

We have to realise that the project of justice will never be completed. In a sense, we will always be arriving: from each subsequent analysis, from generation to generation, we will watch a rich tapestry weave itself in the work we do. And we cannot remain ignorant of what has been left for us from history, be it wisdom or even a lesson we would be foolish not to take to heart from the past failures of others. Despite the flaws that have been pointed out, I think Rawls offered us a keen insight into strong institutions that will safeguard and stand as a check along our journey towards justice. And his thought experiment with the original position speaks to us today, in that we need to continually rethink where we are and reflect on what is most essential to us as individuals and as members of our local and wider communities. While being critical, Sen brilliantly adds value to the Rawlsian doctrine of justice as fairness. And we would be wise to follow this discourse, as it has unfortunately petered out into this new millennium, only to be revived in the very real political and social turmoil we are presently faced with on a global scale. Maybe then we can truly learn and know one another. May we keep the pursuit of justice at the heart of it all.

VI

In returning to the intersection of economics and justice, we find a convergence in the much divergent global discourse on justice. One of the key questions concerning the pursuit of justice in terms of economics is, should states intervene in order to reduce inequalities or should market forces be left as the sole determinant? According to the American economist and political scientist Mancur Olson, 'state intervention is advocated by a "soft-hearted majority" while a "hard-boiled minority" would willingly accept or even rejoice in the inequality'.[52] According to the economists, there will be a trade-off between efficiency, obtained through the market, and equity, that would need to be obtained at some social cost. But what is not clear is whether or not such inequality is unjust, and if it is, what prescriptions there are to redress it.

To address the conundrum, we need to first determine an objective standard of social justice. According to Rawls, as referred to earlier, the answer lies in 'justice as fairness' via the notion of social justice. But libertarians, such as Nozick, contend that justice can only be attained through a minimalist state where there is no room for distributive justice. Both Rawls and Nozick also stipulated that these rights cannot be compromised by the force of economic needs even though they are less extensive. It is this insistence on the unnegotiability of such rights that represents a dubious stumbling block to social justice. In this regard, I am inclined to agree with Sen, who, while acknowledging the paramount importance of fundamental liberties, has argued that other considerations including that of economic needs are just as vital. To my mind, he has posed a stunningly simple, but compelling question: 'Why should the status of intense economic needs, which can be matters of life and death, be lower than that of personal liberties?'[53] The critical issue is not complete precedence, Sen argues, but whether a person's liberty should be deemed to be as important as their other types of personal advantage, such as incomes, utilities, and so on, are. 'Whether it be utilitarianism or libertarianism or Rawlsian justice, there are indeed no royal roads to the evaluation of economic or social policies', he says.[54]

There is no doubt that the modern market economy confers wealth and distributes income in a 'highly unequal, socially adverse, and functionally damaging fashion', to quote J. K. Galbraith, whose brand of capitalism continuously gnawed on the side of laissez-faire advocates. According to him, the intellectual justification and contrivance that defends this inequity cannot be accepted, even if it may be one of the most assiduously encultrate exercises in economic thought. Galbraith's 'humane agenda'[55] aligns with the concept I have advanced since the mid-1990s of the 'humane economy', an essential institution of social justice, that draws its inspiration from the principles of Islam which enjoin that society may pursue commerce to its fullest, so long as justice and fairness—*adl wa ihsan*—in policy and practice remains the chief criterion so as to sustain the long-term well-being of society.[56]

We can also look at this in terms of the issue of ownership and property. According to Locke, 'every man has by nature the right to possess property as his own'. For the 'soft-hearted majority', the advocate of social justice, when taken to its logical conclusion, is really a genus of social mortgage. The poor have a moral claim on the conscience of the nation. In this regard, in the humane economy, the free market stops where Scottish economist Adam Smith's 'invisible hand' is supposed to begin. Smith's invisible hand is mentioned in passing but oft quoted by free-market fanatics, a magical metaphor for how the marriage of individual self-interest and freedom of production and consumption leads to a benefit for the whole of society. Belief that the invisible hand is manifested through the interaction of market forces has often only alienated societies while widening their disparities. For the invisible hand to do what Smith desires, it must instead be manifested through the intervention of the state.

Yet, the onslaught of colonialism and its legacy in postcolonialism, with the plundering and looting of the wealth of subjugated nations, has made it difficult to take issue with the contention that current injustices are the consequences of historical inequalities. They did not disappear overnight. Therefore, the discourse on social justice is invariably linked to the nagging issues of the inequalities of wealth, power, and status for the individual, societies, and nations.

In Renaissance Italy, Giovanni Pico della Mirandola's *Oration on the Dignity of Man* tells us that the dignity of humanity resides in the freedom to be whatever it wants to be. While that was a period associated with moral release, Catholic social teaching intervened to remind us that the life and dignity of the human person is predicated on the belief that the state must play a moral role to ensure social justice. Similarly, the teachings of the fourth-century Chinese philosopher Mencius advocated that activities are to be judged by their moral correctness, not mere economic benefit, a notion which finds convergence with Islam's humane economy where the *maqasid al-shariah* command the ummah to pursue economic prosperity with full vigour, driven by the overarching and ultimate aim of establishing a society that is just and fair.

While we began with a general exposition of the meaning of social justice, we must now grapple with the very essence of the term itself—justice. Coming back to Rawls, we are told that each person possesses an inviolability founded on justice that even the welfare of society as a whole cannot override. We are in danger of seeing a contradiction between Rawlsian justice and social justice. If we do not give more emphasis to social justice, which hinges on the 'welfare of society', we risk sacrificing the 'inviolability' of individual rights founded on the justice Rawls appeals to. On closer analysis, however, we see that society is an association of persons with rules of conduct for the advancement of their own good. The existence of a conflict—as well as an identity of interests—necessitates a set of principles which we call the principles of social justice. They provide a way of assigning rights and duties to the basic institutions of society and they define the appropriate distribution of the benefits and burdens of social cooperation.

Drawing on the useful ideas of utilitarianism from Bentham and Mill, Locke's social contract, and even the eighteenth-century German philosopher Immanuel Kant's doctrine of the categorical imperative—whereby an action was judged as right or wrong by whether, when universalised, it stood as a threat to societal cohesion—we can paint a more complete picture. This is restated in Rawls's *Political Liberalism*, where society is seen 'as a fair system of cooperation over time, from one generation to the next'.[57] Justice also must be intergenerational.

It has been said that this notion of fairness is inclined towards the left, that is, the liberal elite, albeit that we have no reason to begrudge the advocacy of free speech, equality, tolerance, and a resolute commitment to human rights. Freedom need not be restrained within the context of what we know to be encapsulated in any bill of rights. Freedom, here, is of course in accordance with the classic exposition by Isaiah Berlin, that is, freedom is essentially 'not being interfered with by others'.[58]

There is likely no master key to unlock the secrets of any kind of utopian system of income distribution, but some basic formulations for attainment of social justice may be advanced. Governments must be committed to the principle that a more equitable distribution of income is a fundamental precept of the realisation of social justice. In this regard, they should undertake with full conviction integrated plans for poverty reduction in the long run, and value ensuring a comprehensive support system for the poor and the economically marginalised. This is best summed up as 'the empowerment and protection of the powerless'. Regardless of whether the economy is developing or developed in the Rostowian sense, at the stage of take-off or high mass consumption the right of workers to associate and protect their interests must be central. Here, Olson comes to mind for his observation that in reality, many, if not most, of the redistributions are inspired by entirely different motives, not necessarily egalitarian, and most of them have arbitrary impacts on the distribution of income where the outcome is that the rich get richer. We still find instances of scandals in institutions of power and the collusion of established democracies with autocratic regimes. One therefore finds it hard to resist the wry criticism as expressed by Leo Tolstoy: 'The law of man—what nonsense! The truth is that the state is a conspiracy designed not only to exploit, but above all, to corrupt its citizens.'[59]

After each one of my stays in prison, I found myself freed into a dramatic new transition. My first release took me from the turbulent 1970s into a hopeful, yet worrisome, 1980s of growth, progress, and neoliberal ecstasy. The postcolonial struggle be damned—or at least left for another day. I went back to prison at the end of the 1990s, when financial doom and the technological terror of the new millennium left the air nearly unbreathable. And my most recent release in 2018 finds me in a world ruled by the internet of things, social media, and the increasing digitalisation of our lives. Since the beginning of the last decade, the world itself has been flipped on its head several times, struggling to keep up with simultaneous crises of nationalism, greed, and xenophobia, and that's before we get to the economic rollercoasters and pandemics. I have grown rather accustomed to, nearly an expert on, change; and radical changes they have been indeed. Yet, while the images may change, the underlying human suffering and injustices remain and we need to constantly stand on guard against. Sources of evil are so powerful because they are advantaged by their ability to evolve and change. So if we want justice in our futures then we too must adapt our notions. Or else we will lose sight of the faces of injustice standing right in front of us.

At this moment, we face not just the double whammy of political turbulence and our economic woes, but also a concurrent onslaught of compounding and complex crises (some of which we cannot yet see, or keep ourselves ignorant of) that need to be approached and navigated simultaneously and with innovative and creative approaches: the exponential growth of inequalities and divides, the natural by-product of the global capitalist system; the rise of xenophobic sentiment within isolationist and nationalistic fervour; the disrupted lives of migrants seeking refuge from human violence and environmental disaster; the good, bad, and ugly of our digital futures; and, of course, climate change, or rather the climate catastrophe. This sample barely scratches the surface of all the crises we face, both collectively and from country to country and life to life. We must heed the warnings of disastrous inequality exposed by the French economist Thomas Piketty in *Capital in the Twenty-First Century*.[60] We need to be considering the reality of *The Age of Surveillance Capitalism* and our digital rights as elucidated by Shoshana Zuboff.[61] We need to rethink our conventional notions of justice in a technologically driven 'age of extremes', as Mimi Sheller proposes in *Mobility Justice*.[62] It is imperative that we seek green, sustainable ways forward to navigate climate change. Even flora and fauna deserve justice, just as they need water and sun. Plus, there is a whole host of emerging crises on the horizon that we are not currently thinking about, as we are too busy dealing with what is already overloading our plates. We need to challenge our conventional definitions. Poverty now is also immobility. There is digital poverty too. One of the great paradoxes of capitalism shows that while the rich get richer—something relatively easy to observe—the poor are also getting poorer. The second part of this paradox may be harder to conceptualise, but this is precisely what is happening as their right to the mechanisms of upward mobility get further and further from their grasp. That is why we need justice for our times. That is the raison d'être for the founding of a political party that holds Justice (*Adil*) as its namesake. Parti Keadilan Rakyat (PKR), the People's Justice Party. The discourse on justice is not simply an exercise for academia, but a down to earth subject which impacts the whole of society. The pursuit of justice is both the primary motivation as well as a challenge for us all.

The justice we need now is not simply 'fairness', it needs to be about equity, and we need to work out how to see it out in the real world. Justice is not about being impartial, but instead, being impartial to the truth, which does still persist in this world of fake news and alternative facts. And we must remain humble, for we may not have the right answer and even if we find an answer that works, we must not fly so close to the sun (take it from someone who has, and has faced the consequences) and assume it as some universal solution. We must not be led astray, thinking that justice arises through victories: this is the infection of neoliberal capitalism speaking through a corrupted notion. Justice is a balance and involves the efforts of the many. The just world we crave is aided in the formation of a global *Convivencia*. It is incumbent upon us, for it is an objective for all humans to strive for, the alignment that puts all things in their right place. This starts with us not just living next to each other but living by one another and dismissing false stereotypes and manufactured bogeymen. Even more, the imperative for a just balance cannot be overstressed so as to attain a society of humankind that calls for a symbiosis between faith and knowledge and man and nature. This is the essential conceptualisation of the Quranic injunction—*ummatan wasata*.

We are at a particular juncture of human history where climate change, perverse inequality, and technology-induced existential threats should force us to pause, reflect, and rethink. If we do not think about our futures and attune our thinking, it will be too late and we will be left in a cell with no comfort but what comes from prayers.

To live those prayers as justice in the real world, we must endeavour to save democracy and re-evaluate it as an indispensable element of more just futures.

Three

LIBERATING DEMOCRACY

I

Reflecting on the current state of play for democracy, one can liken it to a double-edged sword. On the positive side, democracy is theoretically the representation by the people for the people, it is based on rule of law and protects fundamental rights, and supposedly encourages participation and engagement of the citizens in the political process. On the negative side, there is the risk of popularism, potential oppression of the minority by the majority, or vice versa, and a cumbersome process of decision-making. Looking at the political map of the world that has emerged over the last decade or so, it is obvious that the balance has firmly shifted towards the downside of democracy. Not surprisingly, there is no shortage of recent case studies or reports that could lead us to put democracy, as a concept, on trial.

According to British public policy experts Andrew Adonis and Geoff Mulgan, there are two fundamental weaknesses in modern Western democracies: 'the divorce of politics from society, and of political responsibility from citizenship'.[1] Government is dominated by an elite who offer simplistic, one-dimensional solutions to problems that concern the voters. The typical member of parliament—or its equivalent—is chosen only by a handful of party activists. An electorate of tens or even hundreds of millions is represented by full-time politicians who are the only ones who have a direct say over government and play a direct role in framing legislation. Elections are decided by a few marginal seats. There is something seriously wrong with this representative logic. As citizens are rarely directly engaged in the political process, vote only in elections, and sometimes not at all, they have little direct contact with politicians who sometimes seem to live in an arcane and impenetrable world. Where two or three parties dominate, electors are offered limited choice between catch-all policy programmes which are often vague and confusing, and that parties often abandon in any case once in power. If promises are delivered, they are delivered poorly. Hence the global disenchantment with the democratic process.

But what do we mean by democracy anyway? There is no intuitive or easy answer to this question. First and foremost, one can readily argue that there has never been an example of *pure* democracy in history. The closest we may come to a 'pure' democracy comes from the city of its birth, ancient Athens. And while the democracy at play in this city was pretty fundamental, women, children, and slaves were denied a political voice. Ancient Athenian democracy also played well into the militaristic culture of the city-state, a hypermasculine flaw that would prevent this system of government from attaining the 'common good'. And it had no shortage of critics, including some of ancient Greece's greatest thinkers, Plato and Aristotle.[2] In *Republic*, Plato contends that democracy runs the risk of bringing dictators and tyrants to power. Further, if popularity is taken as the ticket to victory, then incompetent individuals may take the helm of leadership, or worse still, those with a history of moral turpitude may well end up holding the reins of power. Following the experiment in Athens, the governance style would not be attempted again without a tempering of democracy as such. Although the eighteenth-century philosopher Jean-Jacques Rousseau would note the untenability of democracy on the large scale beyond that of a city—like Rousseau's home of Geneva, for example—real politics demanded this of post-Athenian democracies.[3] We see this in ancient Rome and in Vaishali in sixth-century India, both taking on a more representative form of democracy, the republic. The Iroquois Confederacy of pre-European colonised North America is an interesting example, but still required adjustments in order to suit the radical multiculturalism of the tribes involved. Elaborate constitutions balanced by storied histories have us questioning the multiple centuries of work behind the democracies in the United States and France. And the democracies of Western Europe were slow evolutions of Enlightenment thinking, kept just moderate enough to allow the almost contradictory institutions of monarchy and aristocracy to coexist. And regardless of our own judgements on each of these historic democracies, there is a shared pride in the core value of democracy that ties these massively different places together. Yet the question 'does it work?' is never far away.

Indeed, the Greek philosophers never thought it would actually work. Democracy derives from the Greek *demokratia*, from *demos* (the people) and *kratein* (to rule). In its Athenian construction, democracy symbolised rule by and of the people. In the *Republic*, Plato characterised democracy as a 'charming form of government, full of variety and disorder', which ultimately leads to tyranny. Plato instead advances his idea of the 'philosopher king' as the best ruler of a society, contending that democracy runs the risk of dictators and tyrants to power. Going by this logic, democracy could well be a ticket by which popular but incompetent individuals could take the helm of leadership. Worse still, those with a history of moral turpitude could end up holding the reins of power. Plato feared that if people were allowed to make decisions collectively, they would simply endorse their own self-interest, which would result in policies that were nothing more than the lowest common denominator of individual greed and desire for personal security.[4] While Plato opted for the rule of philosopher kings, Aristotle deliberately described democracy as the rule of the poor in their own interest. John Stuart Mill advocated a regulated, 'rational democracy', one ruled by 'an enlightened minority accountable to the majority in the last resort'.[5] In *Democracy in America*, Tocqueville saw a predicament in integrating a democratic political culture with a socially democratic society. He saw that social democracy does not necessarily lead to political democracy in the sense of self-government. He opted for the middle classes but insisted that democratic culture should be institutionalised to prevent government by faceless bureaucracies.[6] Karl Marx thought democracy was the rule of the proletariat.[7]

In modern times, there is growing concern that the democratic process is being hijacked by the rich and powerful giving rise to plutocracies, or more aptly expressed as government by the wealthy. This fear is realised in the perception that Western liberal democracies have been oligarchies of political professionals. They have, for some time, been seen as, to use a phrase common on social media, 'government of the rich, by the rich, for the rich'. But now, in postnormal times, where little can be hidden, it has become manifestly clear. Representative democracy is a product of the rise of capitalism and the decline of English mercantilism. It emerged out of the political philosophy of liberalism; in fact, the philosophy of liberalism and representative democracy are virtually synonymous. The whole idea of the 'democratic rule of the people' was used both to curtail feudalism as well as establish a set of conditions for the emergence of a new kind of political elite. This comprises a coterie of people occupying the corridors of power and, from that vantage point, were able to harness the means to economic aggrandisement. Classical physics of the Newtonian variety had an enormous impact on shaping the content of democratic theory. The emphasis was firmly on the 'laws' of human behaviour, logic, reason, and cause and effect. These fundamental assumptions ensured that the wealthy, educated elites could maintain control of political institutions. Only the wealthy and highly educated had the time and resources to master the skills necessary to pass laws and debate conflicting points endlessly. As in Athens, the first citizens of the new democracies of the late seventeenth and early eighteenth centuries were men. Initially, only landowners had the vote and thus the mandate to participate in public life. Later, non-landowners were also included in the franchise; the abolition of slavery in the nineteenth century allowed voting rights for former slaves and indigenous peoples. In the twentieth century, after a long and bitter struggle, women too acquired the vote and the right to participation in political and public life. But you still have to be well off to go into politics. Consider how many millions, or even billions, have to be spent to be elected to Congress, or the Senate, in the United States.[8] In most non-Western countries, only the very rich can afford to enter politics.

But the problem with the current construction of democracy is not just money. It is also the excessive focus on the individual. Individualism is *the* absolute of liberal democracy: the notion that society is nothing more than the sum of individuals and that the individual is a self-contained, autonomous, and sovereign being who is defined independently of society. The assumption that the individual is prior to society is unique to Western culture: it is the defining principle of liberal democracy and shapes its metaphysical, epistemological, methodological, moral, legal, economic, and political aspects. In non-Western cultures, the individual does not define him/herself by separating from others but in relation to a holistic and integrated group: the family, clan, or tribe, the community or culture, religion or worldview. The Chinese, for example, see the family as an organism linking the past, the ancestors, with the present and the future, the descendants. The individual thus exists not as an autonomous, isolated being but in a living union with his or her ancestors. Muslims see the individual as an integrated part of the society which in a local area is defined by the Friday mosque, and on an international level by the collectivity of all Muslims: the ummah. Society is ontologically prior to the individual and social obligations come before individual dictates. In most indigenous cultures, the individual is defined by the tribe or the clan: the individual cannot be distinguished from the tribe and seeks his or her fulfilment as an integrated part of the whole tribe.

In the Western liberal framework, the individual is constantly at war with the community, feeling perpetually ontologically threatened. The individual's main concern is to keep his or her identity intact, separate from all others, to preserve the boundaries at all costs, to enclose her or himself around with a protective wall. Whereas in non-Western cultures morality is defined by the community or society, in liberal thought the individuals have to make moral choices for themselves. Thus it is rare to find substantive agreement between the individual and the community as a whole. Morality becomes a matter of individual behaviour: the emphasis is not on what is of ultimate value and what ends should be sought, but how whatever ends are chosen ought to be pursued. The goals of liberal democracy therefore focus on providing the individual with all possible avenues to pursue whatever is desired, even if it is, and it often is, at the expense of the community. The government can never seek communal social, cultural, economic, or political goals, such as ensuring equal distribution of wealth, focussing on poverty alleviation, or providing equal educational opportunities for all. The British political philosopher Bhikhu Parekh outlines five liberal arguments which are commonly advanced to justify this position.

Firstly, governments exist because subjects wish to pursue their own goals with minimal constraints. They must, therefore, maximise liberties and facilitate the goals of their subjects. Secondly, 'citizens of a liberal society do not all share a substantive conception of the good life'. Thus, setting goals constitutes a violation of their moral autonomy. Thirdly, economic redistribution of wealth and radical transformation of the social order constitutes a violation of the principles of human dignity and equality. Fourthly, the principle of economic redistribution goes against the conception of wealth ownership, 'for property belongs to its owners and not to the government, and is a product of their labour'. The government is therefore entitled to claim from them only that portion of their wealth that is necessary for the government to pursue collective activities, on condition that the owner consents to it. Fifthly, liberals believe that all social institutions are propelled by certain natural desires in as much as people work diligently and save up for the future, driven by self-interest.[9]

Liberalism, by its very nature, is suspicious of communal concerns and values. This notion is not only the defining value of liberal democracy, but it is actually built into its conceptual structure. This is why in a liberal democracy certain representative individuals are elected to ensure that other individuals have all the freedom to pursue their individual interests. So, strictly speaking, liberal democracy is not so much representative democracy as representative government; and it is not so much liberal as libertarian.

II

Democracy, as history has demonstrated, works well with complexity. Because of this, it often falls victim to association and plays accomplice to a fair share of atrocity. However, its malleable nature and chameleon-level adaptability allow democracy to fit nicely within numerous complex networks. So much so that attempts to excise it from political, economic, social, and even cultural contexts leave many thinkers with nothing more than a bloody mess on their hands. 'Rule by the people' is capable of coexisting besides capitalism, socialism, communism, feudalism, fascism, traditionalism, Marxism, multiculturalism, as well as all manner of religious and ethical mosaic backgrounds. It is capable of finding a comfort as bedfellow to monarchy and rigid social or class hierarchical structures. Democracy readily fits into the complex fabric of a variety of other systems without presenting itself as a contradiction, even when a contradiction clearly exists. It can wear many hats and take on many faces. Democracy has united many people, inspired movements against colonialist sub-jugation and oppression while rallying for freedom and indepen-dence, yet it has also tolerated oppression, state-sanctioned vio-lence, war, apartheid, slavery, even genocide. It has given rise to some of the world's greatest leaders and thinkers, yet it has also given us some of history's most evil villains. Democracy gave power to Adolf Hitler in 1933 just as it gave power to Nelson Mandela in 1994. It does not take too much reflection to realise that in democracy, we have in our hands a chaotic force with the potential to both give and take away.

Democracy in and of itself possesses a not insignificant level of opacity, but when made a vague and confusing concept, denied reflection or the viewing of a critical lens, truly disastrous results await. Malaysia was an amalgam of Great Britain's Southeast Asian territories, imbued with the spirit of democracy, a meta-phorical plutonium that would power it through the tumult of the latter half of the twentieth century and, theoretically, beyond. It was born into the world cleaved in twain by the Cold War. Democracy versus Communism, as we were told. While both these terms are laden with intellectual baggage, squaring them off, one against the other, is an exercise in futility. Very casual reflection makes this abundantly clear. The concepts, while adjacent, do not exactly exist on the same spectrum. Putting aside their ideological complexities, democracy is a system of governance while communism is a system of economics—more precisely, a critical response to what capitalism had become by the nineteenth century. Indeed, communism places its name on numerous political parties across the world and history, but there has been little to no unifying theory of governance behind the various groupings who call themselves 'communist'. Look at the vastly different systems that were in place in the United Soviet Socialist Republics (USSR), the Socialist Federal Republic of Yugoslavia, the People's Republic of China, and the Socialist Republic of Viet Nam. Meanwhile, democracy is happy to be chummy with the whole spectrum of economic systems, from market-loving to market-repressing, from free individualistic enterprise to state-owned economy. What made the Cold War dichotomy work was that you had a cast of characters. The United States, or the West if we are being charitable—the good guys—and the USSR and their rogue allies—the bad guys. Heroes and villains, everything a good drama needs, even if a few of the plots were lost along the way. It truly appeared that the last half of the twentieth century was the dramatic proof that democracy was indeed the superior form of governance.

But in the wings, something rather strange was taking place. The United States, the good guys, as we might recall, used its intelligence services to undermine numerous regimes that, in terms of definitions, fitted what we might call 'democratic'. Of course, this practice already had a deep history prior to World War II. The United States established set boundaries for 'good guys' and 'bad guys', regardless of their democratic credentials, in the Western Hemisphere through the Monroe Doctrine—a policy that made interference in the political affairs of North and South American states a hostile act against the US itself. This policy was re-upped and expanded as the Truman Doctrine—a policy that saw the interference in the affairs of all democratic states by authoritarians or communists as a belligerency against the US. And immediately after World War II, the US deemed it necessary that the only 'good' democracies were the ones that saw to their preferred candidates winning. In 1948, the US assisted Syngman Rhee in winning South Korea's first presidential election, and in return he fashioned the nation into an authoritarian regime he lorded over until he was overthrown in 1961. In 1949, Husni al-Za'im, a man with plenty of ties to the US, overthrew the democratically elected government of Syria. Four days after the coup, al-Za'im approved the construction of the US's desired Trans-Arabian Pipeline (Tapline). In the 1950s, the US twice played foul in Guatemala, again attempted to see their influence expanded in Syria, and of course infamously deposed the democratically elected Prime Minister Mohammad Mosaddegh in Iran, an event for which the chickens would come home to roost soon enough. The 1950s ended with trouble in Cuba when the US-backed dictator Fulgencio Batista was threatened by the young revolutionary Fidel Castro. The US also began meddling in Viet Nam and Cambodia in this ill-fated decade. The 1960s continued with numerous questionable incidents in Africa, South America, the Middle East, and Southeast Asia. Interference by the US and the CIA reached its peak in the 1970s and 1980s, particularly during the presidency of Ronald Reagan, with the funding of rebels in Congo, Angola, Ethiopia, Chad, Honduras, and Nicaragua; the supporting of dictators in Chile, Bolivia, and Argentina; an occupation of Panama; and what the UN called a 'flagrant violation of international law': the invasion of Grenada. And before we knew it, the Cold War was over. Was it truly a titanic conflict between Democracy and

Communism, or a carefully executed strategic agenda for unipolar world dominance? Regardless of the conclusion, the Cold War itself had little regard for any semblance of sanctity for 'democracy' or for what condition democracy would be in at the other end of it.

Overall, in pursuit of its position as a—or rather, *the*—world power, the United States dictated a very specific form of democracy as the 'right' way which all countries should aspire to as their system of governance. Any deviations from the prescription would not be tolerated. Yet it was not simply the way others were to govern themselves that was dictated; how globalisation was going to work was also carefully directed. The Washington Consensus was presented as a fait accompli to the rest of the world. Yet in truth it was a flex of soft power that tied the rest of the world to the International Monetary Fund (IMF), the World Bank, and the US Federal Treasury. The US dollar was to be the currency by which all other currencies would base their value. The US would be the standard bearer of all international trade but would also play world policeman. The United Nations worked on their terms.

In the fog of jubilance pervading the fall of the USSR and the end of the Cold War, one could almost be forgiven for thinking we had reached the end of history. The last three decades have almost reinforced the American political scientist Francis Fukuyama's thesis; perhaps liberal democracy is the highest evolutionary form of human governance.[10] But this observation lacks the nuance that even liberal democracy means something different everywhere it is applied. The point was made crystal clear in the abject, categorical failures that were the US's attempts to create 'democracies' in Afghanistan and Iraq. But the point had already been made with South Korea, a state whose democratic mask hardly hid an authoritarian reality that often competed well with its neighbours to the north. Japan's culture flowed interestingly with democratic structures, but for most of its history, the nation has been a one-party state. Its top-down cultural obedience calls into question the democratic veracity of its electoral system. And Japan's contradictions are rapidly catching up with its history. Likewise, in the West, the supposed inheritors of ancient Greece's romanticised democratic ideals are folding beneath the weight of history. Democracy allows autocrats to prance around publicly displaying their abuse of privilege. All along, fascism has been allowed to return. European politicians fling out democratic principles and vile hatred, often in the same sentence. Far right ideologies and fascists made great strides in the numerous elections of 2024, when over sixty countries had national elections, hosting nearly two billion eligible voters. The results gave dark harbingers for many countries.[11] In the European Parliament, Eurosceptics wreaked havoc winning seats in a parliament they believed should not exist.[12] The last thirty years of US presidential elections came down to the views of a handful of the US's fifty states.[13] People residing in deeply blue (Democrat) or deeply red (Republican) states didn't need to show up on election day. Meanwhile gerrymandering, money politics, and a lack of concern for equity leave the big picture looking pretty hopeless.

In the ugly forms democracy has taken on in history, there is an opportunity for beauty. In democracy's plasticity a challenge is offered up to history. That challenge beckons us to play in the sandbox, navigating the pitfalls of democracy's limitations and course taken thus far, and bring about the next evolutionary form of this governance system that can find a new way and a new context to see to its ultimate ends: a just and inclusive society guided by democratic accountability. While we can wallow in the mess that has been made of democracy by the US, the West, and countless others who have abused its systems, or even cast it into the dustbin of history, baby and bathwater alike, I feel that would be a great disservice to one of humanity's greatest intellectual projects. This is no small task. It will take great effort, but could lead to the greatest of rewards.

Democracy's future will never come about through passivity. The one idea that democracy does not mesh with is conformity or despair. Democracy is an evolving idea and must not be allowed to stop growing, to stop changing. For change is the only constant in all our futures. And we have the power to navigate what course lies ahead for democracy and ultimately justice and flourishing for all humanity. To do this, we need to dispel certain myths and weed the garden of democracy. Once given a bit of tending, we can evaluate the impacts our postnormal times are having on democracy and chart a course forward, so that the dreams and prosperity provoked in democratic societies can be actualised and preserved for the well-being and common good of peoples yet to be born.

III

Before we can set about saving the futures of democracy, we must first dissociate democracy from the myths and circumstantial associations it has accumulated over its history so that we can reform what can be elevated and discard what needs to be left behind. One particular myth has to be debunked so that truth can grant us a window into the spirit of democracy that we wish to take through and beyond our postnormal times. This myth arose recently and has spread in popularity ever since the 11 September 2001 attacks on the United States with its subsequent 'war on terror'. That myth is that Islam and democracy are fundamentally incompatible. Those who perpetuate this belief know little of Islam or little of democracy.

Those most clever at hiding their ignorance of both Islam and democracy make a diplomatic and perhaps, at one time or another, a politically correct push to say that Islam and democracy are incompatible without saying it in those exact words. I wish to address this up front so that we can continue with a reasoned and respectful discourse on the matter. Proponents of this argument will not directly say Islam and democracy cannot work, they will say the Muslim world, as it stands so grossly generalised, is not yet ready for democracy. They lean into the evolutionary nature of democracy and believe that a particular requisite of history is needed before a given culture or civilisation can 'come to' democracy. As if democracy was a cake that required a precise recipe to be followed. They will then say that the West went from the medieval period, the Dark Ages as they call them, and then into a series of periods of reforms that delivered them to the Enlightenment. Thus, the West went from a monarchy and church-controlled society into a secular and supposedly more egalitarian one—a very suspicious assumption. They will then say, the Muslim world—by this they are most certainly referring to a fantasised and most likely Islamophobic vision—must play a game of historical catch-up in order to gain the worthiness of democracy. If only the Muslims would embrace liberal secularism along with a new appreciation for a variety of Western virtues, then and only then could the Muslims have democracy. The first faulty assumption is that all societies must arrive at democracy in the same way. The second is that Muslim societies, in their infinite diversity, would all want the same kind of democracy, let alone anything resembling the democracy of the West, which permits and tolerates irreconcilable difference, rampant and destructive individualism, or opulent greed tempered with fascistic tendencies. And although holders of this opinion would never admit to any discriminatory or racist thoughts against the Other, they could not imagine that God might have revealed many of the same principles enshrined within the popular conceptions of modern democracy to an Arab merchant in the desert, six centuries after the death of Jesus of

Nazareth. Unable to get their heads around that, there can be no chance that those holding this opinion might think of Islam as anything other than yet another religion that simply dropped out of the sky in the first decade of the seventh century. Yet if they could appreciate that the history of Islam is the history of all humankind, a story connected to that of the Holy Bible or the Torah before it, as well as all the revelations made to all of the prophets going back as far as Adam, then they might realise our histories have been and will always be intimately linked. The ancient world was indeed a small place and even today the world is not that big. And although we may take different paths, the belief that truth does indeed exist dictates that we can indeed all reach it, each in our own way. Since we share a past, we most certainly share a future and the sooner we come to this realisation and get past the petty differences that we feel we need in order to feel better about our stations in life, the sooner we can get to the work of saving that future. And with climate change, economic ruination, and total war as existential threats, the regular diet of daily news, we have not got a lot of time for persistent ignorance.

When we further analyse the road taken towards democracy in the West, an interesting divergence arises between Christian Europe and the 'Islamic world'. The church that rose to power in Europe out of Rome, Catholicism, traces all the way back to St Peter, one of Jesus of Nazareth's twelve original apostles. Catholics believe that upon his death, Jesus handed the 'keys of the kingdom' to Peter, thus making him the first pope. From this origin derives the Christian notion of intermediaries. Some Christians believe that the clergy, from the pope all the way down to the common priest, were required middlemen between God and believers. Following the Reformation, when Protestant denominations of Christianity broke off from Catholicism and Eastern Orthodoxy in a variety of fashions, the notion of the intermediary began to fade, if it was not lost entirely. Those less familiar with Islam may believe that our faith tradition must also go through this step of the process. But, in fact, the reliance on intermediates has no credible basis in Islam. Throughout the Qur'an, warnings are made against blind faith in the ideas of other humans. While examples of the righteous life are provided, particularly in the Sunnah, the practices and tradition of the Prophet Muhammad, there is no structure that grants certain humans infallibility or the power of absolution in Islam. 'Say', the Qur'an asks Muhammad, 'I am only a mortal like you' (41:6). The relationship between believer and God in Islam is very personal and often followers are told to be subtle in their faith and not to flaunt their religious adherence or assume any one human is more holy than another: 'There is no compulsion in Islam.' (2:256). All humans are free to choose their own faith as they are all creations of God, and as such demand due respect. Indeed, the Qur'an and Sunnah speak volumes on fundamental human rights and our egalitarian nature, despite the geography and cultures that separate us. And the tradition of Islamic scholarship has embellished these points over and again. Mohammad Hashim Kamali has completed a seven-volume series, beginning in 1999, analysing how many of the tenets of the 1948 United Nations Declaration of Human Rights can readily be seen in the Qur'an and Sunnah.

Both participatory and representative forms of governments are evident in the formative phase of Islam. The Qur'an does not provide a theory of the state. But it does insist, repeatedly and clearly, that community issues should be decided on the basis of shura, or consultation and discussion. The assembly in Medina established the *shura* as the general principle of political activity. It also enacted another central tenet of Islam: decisions should reflect an *ijma*, consensus or the view of the majority. When the Prophet Mohammad wanted to make a political or strategic decision, he would gather the community in his mosque, seek their opinions, and make a decision based on the consensus. This is how, for example, the decisions to engage the enemy at the well of Badr rather than Medina, or to defend the city by digging a trench around it were made. There are echoes here of Athenian democracy: the Muslim community consisted of a few hundred people and the Prophet was able to bring them all together to discuss important political matters. However, as the Muslim community expanded, political structures evolved.

Islamic history is replete with incidences of the ulama, the religious scholars, chastising the unjust and corrupt leaders, and emphasising the notion of community and social responsibility in political matters. The great jurists and founders of the four schools of law in Islam—the Maliki, Hanafi, Shafii, and Hanbali—refused to have their school adopted by the government of their day as the official school of law. Some, like Imam Ahmad bin Hanbal, were imprisoned as a result. The tradition of humanism and dissent, what Nobel laureate Amartya Sen persuasively suggests as the 'argumentative' tradition, although he confined it to the argumentative Indian, has always been present in Muslim cultural history. Both humanism and dissenting pluralism were passed on to Europe from Islam, as George Makdisi demonstrates in his brilliant study, *The Rise of Humanism in Classical Islam and the Christian West*.[14] However, the transition of humanism from Islam to Europe also involved a radical transformation: Europe accepted the ideal but changed the axioms—as was also the case with science and philosophy. The notion of the community and social duties which was so central to Islamic forms of participatory governance was abandoned in favour of individualism.

The birth of democratic ideals, as we know them today, emerged among Muslims at the same time as a movement for reform and renewal of religion and society—more than two centuries ago. I cannot even begin to do justice to the rich current

and cross-current of ideas chosen by the religious scholars, journalists, reformists, men, and women in the nineteenth and early
twentieth centuries that provided today's Muslims with a stall of
reform and democratic ideas. Consider, for example, the tren-
chant criticism of Abdul Rahman Al-Kawakibi of the Ottoman
Empire's despotic role.[15] Or Rifa'a Rafi' al-Tahtawi's admiration
of French democratic institutions, recently translated under the
title *An Imam in Paris*.[16] Or Taha Hussein's lucid exposition on
The Future of Culture in Egypt.[17] And letters of a nineteenth-
century Javanese Princess, Kartini, *From Darkness to Light*,[18] or
the Bengali feminist Rokeya Sakhawat Hossain's *Sultana's
Dream*.[19] Long before criticism became a fashion and feminist
writings surfaced, these provided a constellation of ideas and
infused motives and desires that can only be fulfilled by the
establishment of a free and democratic society.

The noted British historian of capitalism Eric Hobsbawm
described the twentieth century as *The Age of Extremes*. Despite
so much fear and prejudices towards fundamentalists of all religious persuasions, the worst crimes against humanity, Hobsbawm
shows, were all committed by godless fanatics: Hitler, Stalin,
Mao Zedong, and Pol Pot. But the twentieth century, for the
Muslim, was a century of great hopes.[20] Unfortunately, it was
also a century of great betrayal. The great expectations of the
last century issued from the achievement of national liberation.
Muslim countries, one after another, freed themselves from
colonial tutelage: Algeria from the French, Indonesia from
the Dutch, Libya from the Italians, Pakistan and Malaysia from
the British.

Perhaps it is more than a coincidence that Indonesia organised
the Bandung Conference in 1955, the unprecedented and unsurpassed assembly of leaders of the Third World liberation movements, notably Zhou Enlai, Jawaharlal Nehru, Sukarno and others.
I can still recall Sukarno's mesmerising oratory, which I listened to

clandestinely in the early 1960s, at the time when Indonesia launched its *Konfrontasi* (Confrontation) against Malaysia.

Muhammad Ali Jinnah, the founder of Pakistan, was at that time perhaps the most loved foreign leader, not just among Muslims in Southeast Asia but in the Muslim world as a whole. He has been maligned in a number of films, not least the 1982 *Gandhi*, but also in a number of Bollywood productions. But the affection was well placed, as I later read of Jinnah's commitments towards democracy, his horror of corruption, and his stern warning: that the army should never leave the barracks. It is worth noting that the preamble to Pakistan's 1949 Constitution, called the 'Objective Resolution', delegates authority to the country's ruler as 'a sacred trust' from the original Sovereign—God. But this 'sacred trust' gained little traction with a succession of military strongmen—from Ayyub Khan, Yahya Khan, Zia-ul-Haq, to Pervez Musharraf. While there may be grounds stemming from strategic and security concerns, at the end of the day, it is not inconceivable that efforts towards reconcilliation, including with regard to former prime minister, Imran Khan, will prevail. Jinnah did not live long enough to see Pakistan as a civilian and democratic state. After his death, Pakistanis unfailingly and deferentially referred to him as 'Quaid-e-Azam'—the Great Leader. But his ideal of good governance and democracy is yet to be realised. In Malaysia, when independence was achieved in 1957, it was stated in the Declaration of Independence that the new sovereign nation was founded upon the principles of justice and freedom. I think the summary is of somewhat Jeffersonian ideals of freedom and democracy. We will never claim that to be true. Unfortunately, the principles of justice and freedom were forgotten and the provisions of fundamental liberties enshrined in the constitution were progressively compromised and eroded by the ruling clique. However, we have to also acknowledge that the battle cry of our freedom fighters, founding fathers, or liberation fighters echoed democracy, freedom, justice. From Tuanku Abdul Rahman in Malaysia to Sukarno in Indonesia, Jinnah in Pakistan, and others in the Middle East, their sacred oath was to establish independent and democratic nations.

The wisdom given through the Qur'an and Sunnah does not stipulate a particular governance framework; it is simply the ethical compass for Muslims, just as other religious and are ligious humans have their own ethical grounding. Often what democracy is criticised for lacking is this specific ethical grounding. Democracy is the framing, but what resides within that frame? When the ethics are weak, so too are the products of that democracy. Yet, in lacking specific moral foundations, there is a strength in democracy's applicability.

Islam and democracy, rather than being diametrically opposed, complement each other. Islam can be the ethical compass and democracy can give it the vehicle through which to bring about societal prosperity. A narrow approach to democracy demands a secular ethical grounding for the 'best' of all possible democracies, but where the morality comes from should not be an issue so long as the ethics developed actualise and promote those same values and virtues that ensure human flourishing, that uphold justice.

Not only are Islam and democracy compatible, but Islam provides democracy with an edge that can actually help us reform our governance systems in light of the flaws it has encountered throughout its history. There is no shortage of books written espousing Islam's devotion to and love of justice, freedom, equality, charity, and a wide host of other values and virtues embellished by the most ardent of secular liberal democrats. But literature on Muslim democracy is often lacking, making the idea of a Muslim democrat what a medical professional might call a zebra, something exotic and unique, a lightning-in-a-bottle type of occurrence. And while democracy in Muslim societies has taken a far from perfect trajectory through history, it is far from novel. The American professor of law Khaled Abou El Fadl's aptly titled *Islam and the Challenge of Democracy*, the far too sparse literature on democracy in Islam, engages in a discourse around democracy with other great contemporary thinkers in Islam and government from around the world.[21] Shorn of ornamentation, the precepts of Islam, as an ethical system, could serve as a bulwork for democratice practices.

Both Islam and democracy fundamentally require a respect for the rule of law. This is not a rule of law, but the rule of law—meaning that all humans are bound by the law regardless of their background and where no humans are held above the law. Our inherent equality is made practical through the fact that we all are subject to the law and will have to pay for the crimes we commit. But democratic governments, like what is required of all Muslim rulers, gain their legitimacy through free and open contract. In Islam, it is called the *aqd*, or contract, between the people and the Caliph ruler, a concept that was so important to the triumvirate of Western political thought of Thomas Hobbes, John Locke, and Jean-Jacques Rousseau. The Qur'an expounds on the paramount principle of inherent diversity: 'If thy...Lord had so willed, He could have made mankind one people, but they will not cease to dispute' (11:118). Democracy is not a dialogue; it is a polylogue. A framework involving multiple viewpoints, positions and voices coming together for a single purpose.

Mercy is tolerance in its highest form. In Abou El Fadl's words, 'it is a state in which the individual is able to be just with him or herself and others by giving each individual person his or her due'.[22] It is not passive: 'fundamentally, mercy is tied to a state of genuine perception of others'.[23] It is about building what Ziauddin Sardar referred to as 'wisdom communities',[24] the just society. It was Al-Farabi's dream with the virtuous city, an Islamic take on Plato's desired *Republic*, but instead of one philosopher king, the whole citizenry could be a collective of

philosopher kings and queens. In ancient Athens, it was prac-
tised at the Pnyx, the hill where citizens met to discuss matters
of the state. Today we call it congress, or the general assembly,
or parliament. A space where we come to know one another,
demonstrate our mercy, and see out justice for the day, and
perhaps sustain it into the future. Freedom of expression with
mutual respect fosters this synthesis and demonstrates that all
the values of Western secular democracy and Islamic democracy
mirror one another.

In more recent times, a patronising phrase has been invented
to inhibit the progress of emerging democratic states and maintain the pedestal upon which we place Western democracies:
'democratic deficit'. Again, it must be acknowledged that the
phrase came about by way of a noble criticism. In the late 1970s,
democratic deficit was a criticism-cum-warning about the sacrifice or abandonment of democratic principles of member states
in the formation of what would become the European Union.
Following its birth, the phrase was quickly used to bemoan the
less than democratic administrations governing territories of
larger, and formerly imperial, democracies. This applies to the
US's own capital, the District of Columbia, as well as its distant
territories that do not hold the same democratic privileges as one
of the fifty states, or the UK and its overseas territories. And
while democratic deficit still comes up in discourse around
superstates and multinational organisations, it took a nefarious
turn when it triggered the establishment of a variety of democratic indices. These indices have, by and large, sought to mar-
ginalise and distance the 'democratic' credentials of South
American, African, and Asian democracies from those of the
West. Ironically, many of these democracies modelled their own
governance structures and institutions on the very Western
democracies that now chose to judge them. Instead of measuring
the qualities and varieties of democratic accountability or, per-

haps, more loftily judging the quality of governance in a given state (while appreciating the difference in context experience from nation to nation), these indices have been distorted into a judgement of all against a utopian ideal of democracy, a standard that hardly any present democracy could live up to, especially those in the West. And take careful notice of which states are repeatedly mentioned in and the motivation behind these reports, often garnished with their own click-bait titles concerning 'democratic deficiency'. It did not take long for these indices to show themselves for what they really were: yet another academic device to back up the Othering of non-Western methods of governance and to conceal the growing cracks in the façade of 'democratic' superiority that the US and Europe prop up—regardless of how much it diverges from what is revealed when one looks in the mirror.

Yet while we all need to take a long hard look in the mirror, beyond that, looking to the future, we need to come to terms with one critical fact, that the desire to be free is universal. It's neither East nor West; Islamic or Christian or Jewish. It is a universal concern, a moral imperative. It is the human desire to be free, to lead a dignified life, an abhorrence of despotism and oppression that motivate the Muslims, be they Arabs, Malays, Persians, or Africans, to crave democracy. Their desire has been nurtured, accumulated, and betrayed.

IV

While on commission from the French government to study American prison systems in the 1830s, sociologist, diplomat, philosopher, and historian Alexis de Tocqueville made an insightful observation about the democracy he was witnessing in the 'New World'. His account, which would be published in two volumes as *Democracy in America*, began with a survey of the natural and untouched beauty of America just before it was to undergo rapid industrialisation, when the natural frontier was still available for viewing. Statements of the empirical almost act as metaphor. Democracy was a new terrain, and the world was changing. For democracy to realise its full potential, Tocqueville emphasised the need for a 'new political science' to keep the mission and trajectory of a given democracy on the right path. While Tocqueville used the term 'democracy' more loosely than we might prefer, nevertheless, his remarks are astute. The world was on the precipice of social revolution. Old methods of legislating, adjudicating, executing, policymaking, and monitoring were not going to bring about success for this new model. Democracy was a vehicle, but it needed force and direction for it to take human societies anywhere.[25] While Tocqueville's call was timely, it was not heeded, and the attempts at imposing old thinking on the new resulted in corruption and have driven many to despair in the contemporary period.

It is time to repair democracy. If we don't, then modernity will do what it has done with all great ideas, obliviating them in the process of finding the next endorphin rush between nostalgia and whatever rose-coloured fragments of familiar normality we can salvage. And it is not hard to see that in our abandonment of democracy for the 'better' system of governance, we will backslide as a result of our own necrotic imaginations. Socially, most of the world is caught in a tug-of-war over the Overton window, the range of positions and arguments acceptable to the dominant political systems, between a simplistic notion of conservativism and liberalism, both of which are unworthy of the complexity that is human political identity. We pull one way until we grow tired or long for the other. Traditionalism today, punk rock counterculture tomorrow, monetarism followed by austerity (or is it vice versa?), renewed spirituality, and then back to desperate and unabashed freedom. Progress is not even an illusion. It is a delusion. And then authoritarians come in and take advantage of the situation while we squabble among ourselves. Before we know it, we are electing gangsters, murderers, and clowns, election after election, because they simply do something, frankly anything, as we have become ethically numb. Because democracy was allowed to only be a word which could be used to the benefit of whosoever let it pass through their lips. But in practice it was an endlessly complicated bureaucratic nightmare. Inefficiency is always going to be a slight against democracy. But this should not be allowed to be the final straw. Of course, democracy will be less efficient than totalitarian megalomania or corporate, oligarchical authoritarianism. After all, genocide that is not industrial in scale, however running like a well-oiled machine, cannot be regarded as the lesser evil. Dictators and tyrants, well, they just get the job done. We actually say this, like it is not an absurd collection of words. Modernity demands instant gratification and constant update. Patience is not a virtue. But that inefficiency that we place on democracy like a Scarlet Letter, is a necessary sacrifice in order that a common good might just be attained. That justice might just be upheld. We cannot be fooled by modernity, which is collapsing in on itself and has not done many people the good it promised. Only elites benefit. And complacency allows modernity to continue. Indeed, it is easier to comply with the wrath of identity politics, populism, and money politics. It is much easier, as the French philosopher Jacques Rancière put it, to 'hate democracy'.[26] I think more appropriately, today, we fear democracy.

Yet we cannot totally dismiss the problem of efficiency and democracy. While modernity certainly gives us the impression that life is a series of episodes of hurrying along only to then wait and hurry again, the reality is that change itself is changing and we need systems that can help us cope with this reality. Be it illusion or influence of outside forces, contemporary life demands urgent decisions to be made, not simply because we have con-formed to a fast-paced culture, but because major existential threats are just over the horizon. As the American environmental policy analyst Daniel J. Fiorino rightly asks, via the title of his 2018 book: 'Can democracy handle climate change?' Fiorino sees climate change, the existential disaster boiling under our noses, in the same light that we see war and in democratic states.[27] When war approaches, the go-to move is to suspend democracy temporarily. Wartime demands quick and decisive action, some-thing that is seen as impossible in terms of a rule-by-the-people democracy. After 9/11, US President George W. Bush was effec-tively given totalitarian powers by Congress.[28] In Southeast Asian democracies, an emergency is declared and democracy is effec-tively put into deep freeze until the crisis is averted and stability is retained. In Malaysia, this happened following the riots of 1969, as well as more recently in 2020 with regards to the Covid 19 pandemic,[29] where the rule of law and the federal constitution were effectively suspended. A more drastic case has taken place in Myanmar, where democracy is routinely put in the corner as the military seizes power over the country's affairs. We find our-selves in what my friend the former UK prime minister, Gordon Brown, describes as a time of 'permacrisis' of democracy.[30] Thus, the outlook is not ideal. The only agreed upon way to deal with crisis seems to be to suspend what notions of democracy exist in a nation, and there is a general acceptance of temporary anach-ronistic and even deplorable approaches to governance simply so that someone 'gets the job done'. We even spin it as something for 'our own good'. As our postnormal times grow more intense, national governments will have no choice but to act as if we are in total war, backstepping into draconian forms of order. Climate change will soon make parts of the world, as we now know them, uninhabitable. The volatility of global trade, supply chains, mar-kets, and resources will force extreme measures, likely to fan the flames of isolationism and protectionism. Civil unrest and of course good old-fashioned war are certainly not going anywhere either. What will begin as long stretches of holiday for democracy will find its principles and guarantees queuing up in the ranks of the unemployed. And there will never be a shortage of political opportunists waiting to take advantage of the chaos. And in the failure of democracy and the failure of society, both unable to cope with the disorientation of postnormal times, the result will inevitably lead towards the worst-case scenario of democracy—anarchy.

Beyond being an important intellectual exercise, the ramifications will be very real. Democracy needs a vital rethink, but also a reform of its structures so that it can outlast the storm ahead.

Democracy is a vague concept. Vagueness presupposes uncertainty, and it is hard for us to cope with uncertainty. And experience shows that vagueness is easily taken advantage of and corrupted. But the power granted by vague concepts need not only be the power to corrupt. For the power of vagueness can also be an opportunity to balance the needs, some wildly unreconcilable, for effective and strong governance as well as the desires and defence of the people being governed. Before we let the vague framing fall victim to countless complexities, we can examine it at its most basic. Democracy is rule by the people. This requires equality under the rule of law. For this system of government to function, a space is required whereby the people may openly discuss public affairs. Major decisions are voted on and institutions are assembled when necessary to see the work of the government being done.

In studying state responses to disaster and catastrophe, the American political scientist and anthropologist James C. Scott stumbled upon a tangent that led to a whole new line of thinking. His 'intellectual detour' began with Scott studying why the state and nomadic people always seemed to be natural enemies.

He would go on to find that the problem was the modern state needs a sedentary, immobilised population in order to tax it, order it, and conscript an army from it. Also, agriculture provides a good means for a domestic economy. While the pre-modern world always appeared in flux, states came in to draw lines in the sand and organise everything they could in the name of human rights, justice, and protection.[31] Today, our globalised and inter-connected world is pushing not only increased migration but enhanced mobility. It is a challenge for the state, which needs delineation and categorisation. Humanity and contemporary life are simply too complex. He traces similar issues to those Mimi Sheller recorded in *Mobility Justice.*[32] Both recommend a new understanding of the state in an age of flux. Of course, as more natural disasters ignite a wave of climate refugees, which will aggravate the present 'normal' refugee crisis we face with people displaced by war and political repression, we need systems in place to cope with this reality. Yet multicultural states have already dealt with a very similar issue. And we need to appreciate a trend that is becoming a reality in many nations around the world, including some of the most homogeneous countries on earth.

Democracies of the future are going to be more and more multicultural and diverse, and it would be in all our best interests to seek greater plurality in our social and political institutions. This is a prime situation that the vagueness of democracy is well equipped to handle. What is missing from the basic framing of democracy is an ethical backbone. Many ethical backbones can be put in place. Appreciating this, the strongest backbone for a democracy will arise from a plurality of moral sources. Islam brings a host of concepts to the table to complement and enhance democracy. So too does Christianity, Judaism, Hinduism, Buddhism, Jainism, Sikhism, and any other religious ethical world view. Likewise, a wide host of philosophies and traditions can offer a moral basis for running our future democracies: Daoism,

Confucianism, all of the philosophical traditions of the Subcontinent, African philosophy, and even Western philosophies. More indigenous and cultural concepts provide new angles and perspectives for the problems of today as well as those that await us tomorrow. The strongest democracies of the future will be ruled by a plurality of diverse peoples. Practically, this requires a lot of work. We need innovative approaches to immigration and border policy. It requires reform that emboldens representation of the populace in our august houses. And this requires, most crucially, open and inclusive spaces for discourse and polylogue. Principal for this to function properly is a sophisticated respect for freedom of speech. Now, here I do not refer to the mockery of free speech that liberal secularism has made of the institution. This is not freedom from consequence for what is said, but a respect that all may speak their minds and express their opinions without it being used as a source of persecution. This also requires a robust education system that opens our minds to new ideas and perspectives, not so that we may blindly follow the most novel notion, but so that we may analyse critically all that comes across our path. So that we may build the knowledge we need to navigate the future ahead. In this space, criticism, difference, and judgement will not act as the slings and arrows of the citizenry, but the building blocks upon which we lift each other up. Without new ideas, our minds become stagnant, and just like the sedentary demands of the modern state, it will be the immobility upon which future democracy dies.

We must totally rethink our inclusive and plural spaces. They need not be physical. Technology can help us with this. And in our representative emulations of democracy, we must stay true to democracy's principles and remain fair to all our citizens. Gerrymandering is an incredible tool that allows us to update and keep current the necessary number of legislative representatives to ensure that all of the people's voices and demands are made public. But abuse has allowed gerrymandering to perpetuate racism and xenophobia, to tear our communities apart and deny certain voices we would rather not hear. This is a deplorable corruption, and it is incumbent upon all to correct missteps taken in the past and preserve equal representation. Technology can be an aid in this; good data, particularly collected through census surveys, can give us necessary information that can be enacted in policy. But as a tool, gerrymandering is always at the mercy of the government of the day. An interesting innovation is to reserve seats in parliament for minority communities to prevent alienation and disenfranchisement. Many countries reserve seats for female representatives or otherwise marginalised ethnicities. Other parliaments reserve seats for indigenous communities. It is a complex and elaborate problem of maths and sociology, but one that must continually be refined through reform. There is no one way to do democracy, but as democracies, we must strive to always improve upon our present situation. And constructing a solid, inclusive, and open space for political discourse is essential to the success of democracy as a futures-sustainable system of governance.

Beyond this we must look to two major challenges along the road to our futures: technology and money.

Technology, like all new things, can be scary and perceived as a disruption. On the other extreme, there is a utopian propensity to see all new technological advancements as human advancements on some artificial path of progress. Neither view will help us pragmatically engage with the future or appreciate the *realpolitik* at play. Technology can be a crucial aid in helping us attain the higher aims of a society, but we must beware that we do not allow technology to become a crutch on which we are dependent. Technology can offer us real solutions for democracy as well. The challenge of rule by the people only becomes untenable as populations grow and states become larger. But technology gives us the platform, the space, to actualise what we might call a more pure, direct democracy where all voices can be heard and accounted for. There is also an opportunity for open discourse and protection of one's privacy through the opportunities provided for anonymity. But the idea that technology is a tool must not be forgotten. And tools can be used to build beautiful buildings and to tear others down. Technology has shown itself more than capable of dehumanising our futures as well as taking on our biases and hatred.

As the late British physicist Stephen Hawking said, the emergence of Artificial Intelligence could be the worst event in the history of our civilisation. We must heed American cultural critic Neil Postman's warning and not find ourselves at the mercy of 'Technopoly', where culture and knowledge is surrendered to artificial intelligence,[33] or worse, American philosopher Shoshana Zuboff's 'Surveillance Capitalism'.[34] We cannot stop thinking for ourselves, lest we fall victim to the same stagnancy discussed above. And we must resist the repetition of past hardships through future technological means. Technology can lead to a new age of colonialism or bring about genocide on a nigh unimaginable scale. These concerns, however, do not retract from the capacity that technology can bring towards human advancement. Therefore, the mastery of AI is not an option, but an absolute necessity.

And then there is money, or as it is commonly called, money politics. Power is an incredibly complex phenomenon that no shortage of luminaries throughout history have had little trouble writing countless words on its effects on us humans. And just as democracy is capable of enmeshing itself into the complexity of other ideologies and political forces, various sources of power have no trouble accumulating into more compounded sources of greater power. Money is simply purchasing power. But our global capitalist system has turned that power source into a real monster. It demonstrates the thickness of the weeds we find ourselves in as we attempt to seek good governance. The South Korean-born German philosopher, Byung-Chul Han, makes a troubling point about this complexity. The real trouble emerges when the complexity goes so deep that democracy and economic systems become entangled. Instead of the constitution of a nation, the social contract of the people in a democracy being the insurer of our rights as citizens, the market and free-range capitalism become the insurer of our rights.[35] We see this happening in Europe and the United States, and if left unchallenged it will become a global phenomenon: once we are trapped in it, there is little in the way of escape. Our democratic institutions must be equipped to nip money politics in the bud. At this moment, beyond the existential threats that not only lurk over democracy but also jeopardise the future existence of the human race, money politics is the greatest threat to democracy. It is the darkest force of corruption that violates the very basis of democracy. Money can buy one exemption from the rule of law, if threatened, all are no longer equal and the centre cannot hold. This requires systemic reforms in our elaborate governments but also requires a reform of the minds of all our citizens, not to become complacent or remain ignorant to the constant threat the wealthy elites pose to our sacred democracy.

Democracy is spectacularly fragile. And it is no spectator sport; it requires all our active and willing participation. It is not easy and it is riddled with contradictions. All the odds are against us when it comes to this noble pursuit. Federal government versus local governments, public freedom versus private security, liberal versus conservative, our need to develop versus our balanced relationship with the natural world, techno-utopia versus Luddite societies, individualism versus collectivism, tyranny of the majority versus tyranny of the minority. Almost twenty-four centuries after writing the *Republic*, Plato's qualms with democracy remain. But this is not a roadblock. It is a challenge. And in its vagueness and adaptability, democracy can also be the machine by which we transcend these and many other contradictions which have become distinguishing features of our postnormal times. And in our world of great tumult, perhaps democracy is a house of cards, but it is one that we can fortify and defend, the reward being greater social trust and cohesion; the ability to communicate, cooperate, and coordinate; the building of a beautiful space in which we can come to know one another; and a vehicle by which we can attain a share of prosperity and wealth of human flourishing. Rancière aptly encapsulated democracy when he said:

> Democracy is as bare in its relation to the power of wealth as it is to the power of kinship that today comes to assist and to rival it. It is not based on any nature of things nor guaranteed by any institutional form. It is not borne along by any historical necessity and does not bear any. It is only entrusted to the constancy of its specific acts. This can provoke fear, and so hatred, among those who are used to exercising the magisterium of thought. But among those who know how to share with anybody and everybody the equal power of intelligence, it can conversely inspire courage, and hence joy.[36]

In building our democracies so that they may continue to exist in their infinite diversities into the future, we must also not forget the deterioration the last few decades have brought about and not fail to take to heart the lessons history has presented. Malaysia's democratic decline echoes the situation seen in other postcolonial democracies, both those following the Westminster system and those that have taken their own approach to democracy as a form of governance. While having faced the onslaught of its outrageous past, corruption and abuses must not be forgotten, and in our many ways of coming about our democratic states, we can learn from each other's experiences. In seeking a betterment of democracy, a greater rethinking can be provoked. For at this moment, we are stuck in an in-between period. All that we take as normal is on trial, alongside democracy, and it is important that we critically analyse our present condition as things are becoming increasingly postnormal, so that we may navigate towards whatever new epoch we will create and fortify together on the other side of tomorrow's horizon. In light of the foregoing analysis , having established the confluence of democracy and Islam, while taking into account democracy's 'vague immensities' as well as the challenes of AI and future technolgoies, it behooves us to ensure a more comprehensive discourse takes place among the people. And taking into consideration the scepticism and even cynicism of certain quarters of the Muslim community, it is imperative that we focus our examination on the ummah.

Four

RECONSIDERING THE UMMAH

I

Sometime during the evening of 11 September 2001, I could hear commotion from the end of the cell block. I heard the guards speaking rather loudly about some explosions and that America had been bombed. Eventually I flagged down a passing guard who relayed to me that bombs had gone off in New York City and the iconic skyline of the city had been levelled. With no access to any textual or visual media, I remained sceptical for the rest of the night. The next morning, thanks to a scheduled meeting, my lawyers came to the prison and provided me with a fuller picture of what had happened. I was appalled by the extent of the carnage inflicted from the terrorist attack, not to mention the thousands of lives lost. Retiring to my solitary cell, it dawned on me that this violent act of depravity would also trigger untold harm on the Muslim ummah, and fan the flames of hatred and animosity towards Islam and Muslims. This was the genesis of the insidious phenomenon we now call Islamophobia. The least I could do was to put my thoughts on paper: to condemn unequivocally the vicious attack and express my concern for the aftermath.[1]

In prison I experienced the most profound powerlessness. Yet in my ability to read, I was free. And, with my pen, I could speak what others would not, but what others still needed to hear. Islam was not the faith of violent, blood-thirsty warlords as pundits were wont to proclaim. The Qur'an is very explicit on these matters: 'Let not your hatred of others cause you to act unjustly against them' (5:8). A plot was afoot to hijack Islam as a tool of fundamentalism and hate, a gesture I could not abide whether in confinement or not. I penned my reflection and with the help of loyal friends was able to smuggle my words out of prison and into the world.[2]

Never in Islam's history have the actions of so few of its followers caused the religion and its community of believers to be such an abomination in the eyes of others. Millions of Muslims who fled to North America and Europe to escape poverty and persecution at home have become the objects of hatred and are now profiled as potential terrorists. The nascent democratic movements in Muslim countries regressed decades, as ruling autocrats used their participation in the global war against terrorism to terrorise their critics and dissenters.

One is therefore perturbed by the confusion among Muslims who responded to the attack with a misplaced diatribe against the US. At the time in Malaysia, the government-controlled media was deployed to stir up anti-American sentiments, while members of the political elite used a different language for international diplomacy. Certainly, there were and continue to be legitimate grievances against the US and good reason for despondency. But this was not the time for sermonising or moralising over US foreign policy. Had we Malaysians been the victims of such a tragedy, we would find such hectoring tasteless and repulsive.

One wonders how, in the twenty-first century, Muslim societies could have produced an Osama bin Laden. In the past, Islam forged civilisations, men of wealth created pious foundations supporting universities and hospitals, and princes competed with one another to patronise scientists, philosophers, and men of letters. The greatest of scientists and philosophers of the medieval age, Ibn Sina, was a product of that system. But Bin Laden used his personal fortune to sponsor terror and murder, not learning or creativity, and to wreak destruction rather than promote creation. Bin Laden and his protégés were—and those who remain are—the children of desperation; having been incessantly fed on a diet of fanatical extremist religious teachings and finding no recourse for dissent. These people needed space to express their political and social concerns. The need for Muslim societies to address their internal social and political development had become more urgent than ever. Today, the Muslim ummah is more fully engaged with the world on major issues such as governance, the economy, the environment, and civil socity. This places them well within the mainstream of current global awareness and activism, especially amongst the youth. Nevertheless, there is still the existence of fringe elements which still preach the mantra of exclusivism and hatred. And if left unchecked, this could fester into a more insidious phenomenon where it could metastasise into a major trend.

According to Bin Laden, the terror attacks were a result of the undeclared ghost war against Muslims and Islam by the US, pursued through its foreign policy. But the US was also a refuge for dissidents. Many of my most respected friends, great intellects in their own right, had sought out the United States as their home to escape the oppression and killing going on in their own 'Muslim' homelands. What indeed had become of the Muslim world? How did we get from the classical period of Islam, where our ancestors were inventing and shaping civilisation, to a closed-off hive mind following the sinister orders of half-baked religious scholars? And then I remembered a fateful premonition put forward by my late dear friend, the British anthropologist Merryl Wyn Davies, as the Berlin Wall was being torn down, just over a decade prior.

II

Merryl Wyn Davies was a member of a group of critical Muslim thinkers and scholars who called themselves the *ijmalis*—the seekers of beauty—who valued the moral and ethical dimension of knowledge. I joined the *ijmalis* in the mid-1980s. The group met regularly in London and Kuala Lumpur to discuss the issues of the time. In Malaysia, they organised 'intellectual discourses' on such topics as globalisation, the Gulf War, the human genome project, conservation of cultural property, and the future of Islam and Muslims. One historic meeting of the *ijmalis* convened on 9 November 1989 at Davies's home in London, which I was unable to attend, was interrupted by a special report.

While in hindsight the reforms introduced by the Soviet Union's last supreme leader, Mikhail Gorbachev, in the last five-year plan the Soviet Union would have (1985–1990), spelled the writing on the wall for the 'evil empire', no one expected an overnight change. Indeed, peaceful protests cropped up all through the Soviet states of the Eastern bloc, but it was not until Günter Schabowski, the government spokesperson of the German Democratic Republic (East Germany), misspoke at a banal press conference that the flood gates were opened and the tide of change could not be stopped. Schabowski had announced that unconditional travel would be allowed between East and West Germany for the first time since the 1960s when the Berlin Wall was constructed. Caught off guard by a follow-up question from the press, he mistakenly stated that this would be effective 'immediately and without delay', when the brief handed to him stated that this would commence the morning of the next day when all officials had been suitably prepared. The press conference happened in the afternoon and was quickly disseminated to the local news in the 7:30pm daily report, and hit the AP wires within an hour of the announcement. Masses quickly gathered at the already famous Brandenburg Gate. For a while, security forces were able to facilitate an orderly crossing, but before long jubilant crowds gathered and a brick-by-brick deconstruction of the wall was under way.[3]

I am told the *ijimalis* gathered that evening were well fed. Merryl was an exceptional cook. Their struggle for warmth on that cold winter day was aided by a celebration of change rolling over the horizon. And as an *ijimali* gathering was known to go on into the wee hours of the morning, as the sun rose on 10 November, a reality sobered the celebratory atmosphere. Davies knew the Cold War had driven a particular style of operation that benefited the military-industrial complex that proliferated after the end of World War II in the United States. And that machine would be hungry for the next enemy. Davies declared ominously that we, Islam, would be the new 'evil empire' to take the Soviet's place, for the good versus evil narrative was too easy for the masses to consume and far too profitable for the elite to abandon.[4] The West had already had a rough start with the 'Muslim world' at this point, considering the revolution in Iran and the Grand Mosque seizure in Mecca by French forces. But now the new struggle would be for oil, and the likes of Hosni Mubarak in Egypt, Saddam Hussein in Iraq, Muammar Gaddafi in Libya, Hafez al-Assad in Syria, were not the friendliest looking crowd that would now have to be dealt with in this new paradigm.

After the crumbling of the Berlin Wall in 1989 and the unravelling of the Soviet Empire, the Austrian management and business innovator, Peter Drucker, suggested that the world had changed and the new *gestalt* must be viewed as 'configurations' that embrace several aspects of our lives.[5] A year later, American political scientist Francis Fukuyama saw the collapse of the Cold War in a dualistic vision as the harbinger of the triumph of the Western model of liberal democracy, and declared:

> what we may be witnessing is not just the end of the cold war, or the passing of a particular period of postwar history, but the end of history as such: that is, the end point of mankind's ideological evolution and the universalisation of western liberal democracy as the final form of human government.[6]

That unparalleled hubris now lies in ruins.

Indeed, history does not start and stop at the whims of the West, and it did not take long for this to become apparent. Not content to rest on some imagined laurels, Fukuyama's teacher, Samuel P. Huntington, challenged the claims of his student with the publication of a paper in 1993 that carried the same title as a book he would publish in 1996, *The Clash of Civilizations*. Regardless of whether or not Western liberal democracy was the apex of human governance, Huntington noted that the civilisations of the 'East' were incompatible with it, so a clash was inevitable.[7] Since this thesis gave cannon fodder to the US military-industrial complex, it became the narrative of the day. And so, a preordained trajectory began to materialise, taking us from the fall of the Soviet Union to 9/11, and beyond.

A retort to Huntington came from Edward W. Said, the American Palestinian literary and political critic, in his 'The Clash of Ignorance'.[8] Said argued that Huntington's framework was simplistic, reducing diverse societies to monolithic blocs such as 'Islamic', 'Western', 'Chinese', and so on. This approach rode roughshod over internal complexities like sectarian and political differences and perpetuated stereotypes, in total disregard of the shared histories and cultural exchanges that shape human civilisation. Written in the immediate aftermath of the 9/11 attacks, Said's essay carried significance as it addressed the global context increasingly polarised by Huntington's thesis. He warned that such binary frameworks risked exacerbating political tensions and he challenged readers to reject simplistic categorisations in favour of more sophisticated understandings of cultural interactions. Said also criticised Huntington's portrayal of the Islamic world as a uniform entity, highlighting the dangers of bipolar, oppositional thinking, and advocated for recognising the fluidity of identities and fostering dialogue to navigate cultural differences.

Said's critique further invited readers to consider the role of power dynamics in shaping such narratives. By framing Western civilisation as a normative standard, Huntington's thesis reinforced hierarchies that marginalised non-Western perspectives. Said's essay underscored the need to dismantle these intellectual frameworks to foster equitable dialogue and understanding. Huntington argued that a 'clash of civilisations' would dominate global politics because the overriding source of conflict among humankind was not ideological or primarily economic but would be cultural, and that the principal conflicts of global politics would occur between nations and groups of different civilisations, particularly between Islam and the West. As Said puts it,

> The basic paradigm of West versus the rest (the cold war opposition reformulated) remained untouched, and this is what has persisted, often insidiously and implicitly, in discussion since the terrible events of September 11. The carefully planned and horrendous, pathologically motivated suicide attack and mass slaughter by a small group of deranged militants has been turned into proof of Huntington's thesis.

In my earlier critique of Huntington's thesis, which was later published in 1996 in *The Asian Renaissance*,[9] I contended that rather than positing an inevitable civilisational clash, we should be highlighting the commonalities of civilisations, and where there are dissimilarities, we ought to be focussing on the imperative of convergence through civilisational dialogue. In 1997, when I was deputy prime minister, I, together with colleagues including US Senator Bill Cohen, Singapore's George Yeo, and Indonesia's Ginandjar Kartasasmita, felt the imperative to respond to this contentious issue. After a series of engagements, we finally agreed to publish a Charter on 'Celebration of Civilizations'. The Charter declared its belief in a 'celebration of civilizations, where we value diversity whilst seeking unity within that diversity, where we each fortify the values and the ways which make us strong and that make us civilised in our own light'.

This imperative for civilisational dialogue cannot be over-stressed in light of the rising tide of fascism, xenophobia, and Islamophobia. Despite the onward trajectory of societal advancement in this age of AI and quantum computing, the insidious virus of ignorance continues to plague many facets of society. What has taken place since 9/11 and the US-led 'war on terror' has transformed the world. The last two decades, in particular, have seen economic, political, and cultural power shift from the West to the East, and liberal democracy appears to be in an intensive care unit. Fukuyama has since recanted his 'end of history' theory as Europe slouched towards fascism and liberal democracy teetering on the brink. Unipolarity weathering under the weight of the China–US rivalry. Autocratic regimes are again rearing their ugly heads. On the other hand, multilateral entities emerge as they advance in their economic and technological advancement, such as Gulf Cooperation Council (GCC) and the Association of Southeast Asia (ASEAN). Fascism has again returned to Europe, the US appears on the brink of a civil war, Russia is in Ukraine, Israel is wiping Palestine off the face of the map, and China is now a superpower. The United Nations has proven its complete and utter impotence. BRICS[10] countries rise to balance the world order as global discourse seeks to give a voice to the re-emerging 'Global South'. Indeed, the world has become more contradictory,

complex, and chaotic; and we now face the new reality of postnormal times, where uncertainties in social, economic, cultural, and
political life have become the new order of things. Worse, the new
reality, for want of a better term, is not constant but ever changing, configuring and reconfiguring the world.

The postnormal reality that confronts us is well described by
the Secretary-General of the United Nations, António Guterres.
In his speech at the 2025 World Economic Forum Annual
Meeting at Davos, Guterres pointed out that the world had
become 'rudderless' and a 'Pandora's box of troubles' had been
opened: 'we face widening geopolitical divisions, rising inequalities and an assault on human rights'. Two 'existential threats'
demand urgent attention: 'climate crisis and the ungoverned
expansion of artificial intelligence'. Rising sea levels would mean
that the world's biggest ports will be overwhelmed, rising temperatures would lead to more wildfires, and we have pushed past
1.5°C above pre-industrial levels: 'sea level rise, heatwaves, floods,
storms, droughts and wildfires—are just a preview of the horror
movie to come'.[11]

Developing countries are in a dire economic situation, with
some African states 'facing double-digit inflation rates—while
interest payments in Africa are eating up 27 percent of all government revenues'.[12] We could add the emergence of surveillance
capitalism, the problems and challenges of digital economies, the
social pathology of social media, forthcoming pandemics that
could be far worse than Covid-19, the incorporation of different
varieties of ignorance in knowledge production, as well as the
old problems of justice and equality. These are interconnected
issues that urgently need a sense of complexity that is neither a
flirtation with nostalgia nor romanticism. Complexity in our
thinking and approach to problems and issues is something we
desperately need to learn to comprehend because it is pre-emi-
nently the condition in which we live. It is impossible for any of

us to attain a sustainable lifestyle that embraces complexity without also embracing a plural vision of human futures. For this reason, there can be no end to history, but there must be a relearning of the history that has made the world today. Because of this reality, much of the discourse that ended the twentieth and ushered in the twenty-first century had lost an appreciation for the cyclical nature of history, condemning both the West and the rest to an endless and chaotic spin. In order to gain some orientation in these troubled times, revisiting and appreciating the work of such Muslim scholars as the Arab historian Ibn Khaldun and the Algerian philosopher Malik Bennabi is a good place to begin.

The history of cyclical theories goes back to the classical Greek philosophers, such as Aristotle's cycle of regime change and Polybius's theory of *anacyclosis*. The Chinese father of historiography, Sima Qian, propounded a dynastic cycle theory of intriguing comparative schemas of apparently divergent civilisations.[13] But to reach its apogee as a systematic, empirically based study, cyclical theories had to wait for Ibn Khaldun, with his fourteenth-century social and philosophical expositions on the rise and fall of sovereign powers, including civilisations, based on the twin doctrines of *'umran* (civilisation) and *asabiyyah* (tribalism).[14] *Al-Muqaddimah*, the Introduction to his magnum opus, *Kitab al-'Ibar*, could well be regarded as the culmination of the efforts of his predecessors in historiography and social studies, such as the ninth-century Central Asian philosopher Al-Farabi, the tenth-century Persian philosopher Ibn Miskawayh, and the thirteenth-century Persian polymath Nasir al-Din al-Tusi.

Following Ibn Khaldun, Malik Bennabi suggests that

each cycle is defined by certain psycho-temporal conditions proper to a social group: it is a civilisation in these conditions. Then the civilisation migrates, shifts its abode, transfers its values in another area. It thus perpetuates itself in an indefinite exodus, through successive metamorphoses: each metamorphosis being a particular synthesis of man, soil and time.[15]

There is merit in Bennabi's ascription of the transitory nature of civilisation, 'which allows one to discuss not only the conditions of progressive development but also the factors of regression and decadence: the force of inertia of a civilisation'.[16] And it is in this vein of decline that we appreciate the elan of Bennabi's assertion that until Muslim societies free themselves from the six hundred years of 'civilisational bankruptcy' and move towards *islah* and *tajdid* (reform and renewal) predicated on the true Islamic tradition, 'the equilibrium necessary for a new synthesis of its history' will remain elusive.[17]

Bennabi highlights the key impediment before us, we who have dreamed for so long of a revival of the Islamic Golden Age. The South Asian philosopher and poet Muhammad Iqbal takes this proposition a step further in his 1930 book, *The Reconstruction of Religious Thought in Islam*. Iqbal contends that God gave us the faculty of the intellect to free ourselves from the accretion of time and culture. In actuality, this demanded nothing short of 'reconstruction' of the Muslim mind according to the doctrine of *ijtihad*—sustained reasoning. Iqbal offers us a bold and valiant attempt to bring Islamic thought back to the contemporary world so that it may survive and thrive into the future. He gives due credit to Sufi scholars who have 'done good work in shaping and directing the evolution of religious experience in Islam', but laments their 'ignorance' and lack of appreciation of contemporary thought.[18] Iqbal commends and condemns, in opposite ways, the thought of both the medieval theologian Al-Ghazali and the Enlightenment German philosopher Immanuel Kant. He finds an incommensurability between rationalist thought and religious dogma. For Iqbal, both can complement each other and extend the finite into the infinite as we pursue the creation of knowledge.[19] Far from just being an academic issue, Iqbal's quest for intellectual revival of the ummah continues today. And, as the world itself has fallen into a new interregnum of postnormal times, we are presented with an opportunity not just to reflect but to take concrete actions for the advancement of the ummah.

Change is always easier said than done. The challenge is to deal with new metamorphosis—the postnormal transformation that is shaping current and emerging realities. In this transition, the ummah must play its part to mould the trajectory of growth and progress in terms of the advancement of justice and freedom.

Let us first consider the Muslim world. During the period of the Cold War, the world was supposedly ordered into two great but hostile blocs: the First World, also known as the Free World, which in being free naturally embodied all that was democratic, just, and free; and the Second World, or the Communist bloc. Depending on one's perspective, these blocs were either oppressive, totalitarian, and severely restrictive, or capitalistic, reactionary, and imperialistic. The countries in between, argued Frantz Fanon, constituted a third power bloc—the Third World.[20] The 'Muslim World', that is, the aggregate of newly independent Muslim countries, was said to be part of the Third World. There were other categories of division—developed countries, developing countries, and underdeveloped countries; and, sometime later, less developed countries. Sometimes today a line is drawn, or inferred and often taken for granted, between the developed and the 'undeveloped' or 'not-yet-developed', the 'haves and the have nots'. But really, the differences between those who have supposedly made it and those who have not are harder and harder to articulate. It is almost as though the 'developed world' lacks development in certain neighbourhoods while the 'developing world' can equal and even surpass the development of some areas of the 'developed world'. In some cases, the developed world has let its infrastructure go entirely; but looks aren't everything!

The conventional categories of developed, developing, and underdeveloped countries or the first, second, and third worlds are losing their relevance in the face of the weightier concerns. The core, cross-cutting issues afflicting the countries placed in the Third World category—poverty, hunger, illiteracy, disease, climate change, the debt problem, and global militarisation—far from being resolved have become worse. What the sophistication of modern technology and material abundance can achieve for some is even further removed from the life of the poorest than it was at the start of the 'development' decades. But it is important to realise that the three worlds' arrangement was, in fact, an attempt at economic management within one civilisation, that of the West, that embraced and affected all the rest. It made the perpetual accumulation of economic and material resources the major objective of human ingenuity at the cost of too many other necessities, without which material advance loses its meaning and, on the evidence, may be rendered unattainable.

During my university days in the 1970s, the term 'Muslim World' was synonymous with the Third World; the 'too little' countries, in the words of Fanon. But the term was also used in the geographical sense. Conventionally, the Muslim world was the global middle belt stretching from Morocco to Indonesia, and south to north, as far down as Zanzibar to Kazakhstan in Central Asia. To this traditional geographical representation, we added large Muslim communities in the West and other parts of the world. We considered India, which has more Muslims than Pakistan, as part of the Muslim world. The Organization of the Islamic Conference (OIC), as it was then called, introduced the notion of Muslim-majority countries and Muslim minorities. There were long discussions on whether India should be included in the OIC. When we talked of the Muslim world, we meant the general Muslim population of the world.

The notion of 'the Muslim world' has been questioned by the Turkish American historian, Cemil Aydin. In his controversial 2017 study, *The Idea of the Muslim World*, Aydin argues that the term is little more than a product of Western colonialism, designed to sow racial divisions within Muslim subjects of empire and colonies. By the time we enter the twenty-first century, Aydin suggests, the illusion of the Muslim world is deeply entrenched, reinforced by a succession of Islamist and Islamophobic eruptions.[21]

If the Muslim world is a modern concept, then we should not be surprised to note that it is embedded with all the intrinsic ambiguities of modernity—not least imperialism, classism, and racism. Most of Aydin's arguments are based on the 'illusion of unity'—that the Muslim world has never been united, which, given recent history, is almost a truism. However, if the idea of the Muslim world is a modern idea, it cannot be stretched back to the pre-modern times of the early Ottoman Empire or, further back than that, to the formative period of Islam. To suggest that the very notion of a collective Muslim identity is little more than an invention of the colonial powers is not only a grossly sweeping generalisation, but it also denies any agency to Muslims and unfairly labels and consigns Muslim thinkers to the province of racism, chauvinism, or jingoistic xenophobia.

However, we cannot deny that the term has been used by colonial powers to serve their ends, or indeed that certain Muslim politicians or religious authorities have sometimes used it to further their own ends. But this does not mean that it loses its geographical significance. The introduction to Ziauddin Sardar's 1977 book, *Science, Technology and Development in the Muslim World*, has the title: 'What forms the Muslim world?' Sardar is interested in the topographical shape of the Muslim world, and proceeds to examine the science policies of states and communities, with different national and ethnic identities, all claiming to be 'Muslim'. Despite their disunity, which Sardar emphasises, he discovers a worldwide Muslim consciousness.[22] In contrast, the introduction to Aydin's book is entitled: 'What is the Muslim world?'—an entirely different ontological question, which Aydin proceeds to answer with some astute scholarship. But the question 'what is' the reality of the Muslim world does not invalidate 'what forms' that reality, what geographical shape it takes, and what consciousness gives it that form—even though the reality itself may be in a complete and utter mess!

The idea of the Muslim world, I would argue, is intrinsically linked to the idea of the world: what kind of world we wish to make, what kind of world we ought to leave for future generations, and what kind of world would invite the grace of God. How Muslims see the world is how they come to see their own location and responsibility within it. Of course, the idea of the world is based on how we think the world actually works, and that itself depends on our ontological and metaphysical outlook. Which brings us to the notion of the ummah.

III

'The term "Muslim world"', as Aydin notes, 'does not derive from ummah, a concept as old as Islam.'[23] Undoubtedly, the concept of the ummah was problematic for Muslims right from the inception of Islam. When the Muslim community was small, it was easy to see it as a single unit of believers. But the divisions emerged almost immediately after the death of the Prophet—not least with the emergence of the Shi'ites and the Kharijites. The first four caliphs were revered as the rightly guided caliphs of the ummah. They, as well as Caliph 'Umar Abdul Aziz, were considered as the paragons of Muslim leadership following the Prophet Muhammad, setting the gold standard for the administration of state and governance. They were non-hereditary rulers who were, by all accounts, selected on the basis of an electoral process. It is generally agreed that after their reign, governance and the leadership were on the wane. Divisions only multiplied as the territory expanded. What followed, in the shape of the Umayyads and the Abbasid dynasties, was more like empires of antiquity, waxing and waning autocratic tendencies, rather than the system of governance introduced by the Prophet in Medina.

The Abbasids professed to acknowledge the shariah as the rule of life which formed the basis for the Muslim community, the Muslim ummah. Nevertheless, the Abbasids underwent a fundamental shift in creed. So, when the caliph leaned towards the philosophy of the Mu'tazalites, he outlawed the theological school of the Ashari—and vice versa. Even today, this question remains a bone of contention among adherence of the Sunnis. The dispute goes back to the contentious and rancorous 'kalam' debates, which revolved around the fundamental problems concerning the nature of God and God's attributes. The followers of the school of the tenth-century jurist and theologian Abu Mansur al-Maturidi aligned themselves with the Ash'arites. In his Kitab al-Tawhid (Book of Monotheism), al-Maturidi states categorically that iman, faith, consists of the conviction in the heart and affirmation by the tongue. He also subscribes to the doctrine of the pre-eminence of the aql—that is the intellect of capable discernment.[24] Meanwhile the Sufis were frequently declared to be heretics. So different groups were in and out of the ummah from time to time.

The history of Islamic jurisprudence is replete with emotionally charged discourses culminating with charges of heresy, and bid'ah, or pernicious innovation Although Al-Ghazali in his *The Incoherence of the Philosophers* roundly denounced the works of Muslim philosophers,[25] it would be an exaggeration to say that he declared all of them heretics. But just to stretch the argument further, it would be to no avail to say that Ibn Rushd, the twelfth-century rationalist philosopher renowned in the Latin West as Averroes, valiantly came to the rescue of the condemned philosophers, because he himself, having gained the accolade of 'Father of Rationalism', has never been regarded as the ideal referent for orthodoxy.[26] Nevertheless, as American historian Sarah Stroumsa shows in her 1999 book, *Freethinkers of Medieval Islam*, such great freethinkers as Ibn al-Rawandi, who flourished in the ninth century, Al-Kindi, the ninth-century polymath known as 'the father of Arab philosophy', and Abu Bakr al-Razi, the ninth/tenth-century physician and thinker who came to be known in the West as Rahzes, were categorised as heretics—and considered by many to be outside the ummah.[27] To my mind these philosophers placed the faculty of aql as vital in Islamic thought, namely by attempting to integrate Greek philosophy into the mainstream of Islam. No doubt, some orthodox ulama, including Al-Ghazali would cast them outside the ummah in the conventional sense. Nonetheless, contemporary Muslim scholars regard them as contributing a crucial part to the Islamic weltanschauung.

It may well be a category mistake if we seek to define the ummah in terms of what it is, or indeed what it was. The ummah is not an *is* but an *ought* category; and, as an ought category, the ummah cannot simply be based on what is. As a meta concept, it is above the messy, and often unpleasant, reality of the Muslim world—then and now. Moreover, ummah is not about political unity, some utopian caliphate, or a giant polity that enframes the entire Muslim population; nor the demand that all Muslims must express exactly the same confession of faith. As Chandler Barton notes in his review of Aydin's book,

> we must naturally be hesitant to give credence to such a 'No True Musliman' theory because it is not only unrealistic, but also untenable. After all, never in human history has such a hegemonic unity ever existed that the totality of individuals identifying with one particular religion (or any other identifier for that matter) acted or thought in complete solidarity, especially when we are talking about millions or even billions—1.8 to be exact in modern figures—of individuals claiming to be Muslim.[28]

It bears importance here to remember the hadith, 'difference of opinions is a blessing'. It is a misperception to equate unity of the ummah as uniformity of perspectives, approaches, and views. The history of the development of Islamic thought has been underscored by robust contestation of ideas. In practical terms, Islamic governance would warrant inclusivity and accept diversity of perspectives as a source of strength. This would therefore necessitate a governance policy which stresses the importance of tsamuh, tolerance, and incorporate the principle of hasanah, good doing or good deeds, and hikmah, wisdom or reason, in societal dealings and interactions.

As an ought category, the ummah is a metaphysical concept. It is concerned not so much with what the world is, or what political or structural forms it takes, but with what it ought to be. As a metaphysical concept, its meaning cannot be rigidly defined but constantly sought. This, I believe, is what the Qur'an teaches us.

Ummah is a frequently used term in the Qur'an, occurring in sixty-two verses. But the term does not have a single meaning, it changes according to context as we proceed in the chronology of the revelation. To begin with it could simply mean people in general; or more specifically a community. But a more important point to realise is that there is not one but many ummahs. There have been many ummahs in history, and 'God has sent each ummah a messenger' (6:42, 13:30, 16:34, 64). Prophet Abraham represented an ummah himself: 'Abraham was an ummah obedient to Allah, and true to faith' (16:120). The People of the Book, the *ahl-e-kitab*, are an ummah, or at least those who are righteous among them: 'if they had observed the Torah and the Gospel and that which was revealed to them from their Lord, they would surely have been nourished from above them and from beneath their feet. Among them are ummahs who are moderate' (5:66). The ummah can also be a tribe, just like the twelve tribes of Israel: 'there is a group among the people of Moses who guided by truth, and who act justly according to it. We divided them into twelve ummahs' (7:159–60). Then, there is the ummah of the Jinn (7:38), as well as 'all creatures that crawl on the earth and those that fly with their wings are ummah like yourselves' (6:38). But all this diversity of ummahs is not by accident: 'mankind was a single ummah, then God sent prophets to bring good news and warning, and with them he sent the Scripture with the truth, to judge between people in their disagreement' (2:213). The ummah, we learn from the Qur'an, is a dynamic, pluralistic concept with different significance in different contexts.

Moreover, the Qur'an says: 'we have assigned a law and path to each of you. If God had so willed, He would have made you one community (*ummatan wasatan*)' (5:48). It is clear that this verse is addressed not to just one community but to 'each and every' community, dispelling the notion that divine law here (*shir'ah*) refers only to the shariah of the Muslim ummah. This is indicative of God having ordained different ritual and legal formulations for the different religious communities, and each religious community is independent of the laws of other such communities, even if the essential truths and principles are the same.

As such, the ummah does not simply apply to a community of all those who profess to be Muslims. As the righteous among the People of the Book are also ummah (3:115, 5:66, 7:159, 7:168), at the very least the concept suggests that Muslims actively collaborate with Christians and Jews in good deeds and works. The single most important implication of ummah is that it is a moral concept concerning how Muslims should become a network of communities in relation to each other, other communities, and, it must not be left out, the natural world. Manifesting in thought, action, and openness a distinctive moral vision is the raison d'être of the ummah. It is an enduring commitment to the dynamism of a constant set of moral concepts and precepts that creates the contours and ultimate configuration of the ummah.

We should be reminded of the poetic refrain of T. S. Eliot, about 'what might have been and what has been'.[29] And nowhere is the gap between the ideal and the reality demonstrated more profoundly than in Muhammad Iqbal's aspiration, through his poetry, for the universality of the ummah, composed in body and soul of a belief in the unity (*tawhid*) of God, bonded in brotherhood (*ukhwah*) by the message of Prophet Muhammad. The purpose of Iqbal's poetry was to provide a common platform for Muslims—living far and wide, and across geographical, ethnic, cultural, and even temporal boundaries—to come together as an ummah. Indeed, as the late Shahab Ahmed, the noted scholar and author of the monumental 2016 book, *What is Islam?* points out, we cannot 'overemphasise the meaningfulness of the experience of the idea of the universal community of Islam, or of Islam as universal community, in Muslims' conceptualisation of Islam'.[30] It is well and good to proclaim that the ummah is not circumscribed by geographical constructs or that it belongs neither to East nor West nor anywhere in between because it transcends race, colour, or nationality, but ultimately the reality bites hard. I say this less with cynicism than with a deep sense of humility. Thus, when we talk about the ummah, we are not describing the reality of the Muslim world but rather expressing an ideal: that despite the diversity of the Muslim world, differences and contradictions, polities and politics of past and present, the dissensions and discords of history and contemporary times, there ought to be some semblance of unity among Muslims.

This desire to be an ummah stems from a deep-rooted metaphysical and religious concern that binds Muslims, but it does not bind them into a single polity, or even a single community. The ummah is not a cultural entity patterned on the norms of any one dominant group, nor is it the product of cultural contingency. It does not embrace cultural relativism but exists within and is expressed through diverse cultural groups. What binds the ummah, indeed all ummahs, is an ethical consciousness, an awareness that God 'forbids disgraceful deeds—whether they be open or hidden' (7:33). The unifying force of the concept of the ummah is a shared ethical consciousness—whatever the specific beliefs of different individuals who constitute a particular community, or the different polities and politics of different communities, within an international ummah. Moreover, the ummah is not an end point; rather, it is a goal to strive for constantly.

The notion of the ummah has existed as an integral part of Muslim consciousness, seen as trans-geographical in history and as trans-nation-state in modern times. It is a manifestation of the saying of the Prophet that 'Muslims are like a human body, if one part hurts the whole-body suffers'.[31] Ibn Battuta, the fourteenth-century jurist and globetrotter, had a strong sense of ummah consciousness and global solidarity with Muslim communities. This is in fact what enabled him to move from community to community with some ease and without internal angst.[32] Much can be said of other classical travellers, such as the ninth-century geographer, Abu al-Hasan al-Masudi, the tenth-century Turkish intellectual, Muhammad Ibn Hawqal, and the twelfth-century Qur'an scholar from Valencia, Ibn Jubair.

In recent times, the concept of the ummah has periodically played an important part in reviving the spirit of togetherness. For example, after the debacle of the 1967 Arab–Israeli war, King Faisal bin Abdulaziz Al Saud invoked the idea of ummah to bring Muslim states closer together. Despite its shortcomings, the OIC has consistently generated enthusiasm through its discourses on the malaise of the ummah and common determination and commitment to surmount contemporary problems. The notion of the ummah is also constantly invoked by global Muslim charities such as the Red Crescent, Islamic Relief, and

Muslim Aid to galvanise Muslims after disasters to raise money for humanitarian work.[33]

What is urgently needed from institutions like the Organisation of Islamic Cooperation (OIC) is precisely what is needed from Muslim societies themselves. Be that as it may, there are legitimate concerns about the lack of efficacy of some Islamic institutions centred on the limitations of traditions in dealing with contemporary challenges. It is said that our tradition has become fossilised in history and has been transformed into traditionalism: incompatible amalgams of incompatible elements that lack the coherence of a consistently applied dynamic frame of reference. What we have to recover is dynamism, the ability to utilise our tradition as a code for changing things. We need to begin by changing our perception of our own tradition.

That change, I suggest, begins with appreciating that the ummah is not a being but a form of becoming. We need to debate what refines our perception of the ummah and make it more than an abstraction, transforming it into a goal that we constantly seek.

IV

The extrinsic challenges to the Muslim world of today are real, as are the intrinsic weaknesses of the Muslim communities; together they frame the agenda for change. The quality of life in Muslim countries leaves much to be desired. They have one of the highest rates of illiteracy in the world, most notably among women. They are seats of violent social and political upheavals. They present us with the greatest disparity between rich and poor. The dignity of humanity gets mutilated and consistently abused through political repression and rampant corruption. The loss of self-identity is nowhere more apparent than in the Muslim world—where there is a hypocritical abhorrence of

Western tradition and culture in their exhortations, while at the same time an aping of its morally decadent facets and the trivialities of the West in the crudest possible manner. This superficiality was evident even in the Muslim revivalist movements, lending credence to the argument by French political scientist, Bertrand Badie, that the revivalist formula consisted in reinterpreting and remodelling the borrowed elements on the basis of a legitimacy derived from Islam.[34]

Today, Muslim societies, which so superficially absorb and are so deeply affected by the dominant world order, have in several respects become insular, full of contradictions and dichotomies. Conscious of its identity, only to find itself aggrieved, the Muslim world has bred a sense of exclusivity that denies the openness that is an authentic meaning of ummah. It is only through recapturing the dynamic of becoming an ummah that we can open up, liberate ourselves from the stultifying hold of our persecution complex. In seeking to become an ummah, we must see our social structure as an interactive model, a means of relating pluralism within the confines of the diverse professions of a common faith. Ummah consciousness delivers us a universalist outlook that provides the means for existing within a genuinely pluralistic world. It regards intellectual pluralism as consonant with the spirit of the Islamic tradition.

Currently, we are faced with a whole array of challenges for Muslim communities, well-illustrated in the volume *Muslim Societies in Postnormal Times: Foresight for Trends, Emerging Issues and Scenarios*. Problems such as the climate emergency and climate environmental refugees, the degrading of the environment and its impact on liveability, temperature rises, as well as issues with new and emerging technologies such as social media and artificial intelligence, cyberattacks and cyberwars, and genetic engineering, cannot be solved in isolation.[35] They require a coordinated effort in order to be tackled and overcome. Ummah consciousness provides us with a tool both to grasp the truly global nature of these tribulations and navigate our way out to more desirable, sustainable futures. Ummah consciousness can galvanise Muslim communities to work collectively on complex, interconnected problems and issues. The conceptual shift to ummah is also a tool of reason, a source of critical awareness. It calls on us to think differently about our environment because we must now see it as a value—an ethical principle in itself—and through this paradigm of thought to devise new ways of operating that are morally and ethically defensible and sustainable. The ummah, as a network of communities, is required to acknowledge moral and practical responsibility for the Earth as a trust, and its members are trustees answerable for the condition of the Earth. This means ecological concerns and the sustainability of the planet cannot be overlooked. Those countries turning a deliberate blind eye towards these issues need to ponder the dire consequences of their actions. They must be a vital element in our thinking and action, a prime arena where we must actively engage in changing things in rapidly changing times.

Equity and justice are the prerequisites and imperatives of ummah consciousness. This means putting the eradication of poverty at the top of the Muslim agenda and finding means to enable the poor and powerless to work with adequate economic support and dignity. The major challenge is making resources available to assist the poor to attain self-sufficiency, rather than for them to remain in continual dependence. Set against our experience of the failure of the 'development' decades, the applicability of this approach is demonstrable. Of paramount concern is a definitive and comprehensive plan to end the scourge of hunger, famine, want, neglect, and all its horrors are to be abolished.

This does not mean taking on an agenda of reinventing the wheel in terms of the shariah or the Qur'an. It is misguided to make a Muslim Facebook, a Muslim Twitter, a Muslim Amazon, or whatever 'Muslim' version of all the apps available in all the app stores, or even to seek out Muslim AI. Just as it was misguided to create Islamic neoliberal economics or 'Islamic science', which has proven to be ineffective in as much as it only seeks to further isolate our communities from the contemporary world so that we alone may take on the problems of modernity that were imposed by the outside and that in our studies we adopt wholesale. Meanwhile we shun the thought and help of others. This was admittedly a drawback of the 'Islamization of Knowledge' project, launched in the 1970s by the Palestinian American scholar Ismail al-Faruqi, in spite of its pure intentions. The project was in fact laudable as a response of overbearing influence of the West, as it gave a newfound confidence and a sense of cultural empowerment to the ummah. However, as circumstances dictate, the ummah needs a new formulation and paradigm to articulate a comprehensive approach. Such a challenge calls for nothing less than a new synthesis, namely the 'Integration of Knowledge', where knowledge from the West and Islam as well as other cultures and world views come together to form a new synthesis relevant to our times.[36] Ummah consciousness is ultimately a solution to what the renowned Saudi-born Muslim thinker, AbdulHamid AbuSulayman, called the 'crisis in the Muslim mind'.[37]

My old acquaintance, the late AbuSulayman and I had a great chicken-or-egg debate around which strategy was best for confronting the crisis of the Muslim mind. We desired a way to stand against both the *taqlid* (conformity to the teaching of others) of misguided fanatics as well as *talfiq*, the imitation found in grafting Western solutions onto our problems. We needed a new way that brought us back to Islamic values and the Qur'an. We needed to tear down the arid ways of dichotomising good and bad so that we could attain a more sophisticated, moral ethics capable of engaging with the complex, chaotic, and contradictory issues in postnormal times. We worked to become agents of the change we desired. For me, good governance was the key to curing a society's ills. AbdulHamid fervently disagreed. For him, it was a robust education that must come first in order to heal our civilisation. He argued against anyone getting involved in the nasty enterprise of politics. In contrast, I would retort by saying that without good government there is no one to support our new ideas and efforts. Far too many oppressive regimes have stymied the flourishment of the people's minds and their educational systems. I would even invoke the twelfth-century statesman par excellence Salah ad-Din as my prime example of how good governance could change the ummah. Yet, AbdulHamid persisted, without a good education you cannot create the ruling class with the capability to empower educational progress. While our own stubbornness would not see an end to this debate in his lifetime, both of us taking on the career pathways of our convictions, I now see that both ways must be accounted for, *simultaneously*. Ummah consciousness recognises the importance of establishing firm principles for good governance as well as erecting sustainable and resilient educational foundations and infrastructure so that these two can work synchronously to build just futures for all.

Thus, ummah consciousness also makes the eradication of illiteracy a first priority, a moral *jihad*. It is the development tool par excellence, the greatest practical means of enhancing future opportunities and the growth potential of any country. Our concern must then become quality education for life for the new future that we envisage. Appropriate education through appropriate institutions, organisations, and curricula, will demand and facilitate internationalising and synthesising the heritage and fruits of a pluralistic world so that it can be handed on to the next generation as a liveable reality. Only with access to appropriate education can ummah consciousness take root and make possible the ummah of tomorrow, as a personification of the moral principles of Islam endowed with creative, constructive, and critical thought. Just futures for the ummah are not just about material progress but those that manifest in peaceful and inclusive and intellectually progressive ecosystems. Hence, good governance and education should serve as a bulwark against the festering of fanatical and radical world views under the coach of religiosity.

V

The worst nightmare of the late Merryl Wyn Davies, and indeed for all Muslims, in postcolonial times arguably emerged with a vegeance of violent fanaticism during the first two decades of the twenty-first century. All our efforts for education and political reforms, from the 1970s onwards, came crashing down. First, we witnessed the emergence of a radical form of fanaticism, dubbed 'Islamist', that redefined the ummah as an exclusive cult. 'Its own excesses: wanton violence, bullying, unrealistic demands and gross errors of judgement', as described by the Sudanese scholar Abdelwahab El Affendi, led to the nightmare of al-Qaeda in Afghanistan and the Islamic State of Iraq and Syria (ISIS).[38] Then, under the 'war on terror', we witnessed the unravelling of Afghanistan, the destruction of Iraq, the devastation of Libya.

The acts of nineteen men, led by the Egyptian-born hijacker Mohamed Atta, would condemn all of Islam to feed the Western stereotype that Islam was a religion of violence and hate. Our history from the time of the Prophet Muhammad to the classical age, a history that produced great rationalists such as Ibn Sina and Ibn Rushd, brilliant theologians such as Al-Ghazali and Fakhr al-Din al-Razi, and mystics of the calibre of Rumi and Ibn Arabi, was ruthlessly tainted. Osama bin Laden not only saw to the hijacking of four commercial airplanes; he also hijacked our religion, our faith, and tradition. And worse, a world of autocrats of all varieties would exploit this opportunity to oppress their people further. Despite endless conference on the state and plight of the ummah, we failed to arrest the malaise of the ummah that for decades produced the likes of Bin Laden and his proteges. The problem is now prevalent on the global scale.

To promote ummah consciousness there are two important consequences of our recent acquaintance with 'Islamic fundamentalism' that must be overcome. However, there is a general view that we should not fall into the Weberian trap of pigeonholing Islam into stereotypical configurations. Terms such as 'fundamentalist' or 'Islamic fundamentalism' are open to various interpretations and no hard and fast rule prevails. While it may cut across a broad spectrum of organisations and movements that are generally intolerant and exclusivist, some so-called fundamentalists organisations are, in fact, inclusivist or are purely devotional movements. Yet others may be primarily political, some authoritarian, and some violent. Nonetheless, the prevalence of the term 'Islamic fundamentalism' shows, once again, the triumph of reductive labels as a prop of ignorance and a barrier to mutual understanding. Among Muslims, it encourages a confusion that enables redundant and moribund traditionalism to flourish. It enables obscurantism to go unchallenged because it claims a legitimacy that we have not yet learned to debate, let alone deconstruct and think our way beyond. What has come to be seen as Islamic fundamentalism sets a false agenda of peripheral issues as the only topics that get serious and sustained attention. In its conventional understanding, Islamic fundamentalism causes division and engenders unnecessary conflict.

How Islamic fundamentalism has developed among Muslims gives credence to the hysteria of non-Muslim reaction and rejection. The non-Muslim world ignores or misconstrues the genuine concerns of Muslims, to all our detriment. It uncritically accepts all its own stereotypes as well as ignorance of Islam as a vehicle of understanding, to the detriment of all. We even go so far as to dispossess our various communities of their own injustices so that they can become general Muslim injustice, yet we do nothing to resolve the tragedy as it unfolds. In an increasingly interdependent world, we need a new agenda if we are to make peace a reality that is attainable and sustainable, rather than being dragged by our mutual ignorance into crisis after crisis. Fittingly, Edward W. Said's article in *The Nation*, published only six weeks after 11 September 2001, reframed Huntington's thesis and gave it the dressing down it needed a decade earlier.[39]

Certainly, Islamic fundamentalism that is founded on an exclusivist outlook violates the necessary moral meaning of the concept of ummah. It enables some expressions to become Muslim imperialism writ large or writ small. This runs counter to the model of the Medina state under the Prophet Muhammad. Recapturing the contemporary meaning of that model would necessitate that Muslims engage with other people, nations, world views, religions, and ideologies to work for a set of moral objectives that we all agree on, and that we respect the ummah of other people. We have to face our ignorances and admit our uncertainties. It is a concept that first had communal existence in the multicultural and multireligious community of the Medina state, whose written constitution guaranteed the right of continued self-expression and development through its own institutions to its non-Muslim citizens. Islamic history does provide exemplary models of multiracial, multicultural, multireligious, pluralist societies. It is imperative that we recover now, or lose our venture.

The reductionist nature of our view of the world, the dominant neoliberal mode of thought of the past half-century, was a means of perpetuating injustice and the intolerable in the name of laudable objectives. We need to construct a future devoid of one-dimensional reductionism, a plural future where all peoples can flourish and collaborate with fewer false restraints and constraints, fewer misguided impediments. We need to think about the world and ourselves differently to enable positive change to come into being. We need to create the freedom and tolerance for people to think about themselves through their own identity as a moral, sustainable, expressible whole.

The term 'Muslim world' may have been tainted with exclusivist connotations. But the ummah retains its authenticity and power. It does not matter what the 'Muslim world' is, or what form it takes; the ummah is ever present: it is the universal consciousness of Islam and, as such, an integral part of the very being of all Muslims—whatever their sect, ethnicity, nation, or other identity. In these postnormal times, ummah consciousness is an essential requirement for Muslim communities to navigate the great challenges we face. Ummah consciousness will bring our Muslim communities back to the contemporary world in all its rich diversity, but this time with a voice and the agency for change that we always had the capacity for, despite what others have said.

Muslim communities of the world have been rendered more disunited, more fragmented, and brimming with contradictions. We might not be an ummah. But we ought to be. And we need to expand the notion of the ummah to ummahs of other people, as well as the ummahs of flora and fauna of our planet; and learn to recognise them. When cultures and civilisations, or diverse ummahs, meet, they need not clash, or destroy the Earth. We can indeed cooperate and co-create; and fashion an urgently needed new synthesis more appropriate to shaping genuinely prosperous futures for all. For the crisis of all ummahs in postnormal times aligns in our increasingly interconnected world, where Islamophobia and ignorance have been normalised and promoted writ large.

The world, as President Recep Tayyip Erdoğan has stated, is 'bigger than five'.[40] The UN Security Council as presently constituted has now become irrelevant. It used to be the West and the Rest. A body which purports to be democratic and representative of the world has, in reality, ignored the importance and interests of huge segments of our world, such as the Global South and other marginalised states. The question remains open whether this arises by design or out of sheer ignorance. In this vein, the challenge before the ummah is to bring together our myriad of ummahs, transcend the ignorance which separates and rethink its troubling trajectory.

Five

THE ARC OF IGNORANCE

I

Western thought had a rather behemoth learning curve. Nevertheless, as such curves tend to progress, they eventually get where they need to be, equipped with the power to define, and in so doing, to glorify and exalt the road travelled. To this day, university students are bewildered when confronted with cyclical theories of history. In the US, the idea gained currency when the historian Frank J. Klingberg applied it to American foreign policy,[1] launching a long discourse touched on by such American thinkers as the father–son political historian duo, Arthur M. Schlesinger, Sr. and Arthur M. Schlesinger, Jr., the witty political commentator Gore Vidal, and more recently by the political scientist Samuel P. Huntington.[2] The estonishment goes thermonuclear when they learn the famous aphorism, 'those who cannot remember the past are condemned to repeat it', whose attribution is for many, ironically, lost to time. It was actually said first by the Spanish American philosopher George Santayana in 1905.[3] Their classmates in the sciences have a similar epistemological revelation when they come across the philosopher of science Thomas Kuhn and his 1962 game-changing work, *The Structure of Scientific Revolutions*, which applies a cyclical nature to the history of science.[4] Carrying on a bit further and across the Atlantic, the truly astute will read of German philosopher Karl Marx writing of historical materialism, placing a cyclical notion on history along with the interesting precondition of labour, in the late nineteenth century.[5] The fact of the matter is that the genesis of this theory goes to German philosopher Georg Wilhelm Friedrich Hegel, writing at the beginning of the nineteenth century.[6] Yet, the idea of history as cyclical is not a Western idea. Indeed, four centuries before this idea crops up in the 'Western canon', a highly sophisticated cyclical theory of history was developed by the Arab sociologist, philosopher, and historian Abd ar-Rahman Ibn Khaldun in *Al-Muqaddimah*, the introduction of his magnum opus, *Kitab al-'Ibar*, a seven-volume encyclopaedic history of the Arab people.[7]

Even for those students from Muslim societies—from what can be referred to as the 'non-Western' or 'Eastern world', even the Global South—who are not as familiar with Ibn Khaldun's contribution to historiography, many of their histories live this cyclical dynamic.

In as much as dynasties, empires, and sultanates are desitned to rise, they are equally doomed to fall, eventually. This is the essence of the Khaldunian concept of the cyclical nature of history. However, such a conception does not preclude the ability of nations to redeem their destiny through the inclucation of ethics and values. In recent times, the cycles seem less perceptible because of the complexity, gravity, and rapidity of the nature and pace of change. The depths into which we might be presently falling could be far more existential than most have predicted. In the case of postcolonial states, these cycles can also be attributed to the impact of extrinsic forces on the societies and nations that emerged from the ashes of World War II.

THE ARC OF IGNORANCE

In the case of Japan, in the aftermath of the devastating destruction of Hiroshima and Nagasaki, a new face of rebirth took shape in economic advancement that would eventually lead to a recovery of the wider Asian region. As for China, the cycle of history is as unique as it is complex, manifesting extraordinary vibrancy. From Mao Zedong to the Cultural Revolution, the cycle spun into the next phase of exponential prowess under Deng Xiaoping, and after a seeming furlough China under Xi Jinping catapulted into technological advancement becoming a new science and technology superpower. India has experienced its own remarkable trajectory, achieving success in digital transformation and robust growth in human resources. In a similar vein, countries in Southeast Asia, Latin America, and Africa have attained significance progress in their own cycles. Yet others caught in the quagmire of social unrest and civil strife trapped in their erstwhile autocracies.

While recuperating after my surgery in Munich in 2004, I had occassion to contemplate from a different perspective as I transitioned from the solitude of incarceration to the bustle of encounters and engagements with friends from near and afar. It dawned on me, as I pondered over the cycle of past and present events impacting the globe, there is an overarching veil of ignorance that has to be lifted.

II

Ignorance is a powerful entity. It takes on many masks, sometimes appearing benign (sticks and stones), while at other times it is quite homicidal (predator drones and genocides). It travels effortlessly through history. The secret to its success lies in its adaptability and its penchant for evolution. The first two decades of the twenty-first century have been marred by xenophobia writ large. Racism, an evil the West claimed to have defeated by the middle of the 1990s, had reared its ugly face again, demonstrating that it had gone nowhere and only taken on a new mask. Hatred of Asians with all its dastardly roots would make you think it was the age of colonialism all over again, with notions of inferiority and malcontent resurfacing from the sentiments of the generation growing up during and shortly after World War II. The 9/11 attack and the 'war on terror' had provided renewed justification, awakening a sleeping giant of Islamophobia in Europe and allowed the Americans to take it to the level of professionals. Perhaps this age of hate arrived as catharsis for a West that had tried so hard for so long to say it had overcome its own world view; but for us, the Others, the dream of modernity had become a nightmare.

To see how this came to pass, we have to trace back the history of ignorance before it became as brazenly hateful as we see it today. Before Islamophobia and the myriad other words we have for the categorised hate lived between contemporary peoples, there was, seemingly quite innocuous, just ignorance. And like its counterpart, knowledge, ignorance is also constructed. Before there was 'fake news', there were 'fake grand narratives'. They were grand because they moulded world views, disciplines, and the fabric of knowledge. They were false because they were constructed by ignorance. What is known, what we think we know, and what is not known are the result of competing constructs, that of knowledge and that of ignorance. Constructed ignorance becomes pernicious as it begins fabricating views and perceptions of Others—the non-Western peoples and their cultures—even though true knowledge about the Other was known.

The British, for example, knew a great deal about the Malays. Yet, they consciously created the fable of 'slothful natives'. The Spanish dubbed the Filipinos 'indolent'. But as the late nineteenth-century Filipino national hero and polymath José Rizal showed, this ignorant narrative was a product of the system created by the Spanish colonists, an instrument to pacify resistance, a device to keep the Filipinos enslaved.[8] The Spanish described Rizal as a revolutionary: another manufactured ignorance, as Rizal himself denounced violent uprisings and would instead refer to himself as a reformer. He was executed by the Spanish colonists at the tender age of thirty-five, yet had achieved so much in his short life; his knowledge and scholarship were beyond measure and his contributions as a writer, thinker, and artist were titanic. Rizal's life was dedicated to breaking the hold of this narrative through education, as he rightly feared that constructed ignorance would be internalised by his fellow countrymen. Indeed, these colonial projections became so pervasive, and were made so compelling, that they infected the mindset of the colonised elites, which regrettably rubbed off on the masses. In Malaysia, the 'captured elites' who disparaged the masses are exemplified in such works as *Hikayat Abdullah*, by the nineteenth-century Malay writer Munshi Abdullah,[9] and UMNO's *Revolusi Mental*,[10] which promoted the notion that Malay attitudes and negative cultural traits were not conducive to economic development. But the most blatant manifestation of this is Mahathir Mohamad's *The Malay Dilemma*, which purports to lace the colonial mental paradigm with 'scientific' arguments.[11] Its pseudoscientific doctrine has been thoroughly debunked.

The fabrication of Western powers became enduring through a number of rubrics. History (with a capital 'H'): where the history of Western civilisation was presented as Universal History, the apex of human achievements. Anthropology: where non-Western cultures were represented as somewhat inferior, needing guidance, control, and management. Ditto Sociology. And there were also various 'area studies'—African Studies, Asian Studies, Latin American Studies—and 'disciplinary studies' such as Islamic Studies, Chinese Studies, Indian Studies, and Oriental Studies. The cleaving of the world into Occident and Orient

(West and East, civilised and uncivilised, advanced and backward) need not be subtle. The culminating impact of these rubrics was the construction of a vast fabric of ignorance about 'the rest', those other than 'the West'. By the 1980s, this general and widespread misrepresentation of the Other was characterised with a single term: Orientalism.

In the popular academic discourse, Orientalism is associated with the Palestinian American scholar Edward W. Said, who argued that Orientalism was a discourse, 'a political vision of reality whose structure promoted the difference between the familiar (Europe, West, "us") and the strange (the Orient, the East, "them")'.[12] Orientalism derived its legitimacy, and received a boost, from imperialism, anthropology, Darwinism, positivism, utopianism, historicism, Freudianism, and even Marxism. It purported to be a neutral, comparative study of the Orient and Occident but was in fact an expression of power relationships. Said argued that the crucial 'fact' about Orientalist discourse was that knowledge began and ended with the Occident: it knows and parleys about the Orient and Islam, while Muslims can neither comprehend themselves nor have the knowledge and ability to talk about 'others'.

Said's seminal book, *Orientalism*, is a profound critique of Western narratives. His later collection of essays, *Culture and Imperialism*, expanded the theme of colonialism and cultural domination.[13] But Said was not the first to argue or suggest that Western scholars of Islam and Muslim societies, let alone numerous Other societies, were systematically representing the subjects of their studies in a less than favourable light. Indeed, as the Irish writer and academic Fred Halliday has pointed out, 'the critique of Orientalism long pre-dates the publication of Said's work in 1978'.[14] Said was not saying anything particularly new. For example, in his *Western Views of Islam in the Middle Ages*, British historian R. W. Southern described medieval attitudes towards

Islam. In a series of books, such as *The Arabs and Mediaeval Europe*, *Islam, Europe and Empire*, and *Heroes and Saracens*, British historian Norman Daniel provided detailed descriptions and analysis of Christendom and Europe's representations of Islam.[15] But Orientalism was not only a Western study; a number of Muslim scholars had also delineated and examined Orientalism. The 1960s and 1970s saw a number of important texts published on how Islam was represented by Western scholarship. A. L. Tibawi, the Syrian historian and scholar of Islam, argued that Western scholars often projected their own views as though they were facts and then proceeded to draw inferences from them. He offered a masterly dissection of Reverend Alfred Guillaume's translation of the classical biography of the Prophet by Ibn Ishaq, *The Life of Muhammad*. Tibawi showed how certain words were mistranslated to subtly convey notions of violence and misogyny.[16] Often simplistic comparative methodologies were used to expose and show 'defects' within Islam. Hichem Djait, the Tunisian historian and scholar of Islam, offered a philosophical take on Orientalism and suggested that Europe saw its history as unique, and that this perception of 'uniqueness' made Europe 'incommensurable' with other societies, cultures, and civilisations.[17] So, Islam would be seen as inferior by definition and no comparative analysis could be fair or balanced. In *The Myth of the Lazy Native*, the Malaysian sociologist Syed Hussein Alatas showed that European scholars, writers, and colonial administrators consistently represented the Muslims of Southeast Asia in demeaning terms, often describing them as lazy, fatalists, dull, and backward. Much of this representation, Alatas asserts, was 'vulgar fantasy', based on 'untruth' and, in some truly troubling cases, even sophisticated scholarship.[18] Anouar Abdel-Malek, the Egyptian political scientist, argued that European scholarship treated the Muslims as a passive, non-autonomous 'object' of study inscribed by Otherness. Both Islam and Muslim societies were seen as unchanging, buried in history, museum pieces. Arabic, for example, was studied as though it was a dead language.[19] As such, the assumption was that Muslims were not capable of social or moral evolution.

The intellectual history of Orientalism not only reaches beyond Said, but it also has a history that goes right back to the formative phase of Islam. The image of Muslims as depraved, licentious, violent, and unclean can be traced back to the eighth century to the Arab Christian monk John of Damascus, who had an intimate knowledge of Islam. He declared Islam to be a pagan cult, the *Kaaba* to be an idol, and described the Prophet in deragatory terms. The writings and denunciations of John of Damascus became the conventional source for all Christian works on Islam during the medieval period. John of Damascus's judgement of Islam is not surprising: he saw Islam as a major threat to Christianity. Islam presented a theological problem. Why was a new prophet necessary when God's own son had died for the sins of humanity? During the medieval period, Europe was largely rural, feudal, and monastic. In sharp contrast, Islam had produced great cities and architecture, knowledge and learning, and wealth and modes of communication. So, Islam became an economic and intellectual challenge as well. And, of course, there was the military threat. These challenges were met through the production of a picture of Islam that was diametrically opposite to Christianity. Since Christianity emphasised forgiveness, Islam was depicted as being based on vengeance. While Christians turned the other cheek, Muslims had to be violent. While Jesus was the Son of God, 'Mahomet' was the Antichrist. Islam thus became a sinister conspiracy against Christianity. During the Crusades, there was a feedback loop: the images propelling the Crusades, and the Crusades in turn enhancing the representations.

As the religious threat transmuted into a cultural threat throughout the Middle Ages, Islam was commonly perceived and represented as the darker side of Europe. Popular medieval literature such as *chansons de geste*, an early style of epic poetry in France, and the 'Song of Roland' in England, popularised stories of Muslims and 'Saracens' that were based on prejudice and hostility as well as lies and fantasy. And the same images found their way into more sombre literature such as Dante Alighieri's *The Divine Comedy*, historical studies like Simon Ockley's *History of the Saracens*, works of serious thinkers such as Roger Bacon, as well as scholarship and travel literature. Towards the end of the sixteenth century, when the Ottoman Empire was going through revolts and reversals, the West equalled the achievements of Islam. Just think about the narrative around the 'sick man of Europe'. The Ottomans' only solace was to be found in adopting and assimilating what was European or Western. It was Western culture and roots and beliefs about Islam that kept it 'sick' with one foot in the grave. By the beginning of the eighteenth century, Europe had surpassed the Muslim world in military and industrial technology, economic development and civic institutions, and thought and learning. The age of imperialism and empire solidified old myths about Islam as well as creating new ones.

Said's focus in *Orientalism* is on colonial output, although he does mention a few early representations of Islam in passing. As such, he does not offer a broad historic picture of how first Christendom and then Europe created and projected demonised images of Islam and Muslims. So the question of 'where did Orientalism originate?' is neither raised nor answered. Unlike previous scholars who used methodologies of their own disciplines, Said used literary criticism as a tool to deconstruct something specific: 'the Orient'.[20] This is both the strength and weakness of *Orientalism*. By concentrating on so-called literary texts, *Orientalism* ignores what popular culture and fiction had to say about Islam and Muslims. Also, literary criticism presents

Orientalism as an unchanging discourse. This is further demonstrated by the static and repetitive output of the legions of Said devotees—the so-called 'Said industry'. Orientalism is presented as timeless and fixed: just as Orientalism itself saw Islam! Moreover, as the British scholar on representation, Michael Richardson, has pointed out, in Said's thesis the Orient (the object) cannot challenge the subject (the Orientalists) by developing alternative models of representation. In fact, Richardson notes, 'since the object has no real existence, being only a conceptualisation of the subject's mind, it can never be a question of the former acting upon the latter'.[21] The only way out of this impasse is for the subject to represent the object more faithfully. In short, the Muslims will always be at the mercy of the Orientalists. As the British Czech philosopher Ernest Gellner has argued, 'the problem of power and culture, and their turbulent relations during the great metamorphosis of our social world, is too important to be left to lit crit'.[22]

During the 1980s and 1990s, both the Orientalists and the Saidians received support for their positions. The Iranian Revolution, the affair surrounding the publication of Salman Rushdie's *The Satanic Verses*, and the rise of fundamentalism in Muslim societies strengthened the view that Islam was an unchanging, violent, and authoritarian ideology. The advent of postmodernism, with its emphasis on discourse analysis, subjectivity, and dethroning grand narratives, provided support for the academic industry that was building around Said. In the beginning, there was hope that finally Orientalist narratives could be upended and done away with. Emerging disciplines such as cultural studies and postcolonial studies entrenched Said's position and linked it to the French philosopher often associated with postmodernism, Michel Foucault, via theories of discourse and power. Yet, apart from providing the concept of discourse, Foucault is, in Richardson's words, 'a rather minor player in

Said's book'.[23] By now, 'Theory' itself—much like postmodernism—had become an oppressive structure, generating much heat, countless texts, but adding little insight. After all, to say there are no grand narratives, is, itself, a grand narrative.

III

Ziauddin Sardar challenges the limitations of Said's theory in his 1999 book, aptly titled *Orientalism*. Sardar argues that Orientalism is a changing and evolving discourse. The nature and character of Orientalist discourse changed in the mid-twentieth century and then again, quite radically, in the late 1990s and early 2000s. Early and mid-twentieth-century Orientalists were concerned with improving the Muslim world by exposing its traditionalism and making it 'modern'.[24] This can be clearly seen in such works as William Cantwell Smith's *Islam in Modern History*, H. A. R. Gibb's *Modern Trends in Islam*, and Philip K. Hitti's *Islam and the West*.[25] Modernity thus became the yardstick by which Islam and Muslims were measured, and the spirit of Eurocentrism was kept alive by the kind of questions the Orientalists raised. The main thesis, in reality merely a reformulation of the old one, was that Islam was incompatible with the modern world, and the assertion was justified by attempts to prove the intrinsic inferiority of Islam *vis-à-vis* modernity. To give their arguments some validity, the Orientalists often had to present a total inversion of reality. Or, perhaps because of the assumptions buried in their methods of identifying and describing, which were laden with all the old Orientalist values, they could only see reality upside down. So, we find W. Cantwell Smith describing the *Ikhwan al Muslimun* (the Muslim Brotherhood) in Egypt as emotionally bereft folks driven by 'the hatred, the frustration, vanity and destructive fury of a people who for long have been prey to poverty, impotence and fear'. The 'modern world is too much for them, they are incapable of solving modern problems and prefer to intoxicate those who can no longer abide the failure to solve them'.[26] Questions arise as to why Cantwell Smith has nothing to say about the fate of Sayyid Qutb and other members of the Muslim Brotherhood under President Gamal Abdel Nasser. Philip Hitti's works, standard texts in the 1950s and 1960s, presented similar arguments. In *Islam and the West*, he argued that Islam could not make any contribution to the modern world; it would promote only ignorance and dogmas that stifled intellectual activity.

In contrast, the Orientalist discourse of the 1990s and early 2000s saw and represented Islam as a clear and present danger to the West and, by extension, the world. In 1993, Samuel P. Huntington divided the world into 'civilisation identities'—Western, Islamic, Chinese, Hindu, and so on. While Western civilisation was hitherto seen as Universal, Huntington suggested that there was no other Universal civilisation, only cultural blocks, each with its distinctive world view and values, fighting among each other.[27] The most dangerous was the Islamic civilisation, with its blood-soaked borders and culture that was openly hostile to liberal values such as individualism, democracy, and pluralism. A clash was looming between Islam and the West, and the best thing the West could do was either to keep away or to contain Islam. Bernard Lewis, who originally coined the term 'clash of civilization', concurred. In a series of books that fed the Islamophobic mindset, including *What Went Wrong?* and *The Crisis of Islam*, Lewis argued that the West was now engaged in a last-ditch final clash with Islam. Osama bin Ladin, the leader of al-Qaeda, he suggested, was not an extremist but represented the mainstream Islamic position. The Americans, who traced their lineage to the Crusades, could not flinch now but must take on Islam head-on.[28] Thus, the intellectual justification for the 'war on terror' was laid. Interestingly, just after 9/11, Said himself struck back at Huntington in his own article titled 'The Clash of Ignorance', where he largely debunks the 'Clash of Civilization' thesis, noting how it is not necessarily something 'new', and that identity is far more complex than Huntington describes. Said calls the 'Clash of Civilizations' a 'gimmick' that is 'better for reinforcing defensive self-pride than for critical understanding of the bewildering interdependence of our time'.[29] But definitely by 2001, Orientalism had gotten away from Said; but he was right, the clash of ignorance carried on none the wiser.

In the last decades of the twentieth century, postmodern Orientalism had emerged to command the discourse. Given the basic assumption of postmodernism that 'grand narratives' are irrelevant and meaningless, and that Islam itself is a grand narrative, it should not surprise us that postmodern thinkers and writers have not looked at Islam with favour, or with much regard at all. Just in time for Salman Rushdie to use magical realism to deconstruct Islam as a meaningless and warped religion in *The Satanic Verses*. However, despite *The Satanic Verses*, Muslim academics such as Akbar S. Ahmed saw postmodernism as a liberating force—perhaps because of its concern for the marginalised Other, for decentring the subject, for its emphasis on plurality, or its emphasis on irony.[30] But these are side issues. The true irony of postmodernism is that Western culture rediscovers Otherness and its Eurocentric perspective through marginality. It seeks to negate history and historic identity through amnesia. As Sardar argued, postmodernism seeks to consume the Other; its aim is to drain every ounce of spirituality from Islam and render it totally secular. How various tropes of Orientalism became integral to postmodernism has been well illustrated by the American literary scholar Ian Almond.[31] There is one classic trope, that of forgetfulness—for which read erasure. Just as Orientalist historians of science conveniently forget about the history of Islamic science and assume that nothing happened between classical Greece and the Enlightenment, Foucault forgets the simple fact that the world exists outside 'the Occident', sees the Iranian uprising as 'a single people crying with a single voice', and juxtaposes an unchanging Orient against an inventive, moving West. When it comes to Islam, the French deconstructionist philosopher Jacques Derrida too suffers from amnesia; the only place where philosophy can measure up to the challenges of our times, he thinks, is Europe. Even Slavoj Žižek, a philosopher loved by naive undergraduates, influenced by Hegel's deeply embedded Eurocentrism like Derrida, projects nihilism onto Islam. Almond's assessment of postmodern theorists is quite devastating:

> Nietzsche and Foucault seldom appear more European than when they write about the necessity of thinking like an Oriental or the millennium-old immobility of Islam. What Islam also does, however, is reveal the *secular* premise of postmodernity—or rather, Islam shows how the rejection of the transcendental in postmodernity is just as concentrated as it is in modernity. Be it within the pages of *The Antichrist*, Derrida's seminars on religion or *The Gulf War Did Not Take Place*, it is striking how *social* Islam is, how little the God of Islam is mentioned. If Islam has any interest at all for these thinkers, it is as a purely *anthropological* phenomenon, a cultural manifestation, an object of primarily material significance.[32]

A more recent variant of Orientalism may be described as the 'new rhetoric'. It comes in the shape of not scholarly but polemical works, with the aim of persuading the reader that Islam is out of sync with Western liberal and secular values by means of pretentious arguments, truths, half-truths, and falsehoods all wrapped in rhetorical flashes. However, just because the goal is to persuade, rather than downright demonisation, it does not mean that this discourse is less potent. Indeed, any attempt to persuade a falsehood is an act of violence. The rhetoric of the New Atheists, such as Richard Dawkins and Sam Harris, is an obvious example. New Atheism, as British journalist Andrew

Brown notes, began as a social rather than a scholarly or an intellectual movement. It is based on two intellectual novelties. First, 'the doctrine that moderate religious believers are actually more wicked and dangerous than those who burn witches or blow-up children'. Second, 'that the world works according to a few simple and comprehensive explanations'. Gross scientific, pseudoscientific, historic, and sociological explanations are used to suggest that there is little or no distinction between a God-fearing, law-abiding Muslim and a psychotic criminal. Much of the new rhetoric output, such as Richard Dawkins's *The God Delusion* or Christopher Hitchens's *God Is Not Great*, which are aimed as much at Christianity as at Islam, or that of the Somali-born Dutch American writer Ayaan Hirsi Ali, a critic of Islam and dabbler in right-leaning Dutch politics, decried Islam as 'the new fascism' that has to be eradicated.[33] While atheism, new or otherwise, remains in conflict with all religious traditions, it is often pursued with an incapacity for completely shedding its Eurocentric epistemological cloak. And while all religion is 'irrational', some, especially Islam, are more dangerously irrational than others. Overall, their book titles are eye-catching but their words, intended to be provocative, fall short of coherence—rather infantile stuff. But a more sophisticated example, aimed directly at Islam, is provided by the English writer Tom Holland's *In the Shadow of the Sword*.

Ostensibly, Holland, a student of the late Danish historian Patricia Crone, co-author of the highly discredited *Hagarism* (which suggested that Islam was inspired by Jewish messianism, that Prophet Muhammad was a Jewish messiah, and that the Qur'an was revealed and elided in the eighth century), is concerned with the role of God and religion in shaping the history of the religion. But the real aim of *In the Shadow of the Sword* is to examine the validity of 'Muslim sources' and to assess the extent of Muslim scholarship down the centuries. He begins by raising a number of legitimate questions. What do we know about Muhammad? Are the sayings attributed to him reliable? What is the origin of the Qur'an? How much of the history produced by Muslims can be trusted? His answer is to present a revisionist history based almost exclusively on the work of a largely discredited group of Orientalists. In the process, he pours scorn on Muslim scholarship, which is declared unsound, if not totally worthless, and lays into classical Muslim biographers and historians. Dubious, simplistic explanations, based on the work of Crone, suggest that Islam is other than what Muslims say it is. So, the Qur'an was not revealed in Mecca and Medina but in Syria, as Crone once absurdly suggested, or perhaps in Palestine. Mecca was not on any trade routes, so maybe it was portrayed as a 'booming town' by Muslim historians to glorify the city of Muhammad's birth. Given that Ibn Ishaq says in *The Life of Muhammad* that the Battle of Badr was won with the help of God and His angels, Holland claims that he cannot be regarded as objective or be trusted. Ibn Ishaq, the first biographer of the Prophet, must be disregarded; and given that he is a primary source for the biography of the Prophet Muhammad, the whole of the *Seerah*, the traditional collected biographies of the Prophet, is suspect. Since much of what Muslims know about Muhammad is based on Ibn Ishaq's work, the conclusion that follows is that we know next to nothing about Muhammad.[34]

While *In the Shadow of the Sword* has a better mastery of language than your run-of-the-mill popular atheist works, it is not a scholarly work. It is a polemic against Islam masquerading as popular history. Holland does not directly say that Muhammad did not exist; nor that he is simply a product of Muslim imagination. But he does say that 'the total absence of any early Muslim reference to Muhammad' suggests he may not be real. His name on public monuments only appears in 690, around fifty-eight years after his death. This is enough to cast doubt.[35]

The aim is to persuade people that the Islamic narrative is potentially false, and, as such, Muslims know next to nothing about themselves. It is a clever and dastardly strategy used by cheap defence lawyers who sow doubt to help guilty men escape justice. Present a hint of doubt and let the incoherence of the masses unravel the whole enterprise.

The theory and analysis of Orientalism in academia focussed on what we may call 'highbrow' content: academic treatises, serious novels, travel literature, memoirs, and musings cast as 'reports' of colonial administrators. Said made it clear that he had no time for popular culture. Yet, as the Iraqi British expert on Islam in Western popular culture, Anas Al-Shaikh-Ali, argues so convincingly, it is popular culture—films, TV shows, and in particular popular fiction, what he refers to as the 'airport novel'—that 'defines cultural identity and shapes public opinion to an extent that is self-evident and to a degree that is alarming'.[36] As envisaged by Said, Orientalism was a narrow, rather limited discourse. It treated all Orientalists with a single brush. It would be a gross injustice to think that all Orientalists were hell-bent on misrepresenting Islam. There were quite a few who made valuable contributions not just to the scholarship of Islam but also to our appreciation of the rich and diverse history of Islam. Some excelled at empirical work and have left esteemed legacies. One cannot, for example, compare a historian like Franz Rosenthal or Robert Irwin with the likes of Sir William Muir, or treat A. J. Arberry and W. Montgomery Watt in the same way as Philip K. Hitti and W. Cantwell Smith. There are, indeed, 'good' Orientalists just as there are 'bad' ones. Moreover, new expressions of hatred towards Islam and Muslims are also described as 'Orientalism'—which simply muddies the waters. There is, I would argue, not one, single, monolithic, Orientalist discourse. There is a string of discourses that aim to denigrate Islam and cast Muslims as the dark and deranged opposite of

Western liberalism. This string is complexly interwoven with the other discourses around what is and who are the East. Some of them can be described as Orientalism; some not. Some pursue a discussion of the Orient using robust methods of scholarship, some do the same to fulfil prophecies of racism and to slander the Other. However, not all anti-Muslim diatribes can be elevated to the august level of a discourse. And Orientalism is not the only mask that ignorance has worn.

IV

Where Orientalism remains confined within the dignified space of academia, another form of constructed ignorance has taken off from where Orientalism left off, that is now unfettered and capable of spreading hate down to everyday actions and attitudes: Islamophobia. The term is hotly contested but not altogether new. The Spanish historian Fernando Bravo López has suggested that it was first used in 1910 by the French colonial officers Maurice Delafosse and Alain Quillien. It was also used by the French painter Nasreddine (Alphonse-Etienne) Dinet, who painted some of the most memorable images of Mecca in the early twentieth century. Dinet used the term in a biography of the Prophet Muhammad, co-written with Algerian intellectual Sliman ben Ibrahim, to describe the attitude of Orientalists like the twentieth-century Belgian historian Henri Lammens, who sought nothing less than the total removal of Islam from the face of the Earth. Lammens abused the Prophet, describing him as a voluptuous imposter, considered the Seerah to be a novel, and endlessly lamented the Arab victory in the seventh century which led to the contraction of Eastern Christianity. By all standards, Lammens was a nasty, hateful person and Dinet and Ibrahim saw him as someone whose output was inimical to Islam. (I wonder what Dinet thought of fellow French painter Eugène Delacroix, who portrayed Muslims as cruel and obsessed with sex and violence.) The term hovered in the background for much of the twentieth century.[37] It came to the forefront in the 1990s thanks largely to 'Islamophobia: A Challenge for Us All', a report by the Commission on British Muslims and Islamophobia, set up by the Runnymede Trust in the UK.[38] Despite the suggestions that it undermined legitimate criticism of Islam, the term has, to use the words of British human rights philosopher, Brian Klug, 'come of age'. Klug also suggests that Islamophobia is not the same as anti-Semitism. There is no equivalent of the 'hidden hand of Jews' controlling and orchestrating international finance. Neither are the Muslims represented as 'Christ killers'. There is no grand Muslim conspiracy; in terms of both Orientalism and Islamophobia, Muslims would be incapable of pulling off such a trick.[39] Anti-Semitism is, of course, a constructed ignorance worthy of its own deep study. The British writer Antony Lerman's *Whatever Happened to Antisemitism?* and the works of Israeli historian Shlomo Sand have done a good job in critically analysing that particular brand of xenophobia.[40]

Unlike Orientalism, Islamophobia is neither limited to the Western gaze nor to scholarly and literary texts. It is a global phenomenon—as rampant in Europe and America as it is in India, Russia, and Australia. We find it in a plethora of discourses: not just in literature but also in popular airport fiction, not just in identity politics and national debates but also in multicultural sermons, not just in feminism (of all waves) but also in debates on sexual orientations. It is as common in right-wing as it is in left-wing circles. The neoconservatives of the West, the Christian Zionists longing for Christ's return to earth, born-again Christians who replaced 'godless communists' with 'Islamic devils' in their pursuit of US global domination—all provided legitimacy for the liberal portrayal of Islam as a diabolical evil. The connecting arc is clear, and the Islamophobe would see nothing wrong with using the work done by Orientalists to per-petuate and justify their warped world view.

Consider some of the major Islamophobic events of recent times. There was *Fitna*, the 2008 short film by the right-wing Dutch politician and leader of the far right Party for Freedom (PVV), Geert Wilders. The seventeen-minute film was designed to project the Qur'an as a text that sanctions and justifies vio-lence and terrorism against all.[41] This was followed by the Danish cartoon affair, which was followed by the less-known Swedish cartoon issue where caricatures of the Prophet Muhammad, depicting him with a body of a dog, were commis-sioned and displayed in an art gallery. Both the Swedish and Danish cartoons were republished a number of times, in news-papers and magazines. Then we had the Charlie Hebdo affair, which began with the publication of ferocious caricatures of Prophet Mohammad, designed to incite, and ended with an attack on the offices and murder of the editors of the magazine in January 2015. The emerging 'Je suis Charlie' movement estab-lished, as Emmanuel Todd writes, that to be a French Muslim you had to acknowledge not just that 'you had the right to blas-pheme, but that it was your duty'.[42] Disturbingly, mass burnings of the Qur'an have also gained in frequency in recent times. American members of the military and evangelical Christians took to the practice as if it were another common ritual following the 11 September attacks of 2001. Most infamously, the pastor Terry Jones of the Dove World Outreach Center, an ironically named church in Gainesville, Florida, spawned riots around the world when he announced plans to host a public burning of the Qur'an on the anniversary of the attacks in 2010. Then Secretary of State Hillary Clinton had to make a personal call to Jones to talk him down from the demonstration. Twelve people in Afghanistan died as a result of those riots and Jones never got round to actually burning the Qur'an.[43] Qur'an burnings in

Denmark between 2017 and 2023 sparked a national debate about the application of its domestic blasphemy laws, which had lapsed in usage since the 1990s. Sweden was at a loss when a series of Qur'an burnings perpetrated by the far right Danish political party, Stram Kurs, could not be prosecuted under the country's laws against incitement of ethnic or racial hatred. Critique or desecration of religious items was the loophole for that law.[44] In response to these burnings, one of my first acts as prime minister of Malaysia was to print and distribute one million copies of the Holy Qur'an around the world.[45] Islamophobia even entered the realm of Western domestic policy with the powers afforded the US government following the Patriot Act legislation of 2001 and the UK's Prevent programme, an anti-terrorism and anti-extremism campaign. Both policies have been heavily criticised for instigating and perpetuating Islamophobia.

These may all look like separate events, the work of a few individuals or fringe groups with a particular dislike of Islam or need to blame Islam generally for a wrong committed. But there is an assimilationist logic at work here that leads to coordinated and systematic desecration of Islam and Muslims. The 2008 report from the UK's Institute of Race Relations, *Integration, Islamophobia and Civil Rights in Europe*, points out that incidents of Islamophobia are not random and sporadic; the phenomenon of Islamophobia finds its origin in an integration agenda. The report studied six European countries. The media of these countries confines integration within a framework which represents Muslims as an alien threat, leading to a predominance of 'scare scenarios'. This feeds into the fears and conspiracy theories of political parties and other interest groups, which ultimately seek a return to monocultural societies based on cultural homogeneity. Politicians, populists, writers, intellectuals, as well as Muslim and ex-Muslim celebrities who favour assimilation, such as Ayaan Hirsi Ali and Norwegian comedian Shabana Rehman, are then presented as 'expert witnesses' in the integration debate. The entire process not only inflames Islamophobia, but Muslims are also blamed for the social and economic malaise of society and for their own exclusion and marginalisation. In most European countries, integration is simply a euphemism for assimilation, says the report.[46]

The extent of assimilation involved in various policies of 'integration' from country to country, depends to a large extent on the country's particular history with its Muslim minorities. But the driving force for assimilation is the notion of a purist nation and national culture. And much of it bears the familiar undertones of fascism. In Germany, it expresses itself as blood-based citizenship and *Leitkultur* (the guiding dominant culture), and in France as citizenship by birth and earth and *laïcité* (secularism). Norway has the idea of *likhet* (sameness), while the Netherlands has *verzuiling* (vertical separation of citizens into religious and political groupings). One would expect the extreme right to embrace such notions. But the report finds that centre-left parties also use these racist sentiments in their political strategies. European left and centre-left parties may be liberal when it comes to immigration, but when it comes to Muslim communities they fall prey to Islamophobic tendencies, 'nourished by a mixture of feminism and secularism'.[47] Thus, Islamophobia emerges not from a reasonably lucid discourse but from an irrational fear of being swamped by people with an inferior culture and values.

The irrational absurdity of Islamophobia reaches its peak where the sentiment used to demean a people, its cultures, and its values as backward, in the same breath gives legitimacy to crazed conspiracy narratives that cast Islam as a plot against the West. They may be inferior, but the Muslims are out to destroy the West through a variety of nefarious means such as accelerating birth rates, immigration, and introducing the phantasmic

'Shariah Law'. The same people they have claimed to be the savages of the world, living in 'stone-aged' conditions, are suddenly the new conquerors and political back-door gatekeeping elites. And now they will stop at nothing less than the creation of 'Eurabia'. 'As a conspiracy theory', notes the Norwegian social anthropologist Sindre Bangstad, 'it is non-refutable on factual and empirical grounds to those who happen to believe in it, for those who do argue against it are often cast as part of the conspiracy itself.'[48] The term 'Eurabia' was first used by the extreme right-wing Italian feminist Oriana Fallaci in 2004.[49] It was later systematised by the nonagenarian far right Cairo-born Swiss Israeli author Bat Ye'or (pseudonym of Gisèle Littman) in her 2005 book, *Eurabia: The Euro-Arab Axis*. It was readily embraced by the extreme right in Europe and the US.[50] A string of books with Eurabia in the title have been written by French, Dutch, Norwegian, and Belgian right-wing conspiracy theorists. Not to be outdone, the American conspiracy theorists—such as Frank Gaffney, Pamela Geller, Robert Spencer, Steven Emerson, and Brigitte Gabriel—have produced an avalanche of books propagating Islamophobia, xenophobia, nationalism, extremist Protestantism, Zionism, and racism. Despite this they were seen as 'fringe' writers. But as Abigail Hauslohner pointed out in the *Washington Post*, the election of Donald Trump as the Forty-Fifth President of the United States, brought them into the mainstream.[51] Perhaps the biggest champion of this thesis is the foaming-at-the-mouth right-wing British journalist and commentator, Douglas Murray. He has provided intellectual justification for conspiracy narratives in his book *The Strange Death of Europe: Immigration, Identity and Islam*. The point to note about these conspiracy narratives is not just that they are based on an extreme, fanatical hatred of Islam but they also actively seek the destruction of the very House of Islam.[52] These authors have served as cheerleaders for the re-emergence of not just far right but fascist movements in Europe and the US. And these movements no longer exist on the periphery or as fledgling organisations. They are winning seats in various parliaments, even entering into coalition governments. The parliament of the European Union is infested with politicians of this ilk.

Yet, Islamophobia not only arises from the outside, but also from the inside. A fair discourse of Islamophobia cannot take place in the absence of an objective interrogation of Muslims themselves. It cannot be denied that the propensity towards violence on the part of some Muslim groups, due to ignorance, or distorted views of Islam, has also contributed to the rise of Islamophobia. The ignorant actions of Muslims as individuals as well as within our communities can create just as much Islamophobia as has been produced by others. This ignorance is like a festering disease born of distorted interpretations of the Qur'an, the conflation with violence, terrorist acts accompanied by outward Muslim displays of religiosity. And these problems will persist unless we address them in a rational and concerted way. A true discourse of Islamophobia cannot take place in the absence of introspection from Muslims themselves. It cannot be denied that several major factors contribute to Islamophobia, such as a propensity for violence due to hypersensitivity (an effect of the phenomenon of 'princeling' parenting and other modes of propagating fragile masculinity within our communities), intolerance due to a lack of education, and ideological rigidity. Our own extremist and fundamentalist groups, often conforming to close-minded, xenophobic tendencies, are fostering the Islamophobia narrative and often doing the most damage in cultivating ignorance. Islamophobia is not just a product of internal and external social dynamics; the world around us is changing at such a pace, in such a chaotic manner, that even as we work among and between ourselves, we must be wary of larger looming threats.

Ignorances, conspiracy theories, and blatant lies are taken to a new level in the age of Post-Truth, where fake news can spread anti-Muslim narratives at super speed thanks to social media and our hyperconnected lives. It is not a new phenomenon that conventional, established news sources, both networks and online or print media, have some degree of bias and their leanings are not subtle. But now, new alt-right websites and news sources such as Breitbart, Infowars, Fox News, and GB News specifically push anti-Muslim and other xenophobic conspiracy theories. Network predelictions have pushed many to pursue more independent means. Some prominent journalists have moved to more independent formats, taking more objective perspectives. The ability to share their content across multiple social media platforms represents a quantum leap for the dissemination of these narratives. This is taken to an industrial scale when troll farms or cybertroopers, something that all countries and many influential individuals have access to (and, by common parlance, should never leave home without!), work to perpetuate rapid-fire content beyond the traditional notion of 'trending' or 'going viral'. The cycle is perpetuated by such platforms as X (formerly Twitter), where tweets containing falsehoods are 70 percent more likely to get retweeted than verified truthful tweets. When reputable and respectable news sources then share what initially started as lies, opinions, or conspiracy theories, then the quote made famous by the chief propagandist of the Nazi Party of Germany, Joseph Goebbels, becomes all the more prescient: 'A lie told once remains a lie, but a lie told a thousand times becomes the truth.'[53] It makes me wonder how many times a lie needs to be retweeted before it ends up on the front page of once respectable newspapers such as *The Washington Post*, *Times of India*, *The New York Times*, or *The Wall Street Journal*, or is broadcast on what were hitherto regarded as trustworthy sources, the BBC, Sky News, CNN, or France24? Not many from my reading! And, sadly, many of these lies and conspiracy theories that are going viral are Islamophobic at their heart. Indeed, some newspapers, such as the UK's *Daily Telegraph* and *The Mail*, and a host of newspapers in India, push a regular diet of xenophobic, anti-Islamic rhetoric.

All this suggests that the anti-Muslim landscape has changed: it has become complex, industrial, global, and regularly sprouts new varieties. There is an arc of anti-Islamic discourses and narratives from John of Damascus to Orientalism, neo-Orientalism and postmodern Orientalism to Islamophobia and new rhetoric, all the way to conspiracy theories, false news, and post-truth bile. As Al-Shaikh-Ali states, 'the historical Islamophobia is informing contemporary Islamophobia, which, in turn, is affecting individuals, communities, and nations by sowing the seeds of future conflict and instability'. The seeds bear fruit, and outbursts of Muslim hatred and accompanying discourse/narrative appear whenever the Occident or Christendom, Europe, the US, or the West, feels a real or perceived threat to its power and hegemony. This often triggers a feeling in the West that necessitates an extension of its influence. For example, during the Crusades, the imperial expansion of Europe, and the colonial period; after the 1857 Independence struggle in India and, more recently, after the emergence of OPEC, the Iranian Revolution, the Rushdie affair, 9/11, ISIS, even the global refugee crisis and the Covid-19 pandemic. Before too long, climate change may even be used as an excuse for the West to flex its muscles and perpetuate further Islamophobia. Every now and then, there is a turning point before which things are relatively calm and after which change is rapid and the floodgates open. One of the major turning points in recent times occurred, as Al-Shaikh-Ali notes, in the 1970s, after which we had a string of interconnected events that fed on each other and accelerated the disparagement of Islam and Muslims:

> the 1967 and 1973 Arab-Israeli wars, the oil embargo, the Lebanese civil war, the Iranian revolution, the hostage crisis, the recession of the

early eighties, the two Gulf wars, as well as the tragic events of 9/11, and the invasion of both Afghanistan and Iraq, focussed global attention on the Middle East and Islam and Muslims as never before.[54]

V

Two key observations can be taken away from this historical analysis. First, the underlying motivation is always the same: fear. Fear that the Christian/European/Western culture and values are not the Universal with a capital 'U'. Fear that they are not the Truth with a capital 'T'. Fear that they are not the beginning and end of Civilisation, Progress, or globally accepted as History. Fear that global power is shifting towards Asia. Fear that the world has become complex and is not amenable to standard Western answers and solutions. Fear of collapsing dominant paradigms. Fear of the increasing diversity and multiculturalism of our planet. Second, this fear is rooted in ignorance, not simply the not-knowing, but the refusal to know. The arc of ignorance has evolved from anti-Muslim fear of the Other to Orientalism to Islamophobia in a variety of shades to allow for leaps of logic and to sidestep contradictory sentiments. Notice how much passionate anti-Muslim and Islamophobic revulsion comes from paranoid right-wing politicians in Europe, evangelical and even 'New Age' Christians, unhinged commentators and broadcasters, YouTube gurus and self-made influencers. Where this is going, they don't need logic or rationality. And regardless of the contradictions that stack up, there is no slowing this speeding train. Consider how many respectable European intellectuals of the left and the right use the rhetoric of 'freedom' and 'human rights' to deny Muslims their freedoms and human rights and to create a political climate and social atmosphere in which Muslims can be easily demonised. Ponder how Western culture is privileged at every opportunity by every discipline: from anthropology to political science to history of science to history of art; and by every international institution. Anti-Muslim racism is not something limited to scholarly texts on Islam or literary novels and poems, the works of 'the Orientalists'. It is now the staple diet of popular fiction, trendy history, tabloid as well as serious journalism, cinema, television, advertising, online games, far right websites, YouTube channels, conspiracy theories, fake news, troll farms, packs of cybertroopers, social media posts, stories, and feeds—it is everywhere, in multiple forms: it is in the postnormal air we breathe.

It is unlikely that the arc of ignorance targeted at Islam and Muslims will end with Islamophobia. As a trend, it is likely to escalate. Placed on an S-curve, this trend remains in the early stages of growth. New communications technologies and avenues from new websites to new social media platforms will play an important part in driving this trend and globalising it. Emerging technologies, especially artificial intelligence (AI), but also genetic and biotechnologies, will take this trend beyond what can be imagined at this moment. Islamophobia is truly a complex trend with social, cultural, and political dimensions. It runs parallel and is tethered to trends in the rise of extremist thought, far right politics, and fascism in the West and beyond. We would be wise to anticipate the Islamophobic implications of culture wars, cancel culture, and neocolonialism resulting from the conflicts between the US, Europe, Russia, and China concerning the future of Africa and Asia, as well as the communities threatened in our age by 'global boiling'.[55] We have seen what is happening to the refugees of war-torn Muslim societies, but what of those made refugees when climate change makes their homes uninhabitable? And Islamophobia is a multiple direction expressway. It not only comes from the outside but also from within. Muslims also can, and do, actively contribute to Islamophobia and the exacerbation of the arc of ignorance through destructive acts of senseless terrorism, through the dissemination of extremist and fundamentalist interpretations that sully Islam, through the spreading of dangerous conspiracy theories and the abandonment of reason, and through the teaching of constructed ignorance to our youths, condemning our futures to the will of others. We cannot rest upon our laurels if the trend partially dies, for re-emergence is likely and with greater vigour if we do not anticipate the forces that seek to lead us astray and ultimately wipe us from the face of the Earth.

The genocide in Palestine presents for us a real example of how bad this trend can possibly get for us Muslims. By July 2025, after the second year of what is being called the Israel–Hamas war, at least 60,000 Palestinians had been killed, and over 17,000 of those killed were children. Almost 100,000 had been injured in Palestine, while almost 10,000 remained missing. Calling this a 'war' suggests some sort of parity between aggressors. With Israel's 1,139 people killed and at least 8,730 injured, the notion of 'equal' does not appear to belong in this conversation. In Gaza, according to reports from *Al-Jazeera*, 87 percent of housing units, 80 percent of commercial facilities, 68 percent of farmland, 68 percent of roadways, and 87 percent of school buildings have been damaged. Hardly any hospitals remained operational. Simply put, there were no 'safe' places for ordinary people to go to. Aid was constantly blocked. At least 163 journalists were killed; many deliberately shot.[56] As Palestinian infrastructures were decimated, new Israeli settlements (colonies) popped up along with state-of-the-art military infrastructure and surveillance technology. The completion of the Philadelphi Corridor and other military installations in the Gaza Strip will turn the territory into a surveillance police state under the ever-watchful eye of the Israel Defense Forces (IDF). The most advanced weapons systems available were used to target the leaders of Hamas anywhere in the world where they might be located at any time.[57] The most destructive weapons available were used in the systematic annihilation of the Palestinian people.

On the whole, Muslim countries are powerless beyond their ability to help the dispossessed Palestinian people in their suffering. Those who manage to seek refuge elsewhere fall prey to the stereotypes of 'burdensome refugees'. Israel stands with the support and military aid of the US; Iran stands with the military aid of Russia. The international community was and is impotent by its own designs. Much of the media heavily censors what is going on, what can be said about what is going on, and has banned the usage of language that describes what is actually going on, that is, calling a genocide a genocide. The West has virtually outlawed anti-Semitism, which has been redefined as Israel's right to occupy and colonise Palestine, and any criticism of Zionism, Israel, or its allies. Violators will be socially cancelled, or worse, prosecuted. And all of this continues unhindered, as we watch a genocide in real time through inescapable social media streams, reels, stories, and other such videos, photos, and accounts on our always undercharged smartphones. This is classic, unabashed Islamophobia. An allowed, enabled, and even empowered genocide against the Other. The arc of ignorance certainly does not bend towards justice.

It would be absurd to ask how we can be reconciled with the reality placed before us. But to despair would be the ultimate defeat. It is our duty to study, deconstruct, and develop approaches of countering these waves of anti-Muslim, ignorant hatred. In seeking new approaches, it is important not to dismiss all that came before. Old-fashioned Orientalism can, of course, still be dealt with in the old-fashioned way: forensic scholarly analysis employed by scholars in the vein of Normal Daniel and A. L. Tibawi; literary criticism, used so affectively by Said; post-colonial approaches and methods and tactics used by numerous cultural studies academics—all of these are as valuable today as they have ever been. Islamophobia is now being documented in detail and studied as a trend: the annual European Islamophobia Reports by the Turkish Foundation for Economic, Political and

Social Research (SETA); the annual Islamophobia Report by the Council on American-Islamic Relations (CAIR); and websites such as Tell MAMA (Measuring Anti-Muslim Attacks) in the UK are excellent examples.[58] The very fact that Islamophobia is now seen as a trend suggest a methodological shift is taking place in studying and monitoring Islamophobia.

To comprehend the potential threats we face, it is essential to realise that the world has changed drastically over the last few decades: we have entered postnormal times, where everything is connected to everything else and everything is complex; contradictions and uncertainties abound; and things can multiply in geometric fashion and lead to chaos. The genocide in Gaza demonstrates the confounding nature of postnormal times. Orientalism may have been the 'norm' before the age of post-truth. But there is nothing normal about conspiracy narratives or troll farms and cybertroopers feeding anti-Muslim fear and hatred to countless news outlets—shady as well as 'respectable'—or endless social media feeds inciting violence against Muslims or AI bots spouting racist chants. So, we are in a totally new, uncharted territory where we need novel ways of classifying, fresh approaches to study and analysis, and new disciplines to tackle historic, current, and the coming tsunami of ignorance that is fuelling anti-Muslim bile.

Beyond the conventional approaches to the arc of ignorance, other small efforts seen through history can be examined and their spirit replicated in other fields and instances. In 1937, the Belgian historian Henri Pirenne penned the seminal work *Mohammed and Charlemagne*. Pirenne focusses on the biographies of two historical figures about whom, in terms of academic historical research, little is known. By exploring the worlds they inhabited, he seeks a new approach to geographical and periodic considerations of history between the East and the West. He challenges the view that Rome fell to Germanic invaders and attributes the ending of the Roman Empire to the expansion of Islam into Eastern Europe, northern Africa, and the Iberian Peninsula. This historical analysis challenges readers to see how without the advent and expansion of Islam, there may not have been a Europe as we see it today.[59] Further contributions challenging the Eurocentric view of history will temper attitudes towards the demonisation of Muslims. The late British anthropologist Merryl Wyn Davies, with her work *Knowing One Another: Shaping an Islamic Anthropology*, engages the West and Islam, asking for a new integrated approach towards knowledge creation. This book is largely focussed on the project of taking the colonising power out of the discipline to make it a more open field towards mutual understanding.[60] It is also a pillar on the road towards greater 'integration of knowledge' in the phrasing proposed by Sardar, requiring a synthesis of the best of East and West and an appreciation of not just each other's cultures but also ways of knowing, being, and doing.[61] Of course, along the way of integrating our world views and building more inclusive and multicultural knowledge, some of the past needs to be given a dressing-down, to be acknowledged and transcended. We know ignorance can change and evolve; so too should knowledge.[62]

However, we need to appreciate that the ignorance we face today is not simply the lack of knowledge.[63] There are, not surprisingly, different varieties of ignorances: factual ignorance; object ignorance; practical ignorance; technical ignorance; culturally based ignorance. Racism and xenophobia are themselves a form of ignorance. There is existential ignorance about the consequences of our behaviour that threaten our planet. In the past decade alone, a new dictionary of terms signifying ignorance has emerged: misinformation, disinformation, post-truth, toxic, brain rot, group think—to mention a few. A host of different types of ignorances are explored in *The Routledge International Handbook of Ignorance Studies*.[64] Here, we are specifically talking about postnormal ignorance: an explicit product of a globalised world of complex networks and instant communication, where prejudices and preconceptions multiply rapidly and bigotry and jingoism can jump to chaotic proportions. Indeed, a new discipline, agnotology, is emerging to study certain varieties of ignorance. But it is limited to such questions as how we know, what we do not know, and why we don't know what we do not know. It needs to develop to incorporate issues of how ignorance is manufactured and spread, what role it performs in politics and cultural supremacy, and who benefits from its global dissemination.

In postnormal times theory, ignorance is dissected into three categories. First, we have *plain ignorance*: the ignorance we meet and sometimes overcome in everyday life and learning. We find that we do not know something, and we seek the knowledge we do not have. There must be an awareness that we do not know before we can embark on doing something about our ignorance. Second is *vincible ignorance*: this requires some effort to overcome, and sometimes can only be resolved in the future. It requires investigation, research, dialogue, discourse, and even polylogue to tease out the multiple perspectives at play in this type of constructed or manufactured ignorance. The third category is *invincible ignorance*: this is the deepest level of ignorance that resides at the level of one's world view. To overcome it requires shedding one's outlook and world view, unlearning what you think you have learned, while also invigorating our creative and imaginative potentials so that we can seek innovative solutions.

Islamophobia incorporates all three varieties of postnormal ignorance. In its plain ignorance form, it manifests as racism and bigotry towards Muslims. It can be incorporated into certain policies, such as the ban on the hijab in France,[65] or profiling people with Muslim names at airports, or outright discrimination in employment. The 'Arab terrorists' of Hollywood films, and the Christian evangelical 'Left Behind' series of books,[66] are also good examples. As vincible ignorance, Islamophobia often emerges as confirmation bias—the tendency to favour reports and information that confirm one's own prejudices, standard beliefs, and what could be called values. This type of Islamophobia can have disastrous consequences. A false claim on social media can lead to riots, as we saw in the July–August 2024 violent attacks on immigration centres and mosques in England.[67] A rumour on Facebook can lead to genocide, as we witnessed in the case of the Rohingya in 2016.[68] Communal violence in India, where hate speech targeting Muslims has become the norm, is frequently initiated on X.[69] This vincible ignorance requires determination and constant struggle to dislodge. For it is not just a question of social media being weaponised; rather, social media has now become the main weapon in promoting fear and loathing. The battle here is a long-term one and has to be fought both with policy and education. Finally, Islamophobia of the invincible ignorance type presents us with a formidable problem. It is deeply rooted in various Western world views, belief systems, and supremacist outlooks. The prescription for its removal requires a transformation in the dominant paradigms of the West, which are already crumbling.

Let me provide two illustrations.

First: During a state visit to Germany, Chancellor Olaf Scholz welcomed me at the Federal Chancellery. I was accorded an official welcoming ceremony and inspected the guard of honour mounted by the Wachbataillon of the Bundeswehr (German army) as the national anthems of Germany and Malaysia were played. Then came the press conference. Chancellor Scholz strongly defended Israel's right to defend itself following the 7 October 2023 attack by Hamas and reiterated that Germany bore a special responsibility for Israel and supported it unconditionally. There was no admission that the entire world, bar the US and a handful of European states, regarded what they were witnessing as genocide. No mention that the International Court of Justice (ICJ), in a landmark ruling on 26 January 2024, had acknowledged the violence in Gaza as a plausible case of ongoing genocide and ordered provisional measures.[70] No awareness that a comprehensive report from 24 March 2024 by Francesca Albanese, the UN Special Rapporteur, on the situation of human rights in the Palestinian territories occupied since 1967, concluded that 'there are reasonable grounds to believe that the threshold indicating Israel's commission of genocide is met'.[71] Or indeed, that almost every international organisation, from the UN Relief and Works Agency for Palestinian Refugees (UNRWA) to Amnesty International and Human Rights Watch, had declared the 'war' to be nothing more than genocide. Not too far away from where the press conference was being held, people wearing the keffiyeh were being arrested. Students demonstrating on behalf of the Palestinians, including children as young as eight or nine, were being chased and beaten. Protesting academics exposing the long history of Israeli atrocities were being labelled as anti-Semites.[72] It was as though the whole process began on 7 October 2023! Chancellor Scholz downplayed decades of oppression and atrocities committed against Palestinians since the Nakba in 1948. In response to questions from the media, I said: 'Where have we thrown our humanity? Why this hypocrisy? Why this selective and ambivalent attitude towards one race and one another? Is it because they are coloured or they are a different religion?'

Hypocrisy has been a prime Western value for almost a century. But one would expect that Germany would know a great deal about genocide, having been culpable of not just the Holocaust, but also the 1904–1908 Herero and Namaqua genocide in West Africa and the Romani genocide of World War II. But there is more at play here. Unconditional support for Israel, no matter what it does or how many atrocities it commits, is an intrinsic part of Germany's contemporary world view. The support for Israel is a way for Germany to redeem itself from its culpability for the Holocaust. Or, as the German Swiss psychologist and philosopher Karl Jaspers asked in his 1947 book, how is 'the question of German guilt' to be answered?[73] It comes in the form of German redemption theology, so clinically analysed by the Bosnian German sociologist Adnan Delalić. Germany's hypocritical stance, writes Delalić, 'on Gaza and rampant domestic repression speaks of guilt for the Holocaust that makes Germany behave the way it does'. Through its redemption theology, 'Germany imagines itself as emerging from the Holocaust as purified from Nazism and Antisemitism.'[74] Or, as Australian scholar Dirk Moses puts it in 'The German Catechism', it is 'a redemptive story in which the sacrifice of Jews in the Holocaust by Nazis is the premise for the Federal Republic's legitimacy'.[75] The Holocaust 'thus rendered as redemptive violence' leads Germans, the principal anti-Semites of history, to become the arch-protectors of new Zionist Jews.

The sheer depth of this ignorance, transformed into a perverse faith and world view, makes it invincible. It cannot be overcome, let alone replaced with sensible, objective knowledge, without totally abandoning the world view it is based on.

Second: At the 2023 Asia-Pacific Economic Cooperation (APEC) conference in the US, prime ministers and presidents from twenty-one countries gathered in San Francisco. These included leaders from China, Indonesia, Thailand, Australia, New Zealand, and the US. At an evening dinner, the then US President Joe Biden asked the gathered world leaders to condemn Russia for its crimes against humanity. Many of the countries attending, including Malaysia, had condemned the invasion of Ukraine. So, I asked the President why he was being selective in his condemnation. How could the killings and destruction wrought by the Israelis in Gaza be any less blameworthy? Biden remained reticent.

THE ARC OF IGNORANCE

To understand the ostensable American rationale in its foreign policy towards Israel, the general view derives from two perspectives. There is the fundamental belief of Christian Zionism that Israel is a fulfilment of biblical prophecies and that the gathering of the Jewish diaspora in the Holy Land is a criterion for the Second Coming of Christ. Thus, Israel has to be defended at all costs. But there is also a bigger 'Judeo-Christian' issue here: American Christianity has internalised the perception of exiled Jews; unconditionally supporting them is a sign of repentance and potential salvation. The secular modern notion of the 'Judeo-Christian', according to Adnan Delalić, quoting the Israeli scholar of Judaism, Amnon Raz-Krakotzkin, has now become

> a sign of repentance and reconciliation, symbolising the end of the long history of Christian antisemitism that culminated in the Holocaust. However, the Judeo-Christian, above all, serves as a marker of civilisational difference, in particular against Muslims and Arabs: the secular Zionist, the figure that most represents the now fashionable 'Judeo-Christian', has been constructed through a distinction from the East, from the Arab, and from the historical-exilic Jew.[76]

Again, we have an invincible ignorance that cannot be overcome unless the foundation on which it is based is jettisoned.

The construction of 'Judeo-Christian' heritage as a superior miracle, that consigns the history of all other cultures to minor tributaries, is the world view that has to be dispatched if we are to create a world based on knowledge, equality, and justice. It is not as though some sporadic dark cloud of evil has suddenly descended and started to spread hatred and prejudice. The rise of Islamophobia and the rapid spread of fascism around the world is a consequence of long-held and dominant world views with entrenched beliefs, attitudes, laws, and policies that have created hierarchies of people and division, and sought to isolate and separate one group that would be defamed and denounced, to define them as inferior and then eventually to eliminate them in the name of progress.

Modernity has played this part for centuries; it declared all traditional societies to be, by definition, inferior. By declaring all 'grand narratives' except liberal secularism as meaningless, postmodernism tried to achieve the same goal. Such supremist notions must now be consigned to the annals of history.

No single culture has all the answers to the problems of postnormal times, and some of the ignorances we face cannot be overcome by one individual or community and cannot even be resolved in one generation. The challenges of confronting the postnormal anti-Muslim paranoia—in all its forms as Orientalism, Islamophobia, conspiracy theories, digital pathologies, and emerging cyber manifestations—are both urgent and complex. Often this makes us feel like we are lost in a dark room without a torch. But it is possible to conceive a world where the accent is firmly on knowledge rather than rampant, deep-seated, and multilayered ignorances. Knowledge versus ignorance is not the good versus evil dualism we often characterise it as. It is far more complex and will require complex approaches that seek resolutions by transcending supremist ideas and notions, debunking nefarious world views and outlooks, and navigating societies towards an appreciation of diversity and difference.

An awareness of the arc of ignorance is the key towards rethinking ourselves in the pursuit of freedom and justice. This calls for a profound realisation of our own inadequacies, self-serving tendencies, as well as our own lack of humility and self-criticism. Bereft of this, the path towards rethinking ourselves may well be illusory.

Six

RETHINKING OURSELVES

I

Dante Alighieri's fourteenth-century narrative poem *The Divine Comedy* is a journey. It is a universal and timeless drama of the human predicament. At its core, the poem is the experience of the clash between good and evil. According to the Spanish American philosopher and writer George Santayana, writing in the early twentieth century, the rich symbolism in *The Divine Comedy* had been devised for a purpose: 'and this purpose, as the Koran, too, declares, had been to show forth the great difference there is in God's sight between good and evil'.[1] Fitting, I think, that the poem is also an allegorical take on Dante's own foray into medieval Florentine politics. Florence at the time was on the border between the Papal States and the Holy Roman Empire of medieval Europe and thus the epicentre of many dastardly plots between popes and emperors. While Dante, as a young civil servant, was on a mission to Rome, Florence was sacked, and his faction was put to the blade. He and others outside the city at the time of the sacking, were told not to return. Dante's journey left him with his own metaphorical and literal collection of bumps, bruises, and daggers to the back, ultimately landing him in the exile where he would spend the rest of his life. *The Comedy* was a wonderful opportunity for Dante to get the immortal vengeance good literature affords against one's enemies as well as to help him cope with the trauma he endured. It must be quite cathartic to be able to send your political rivals, corrupt officials, and a handful of popes to hell, literarily. The cast of hell in *The Comedy* does not just give us insight into Dante's politics, but it does give us a window into the xenophobic nature of the fourteenth-century Florentine mind. So much so that many human rights organisations, including groups in Italy, have clamoured for this great literary work to be removed from school curriculum, or to be used with great caution because of its 'offensive and discriminatory nature', particularly singling out the infamous depiction of Judas being endlessly chewed in the teeth of Lucifer. The Prophet Muhammad is also graphically described in a similarly deprecating manner. Consequently *The Comedy* is condemned as both antisemitic and Islamophobic.[2] On the other hand, they are literary critics who regard this work as one of the gems, not just of Italian literature but, as Harold Bloom puts it, as an essential centre of the Western literary tradition. Further, Dante's depiction of the well-known Islamic philosopher Ibn Rushd (known to Dante and many in the West as Averroes) is said to demonstrate the influence of Islamic philosophy on medieval thinking. Likewise, his eschatological forays—death, judgement, the afterlife—are viewed by literary critics as bearing uncanny parallels with the mystical expositions of the great Muslim Sufi, Muhyiddin Ibn Arabi. But beyond the elaborate details of the story, it also took the titanic, celestial, good-versus-evil encounter and made it real, practical—something John Milton would do for the English a few centuries later with *Paradise Lost*.[3] After the ink had dried on Dante's words, good versus evil was no longer just the thematic glue of theology, myth, and fantasies. It was the real, lived drama of our contemporary lives.

Unfortunately, today, in the final analysis of the intellectual sidestep that was postmodernism, that classic struggle of good and evil has been all but pacified. It denied 'grand narratives'—that is, anything and everything that gives meaning to our lives, from religion to science, history to tradition—and relativised everything, evil is now merely an absence of good, a glitch in the matrix, something that will pass like the common cold. The desolation of postmodernism even found a victim in 'truth'—once one of the greatest pursuits afforded to humanity, now completely eviscerated. Ultimately there has been a failure to respond to the problem that was and continues to be modernity. Evil very clearly exists in our world. It is all around us. Genocide—but not just *a* genocide—numerous genocides happening simultaneously all around the world, broadcast live by brave journalists who can get to where these atrocities take place, or even by the smartphone-wielding, nameless witnesses who upload their accounts to the omnipresent cloud. They know there is truth and that the truth is this: evil does indeed exist and thrives in our present moment of instability. Instead of pressing on in the struggle to end hate, it is easier simply to deny humanity to certain groupings of humans than to admit that our attitudes, cultures, and desires are often undercut with xenophobic, racist, ageist, and sexist undertones. Tyrannical populists use lies to emotionally blackmail the people into giving them greater power. Hesitation allows the evils of climate change to rage on. Evil never looms far from discussions of progressive, innovative technologies and artificial intelligence. And somewhere between two infamous quotes, one attributed to the chief propagandist of the Nazi Party, Joseph Goebbels, in 1940s Germany, 'a lie told once remains a lie, but a lie told a thousand times becomes the truth',[4] and the other to the nineteenth-century French essayist Charles Baudelaire, 'the greatest trick the Devil ever pulled was convincing the world that he didn't exist',[5] we find the evasive mask of evil in our contemporary world. The American physicist J. Robert Oppenheimer once quipped, 'the optimist thinks this is the best of all possible worlds. The pessimist fears it is true'.[6] Our reality goes beyond optimism and pessimism. Yet, I believe that there is still *real* good in this world and it can ultimately triumph over the equally real evil we find all around us.

Both good and evil are complex. Both change with time and come in different shapes and many disguises. Shakespeare understood this. In his comedy *As You Like It*, he gives these lines to the melancholy Jaques, a narrating character:

All the world's a stage,
And all the men and women merely players;
They have their exits and their entrances;
And one man in his time plays many parts

(II, vii, 146–49)

This fittingly exemplifies the complexity we find in our contemporary societies. Often fiction simplifies its characters to the point of being only two-dimensional, good guys or bad guys. Beyond this they are simply set-dressing, or as is gaining popular parlance with the upcoming generation, NPCs (non-player characters). But true literature delves into the rich complexity of its characters. People, like characters, are infinite, complex collages of motivation and, indeed, play many parts in their time.

In *Julius Caesar*, you hear yourself telling Brutus why he should not have made that fatal error of allowing Mark Antony to address those fickle-minded Romans. And then it dawns on you that you yourself might have suffered the same overweening confidence in the goodness of your cause to resist injustice and tyranny. The nineteenth-century English critic William Hazlitt sums up the argument by noting that tyranny and servility are to be dealt with after their own fashion, otherwise they will triumph over those who spare them. Reading *Macbeth*, you tell yourself that the 'air-drawn dagger' should be haunting your conspirators, assailing them with 'the stings of remorse'. Usurper, murderer, and tyrant, that's what Macbeth is. In *The Tempest*, you look around and find yourself surrounded by four walls; what else is there to do but to take a flight of fancy and start playing the part of Prospero? This one you can definitely relate to. It's the story about freedom over tyranny, the triumph of light over darkness. It starts with incarceration and ends with freedom. And between the idea and the reality you have to settle for Ariel instead, bending to the tasks at hand, do your time before the time is out. And as the end draws near, you gain freedom with the rediscovery of virtue within yourself. But we see tyranny in its most ruthless manifestation in *The Winter's Tale*, unleashed on the saint-like Hermione. There is neither an Edmund nor an Iago to lay the blame on for Leontes's state of mind. Is there a way to rationalise the character of this jealous tyrant? Is it the tyrant in him that makes him so irrationally jealous or is it just the jealousy that transforms him into a tyrant? Or does the answer lie in Shakespeare's metaphysics?

We could say, like the late American literary critic Harold Bloom, that with *King Lear* we are at the very centre of canonical excellence,[7] just as we would be if we traversed the cantos of the *Inferno* or the *Purgatorio*. But above all, it is the harrowing barrenness of the final scene that made it particularly compelling for me to read the play over and over again, in those long hours of solitude, and to read it with intense attention. Yet it is in defeat that we find victory, as we may gather from Lear's speech to Cordelia after they have lost the battle:

> Come, let's away to prison;
> We two alone will sing like birds i' the cage:
> When thou dost ask me blessing, I'll kneel down,
> And ask of thee forgiveness: so we'll live,
> And pray, and sing, and tell old tales, and laugh

At gilded butterflies, and hear poor rogues
Talk of court news; and we'll talk with them too,
Who loses and who wins; who's in, who's out,
And take upon's the mystery of things,
As if we were God's spies; and we'll wear out;
In a walled prison, packs and sects of great ones
That ebb and flow by the moon.

(V, iii, 8–19)

Needless to say, depending on your state of mind at any given time, with Shakespeare, you can be anyone you choose to be. When the nineteenth-century English poet John Keats was suffering from bouts of depression, he wrote to his friend, the painter Benjamin Robert Haydon, who chided him. In reply, Keats says: 'I never quite despair and I read Shakespeare—indeed I shall ... never read any other Book.'[8] And this leads us to *Hamlet*.

According to T. S. Eliot's theory of 'objective correlative',[9] *Hamlet* is a failure. Hamlet (the man) is dominated by an emotion which is inexpressible, because it is in excess of the facts as they appear. It is a feeling which he cannot understand; he cannot objectify it, and it therefore remains to poison life and obstruct action. In conclusion, Eliot says, we must simply admit that in *Hamlet*, Shakespeare tackled a problem which proved too much for him. But *Hamlet* needs no 'objective correlative', and this is what happens when we keep hoping to be wrong about Shakespeare with each new interpretation brought to the table. The nineteenth-century poet and critic Samuel Taylor Coleridge, perhaps having foreknowledge of the self-induced intellectual conundrums that might be caused by *Hamlet*, summed up the situation as follows:

It has been too much the custom, when we could not explain anything that happened by the few words that were employed to explain everything; we passed it over as beyond our reach: they were looked

upon as hints which Philosophy could not explain: as the terra
incognita for future discoveries; the great ocean of unknown things
to be afterward explored, or as the sacred fragments of a ruined
temple, every part of which in itself was beautiful but the particular
relation of which parts was unknown.[10]

Indeed, it is this *terra incognita* in *Hamlet* which, in the language
of transcendence, will remain hidden to the uninitiated; but it is
not unknowable, it is but a hidden treasure waiting to be discovered. It may be more accurate to say, therefore, that in *Hamlet*
Shakespeare tackled a problem which proved too much for the
audience at large to handle.

This calls to mind the observation made by the twentieth-
century Sufi teacher and scholar, Martin Lings, that to be present at an adequate performance of *King Lear* is not merely to
watch a play but to witness, mysteriously, the whole history of
humanity.[11] As Shakespeare matures, he becomes more focussed
on the question of religion, not in the narrow sense of a mode of
worship but in its most universal aspect, which is man having
the right attitude of the soul towards God. He places himself at
the very centre of the ancient world. For him, Apollo is not the
god of light but the light of God. Character after character is
developed to a state of virtue which is pushed to the very limits
of human nature. King Hamlet is purified in Purgatory, but he
is also a symbol of man's lost Edenic state, spoken of by young
Hamlet in the following terms:

A combination and a form indeed,
Where every god did seem to set his seal
To give the world assurance of a man

(III, iv, 60–62)

The pious man looks at the story of the Garden of Eden objec-
tively but imagines the Devil to be harmless, unaware of the extent
of his own subservience to him. The mystic, on the other hand,

looks at it subjectively and knows that most of what seems neutral is harmful. *Hamlet* transcends the idea of salvation, that is, simple piety in the conventional sense, and shows that Shakespeare, having drunk from the fountain of esotericism, knew, as Lings puts it, where to 'take upon us the mystery of things, as if "we were God's spies" and tread the path towards sanctification'.[12]

Whether it is Islam, Christianity, Judaism, or other religions, dogmatic faith can lead not just to bigotry, but may, when compounded with the elements of political and social discontent, cause us to express ourselves through violence and bloodshed. But if moulded under the hand of the universal wisdom, it could be a force to free us from ignorance and intolerance, injustice and greed. To use the language of the Gospel of St John, this perennial wisdom is the light that 'shines in darkness', although 'the darkness comprehends it not' (John 1:5). It is also alluded to in the Qur'an with striking imagery of the light of a lamp, 'lit from a blessed tree, an olive neither of the East nor of the West, whose oil is well-nigh luminous, though fire scarce touches it' (24:35).

Shouldn't this be the light to illuminate our path by imbuing us with ideals that are universal: a message of truth, justice, compassion, and above all, the liberty and dignity owed to all humankind? We talk of globalisation and the end of history, but we remain a world torn asunder by the practice of polity identified solely with the exercise of power, and leadership that is increasingly divorced from ethical concerns and morality. Enduring peace and harmony of the world must be built not upon hegemonies but on mutual concern, trust, and respect. We must discard our loyalties for the parochial and break free from the chains of outmoded mindsets; we should, like Hamlet, be 'a little more than kin, and less than kind'. For more than a century, Rudyard Kipling has had his say. Let us renounce his 'Oh, East is East, and West is West, and never the twain shall meet',[13] and instead, like Prospero, proclaim a 'fair encounter, of two most rare affections'.[14]

RETHINKING OURSELVES

Navigating the very strange world we find ourselves in requires that we rethink ourselves.

II

Psychologists will tell us we think about how we identify ourselves, or how others perceive us: who we are, perhaps even where we are coming from and where we are going. Some psychologists suggest that we do not think about ourselves at all but that society determines what we think ourselves. In my prison cell, self-reflection often led to the question of what it means to be really free. When Walt Whitman described democracy as a young giant exposed all over to the life-giving air,[15] he also meant that in such a democracy every citizen was free to think and feel for himself. But what does freedom mean in the age of social media, mass surveillance, excessive data-farming, fake news, post truth, and artificially induced desire for consumption and thought control? In the land of Shakespeare, thought control was introduced in the midst of the Civil War in 1643, prompting John Milton to write *Areopagitica*. In what is generally regarded as the earliest indictment against censorship in England, as well as his best prose writing, Milton writes:

> Truth and understanding are not such wares as to be monopolized and traded in by tickets and statutes and standards. We must not think to make a staple commodity of all the knowledge in the land, to mark and license it like our broad cloth, and our woolpacks.[16]

In contemporary Western societies, the tension between the ultimate value of 'freedom' in its broadest sense often comes in conflict with the idea of 'equality'. In his widely cited essay, 'Two Concepts of Liberty', the British political philosopher Isaiah Berlin divided freedom into two categories: negative and positive.[17] Negative freedom simply amounts to absence of interference, say from laws, regulations, social norms, or coercion from others. Positive freedom is the ability to control one's own destiny—this means the individuals must have equal opportunities, equal access to resources, to education, to employment. However, Berlin warns, this positive freedom can lead to tyranny—to dominate and suppress the individual. But those who benefit most from freedom of either kind are not always the weak, the marginalised, and the oppressed, but mostly the rich and the powerful. For me, it makes little sense to talk about freedom in the face of unparalleled inequality, where the vast majority of people do not know where their next meal is coming from. Freedom must also include the freedom to be represented honestly and justly, which has been a daunting task for Western societies for centuries. Moreover, freedom does not mean total liberty from truth and objectivity.

Of course, arguments for the constraints of freedom have been used by autocrats and tyrants to achieve their goals. For example, they will contend that the freedom to criticise the powers that be must also be curtailed because it causes political instability, which in turn may lead to insurrection and disorder. This pretext has been used habitually by petty despots and aspiring autocrats alike, some citing religious sanction for legitimacy. Of late, it is also being used by democracies as legitimate grounds to erode the basic freedoms of the people. Consider, for example, how the 'war on terror' led to the suspension of so many civil liberties which are supposed to be the hallmarks of a constitutional democracy. In this regard, it is fashionable in many non-Western states to invoke the virtues of traditional values and condemn the blind imitation of Western concepts: consensus is better than individual freedom. The opinions of the state must prevail over those of the individual because of the need to protect public morals and to maintain peace and harmony. It seems hardly worth pointing out, particularly to tyrants and autocrats, that those who hold positions of power also carry a moral responsibility to listen to the people. To curtail the freedom of individuals is not just to rob them of their freedom but to undermine their dignity, and the right and responsibility they have to reason and think. A society without individual freedom is a truncated society; it may be economically wealthy but it is also humanely poor.

Each time I regained my freedom, in 1976, 2004, and 2018, the world outside that I returned to had changed beyond recognition. Kuala Lumpur, the city I called home, transformed radically into a mega conurbation. Where once nature and human development played out in a balance of a handful of neighbourhoods with a sprinkling of tall buildings, connected by poorly lit jungle highways, now, in the blink of an eye, concrete jungles connected skyscrapers and construction projects by way of layered and overlapping highways, as waterways and flora filled in what spaces were left behind. The acceleration of technological development was most stark to witness. Payphones were replaced by the first mobile car phones, that weighed a tonne and never held a signal; then came my trusted BlackBerry that only lasted a minute before it was made redundant. Almost every week there is now a new queue at every one of our innumerable malls for the latest gadget. The queues we used to see have mostly vanished, as most sales, banking, and bureaucracy have moved to the digital sphere. VHS and DVD collections collect dust as there are no viable machines to play them on. Instead, everything is streamed. We watch less and less television and more and more Netflix and YouTube, and now TikTok and our social media feeds. CNN, the BBC, and Al-Jazeera compete with a string of other global news channels. You can now watch anything, anywhere, on any device. We no longer talk on phones. We do not even text. Now we WhatsApp or tweet on X, which is no longer Twitter. One moment newspapers filled our convenience shops, the next everyone seemed to have a blog. Now everyone has their own profile, or rather brand, on multiple social media platforms. And now those convenience shops only seem to have devices, oddly marketed with hyperbolic colours to youth, for vaping. We get our news mostly online; and drive everywhere with the help of a GPS via Google or Waze. We do not hail a taxi anymore; instead, we get an Uber, or more specifically in Malaysia, we Grab! We do not go out for food; food is delivered to our doorstep. There is an app for everything. Western popular culture gave way to Japanese popular culture (JPOP) which in turn has given way to Korean popular culture (KPOP), and I am told Viet Nam and Thailand are making way for VPOP and TPOP. My grandchildren roll their eyes as I attempt to keep alive my love of P. Ramlee, the brilliant twentieth-century Malaysian film-maker, actor, and musician, and the music accompanying the world of South Asian films from my youth. Worst of all, the solar system, I was told, had been reduced from nine to eight planets; Pluto had been 'declassified'. In my absence, the world had shrunk, communication had become both instant and omnipresent, and accelerating change was modifying human behaviour.

That new digital technologies had an unpalatable side was brought home to me when I was trying to log on to a website I had not used for some time. It asked me to confirm that I was human—and not a robot. I had to tick boxes with cars and traffic lights! Reality had been transformed: nations and communities were addicted to 'Reality TV', constructed and mediated, from the bickering of 'Big Brother' to the manufactured fame of people who were famous for just being famous—by simply appearing on reality shows. Now anyone with a social media profile and a bit of gumption could be a celebrity via the route offered in being an 'influencer'. In 2008, the election of Barack Obama meant, it was said, that the US was on its way to becoming a 'post-racial society'. Eight years later, I discovered that white supremacists were described by the new president as 'very fine people'.[18] Nevertheless, in an extraordinary demonstration of the power of populism, Trump reclaimed the office of the President of the United States in 2024. Populism, a term I knew only from reading the history of the first half of the twentieth century, had now become a global phenomenon: it swept religious fanatics, right-wing bigots, semi, and neo-fascists into power.

Populist parties and causes gained ground all over Europe, even in places once considered to be a fortress of liberal values. The European Parliament, far from being a bastion of liberal and humanist values, had become an incubator of extreme right-wing parties. In prison, I read the first 2012 issue of *Critical Muslim* entitled 'The Arabs are Alive', focussing on the hope generated by the Arab Spring.[19] But in less than a decade, the Middle East was in the grip of a deadly winter. All hope had diminished. The web and social media, far from liberating us, had unleashed the politics of hatred, ushered in new waves of criminality, social strife, and discord.

What one could label as old and new problems were blending. Throughout my political career we have known there were issues with capitalism, and especially the brand much of the world had accepted following the Cold War. The 1997 Asian Financial Crisis that bookended my first term as Malaysia's minister of finance, found its origin in the same structural problems that the Global Financial Crisis of 2007–2008, taking place only a decade later, would underscore. While that was considered the most serious crisis since the Great Depression of the 1930s, now each subsequent crisis is simply compared to the last. There were many lessons put forward to be learned, not just about banking but also about sub-prime mortgages, insider trading, currency manipulation, and hedge funds. Likewise, foundational problems of class, privilege, and equity were constantly hinting at deeper structural contradictions in the way we went about everyday life.

But lessons are seldom learned. The bankers were rescued, some meaningful regulations of the banking sector were introduced as a bare minimum, and austerity was imposed on those who were already facing financial hardship. New technologies such as fintech, blockchain, cryptocurrencies, and the use of AI in banking provided new opportunities for the banking and financial sectors to manipulate the system to their advantage. Capitalism has now become unhinged; it has, as David Simon, the creator of the celebrated HBO television show, *The Wire*, suggested, become a 'horror show'.[20] A number of new terms are now being used to describe capitalism, reflected in the titles of some recent works: Shoshana Zuboff introduced 'surveillance capitalism', Naomi Klein spoke of 'disaster capitalism', Guy Standing noted 'corrupt capitalism', Grace Blakeley gave us 'vulture capitalism', Matt Stoller 'counterfeit capitalism', Andrew Manno 'casino capitalism', and Kimberly Kay Hoang 'spiderweb capitalism'. All of these followed the French economist Thomas Piketty's stunning study, beginning with the seminal work *Capital in the Twenty-First Century*, that exposed and verified our fears that inequalities were indeed inherent to our systems of capitalism.[21] All this suggests that corruption is not part of the system, rather it is the system. The Malaysian sociologist Syed Hussein Alatas had already made this point in the 1960s![22] The abnormalities and contradictions of capitalism are intrinsic to the global banking and financial system, which has become too complex, too interconnected, too contradictory, too steeped in deep uncertainty and ignorance to be anything else but debased. As the Dutch economic writer Joris Luyendijk points out, the whole banking and finance system is 'highly dysfunctional, deeply entrenched, and enormously abusive, both to its workers and the society it operates in'.[23]

For sure, it is time, as the title of the book by British economists Michael Jacobs and Mariana Mazzucato suggests, for 'rethinking capitalism', or, as suggested by the title by an international network of scholars and students pushing for pluralist economics, it is a time for 'rethinking economics'.[24] But that in itself is not good enough. We need to abandon the mode of thought that capitalism instils; capitalism shapes the way we think about economics, development, and progress. Look at what it has done to the once noble pursuit of Islamic Economics. It has made Islamic Economics a subcategory of capital 'E' Economics, which we all know is pronounced 'Western neoliberal economics'—a plague against the notion of prosperity. We need to transcend some of the basic contradictions in orthodox economic theory and the colossal failure of policies based on it. The very notion of 'economic freedom', for example, gives highest value to property rights, and even regards democratic elections as enemies for they might work actively against economic freedom. Economics, as the economics undergraduates at the University of Manchester, who rebelled and declared their discipline to be irrelevant to contemporary needs, claimed, has become the supreme ideology of our time. Economics, the students argued, claimed too much knowledge in the age of uncertainty, fragility, and multiple types of ignorance; it placed too much power in the hands of technocrats who shape policy, driven by their own desire for profit and to line the pockets of their families and cronies.[25]

The ignorance surrounding AI was bought home to me when we began crafting the New Industrial Master Plan (NIMP) for Malaysia. We wanted to set the course for navigating our digital futures, to make our country advance strategically in production and manufacturing for high-capacity service industries. We gave top priority to Malaysia's digital transformation across the board. But, as we soon discovered, the terrain ahead was rough. As a wave of AI advancements take on global significance and show little sign of slowing in the near future, Malaysia's efforts to surge ahead with an appropriate ecosystem with sufficient human capital and a strategic supply chain were not going to be easy. Nevertheless, we succeeded to some extent and the plan has recently made Malaysia a magnet for global technology players. After meeting some of the captains of industry in this sector, I have to admit I was taken aback by their attitudes and approach.

In the traditional way of transforming an economy, the equation is relatively simple. You need access to raw materials, the technology for processing or manufacturing, and the skills to operate and manage the whole process. A clever manoeuvring of training and borrowing had allowed agrarian and trade-dependent economics to give way to industrialised producers—that is, manufacturing building components in a controlled environment and assembling them on site. Economies, it was thought, could make quantum leaps with a bit of access and a few years for things to establish themselves. Today, this mentality is fraught with future peril. The world is far more complex and chaos is now a major player. To take a technological product, such as AI, and introduce it to your economy would create a whole host of problems down the line. You cannot simply ask one of the major AI firms to come to your country, bring their asset, and train your workers on how to work with it. AI takes on the prejudices and contexts of its creators. We have seen how it can show bias, even become racist or xenophobic. This is even the case when it is unintentional, such as how facial recognition and replication programmes can work out greater details of peoples with fairer complexions, are often not able to tell people of darker complexions apart, or even to differentiate them from animals. How can this be? Well, you need only look at who is developing the technology in the first place. The less diverse the crafters, the more limited the scope of the craft.

So, when I spoke with technology executives, I pointed out that I did not simply want a product and training modules for Malaysians to adopt wholesale. We needed to build a system where Malaysians learned how to utilise the latest technology, but that also empowered them to develop their own advancements and products. I asked, how do we build indigenous capacity for our digital futures? They responded with a stock answer: the old way of transforming technology. They told me, AI is just a machine: you deposit your inputs and it delivers outputs. There seemed to be little or no awareness of the characteristic values and biases of the technology. This is not good enough. This is why I emphasise not only the need for more STEM and advanced technological education, but that we must simultaneously uphold and reinforce education of social sciences and the humanities, so that issues of values, ethics, cultures, and sociology can be the consideration of those who develop the technology on which our people are becoming increasingly dependent. I not only posed this challenge to the captains of industry, but to my own cabinet ministers and civil servants. No one has the answers, but if we take a more pluralistic, societal approach, the sheer diversity of inputs will enable us to plot more appropriate and sustainable next steps.

As we advance Malaysia's digital transformation, we are also considering the wide applications of blockchain technologies and digital commerce through digital currencies and wallets. Our banks and financial institutions have to be prepared for this change; if they are unprepared, they will be swallowed up by the waves of change. But in the loss of control these technologies usher in, they also give greater access and agency to the people. So we need to take account of all sides to determine the best way forward. Only through doing this can we ensure our ethics and values live on in this digital future. As we continue to explore our national AI strategy and digital transformation, we are also looking at how shariah-compliant financing and halal economics can carry us forward. As we continue to move forward, we are guided by our NIMP with the strategic thrust the country needs to be technologically advanced, so that we may be productive in the manufacturing and the high-capacity device industry. In this regard, digital transformation occupies the top priority. As the wave of AI advancement takes on a global significance, naturally Malaysia is also moving ahead. With the ecosystem ready, and a human capital and a strategic value chain in place, Malaysia has become a magnet for big technology players. But the aim is not just to put our values and ethics out there, but to look for new approaches to problems every nation faces.

How to regulate emerging technologies remains one of the greatest contemporary challenges for every country. We can neither trust nor depend on the ideas of one or of others; we all must be engaged in a discourse around challenges that will have tremendous ripple effects on our futures. And we cannot afford to leave anyone behind in this progression.

The technology determinists and the 'econocracy' have evolved a mysterious language that serves as a barrier to understanding reality on the ground and to allowing the public to contribute to the discourse.[26] The technocrats talk of 'singularity'—where humans and AI become one—with bated breath and unbridled joy. Faceless economists make social and political decisions, undermining democracy and leading to rampant inequality. Development theory lumps human rights with consumer rights, as though both had equal value. As the German Catholic sociologist Wolfgang Sachs asks,

> How can one treat the basic social rights to food, housing and health as being at the same level as the consumer demand for SUVs, real estate and stocks? What do the Mapuche in southern Chile have in common with the Wall Street bankers, or the cotton workers in Mali with the start-ups in Shanghai? Not much, expect that they are united in the mirage of development.[27]

This vision of progress, described by the British philosopher John Gray as 'the moth-eaten musical brocade' (quoting Philip

Larkin's poem 'Aubade'), has turned out to be inherently non-distributive—it does not effectively transfer wealth either between the rich and poor nations or within nations and society.[28] The very idea of perpetual, linear, open-ended progress—a specifically Western notion—has now become untenable, unjust, unsustainable, and inherently injurious to the planet and therefore to the future of humanity. We need to see capitalism not so much as a distinct entity but as a multilayered system that is nourished by certain disciplines and widely believed concepts imagined as universals—all of which produce a particular mode of thought. Far from being a technocratic exercise, rethinking capitalism requires us to rethink a great deal of ourselves: our mental outlook, our way of conducting business, our modes of socialisation and respect, what we actually need and what we insatiably desire, what we think is a 'good life', and how we construct community and relate to others—in short, what it means to be human and how we conduct the business of life for ourselves, for our families, for our communities, and for our planet!

Both life and our humanity are being transformed and put in danger by recent developments in biotechnology and the evolution of artificial intelligence (AI). This was brought home by two exhibitions that were held in London: the permanent Wellcome Collection exhibition titled 'Being Human' and the 2019 exhibition, 'AI: More than Human', at the Barbican Centre. One of the first exhibits one encounters on entering 'Being Human' is a DIY CRISPR gene-editing kit. The accompanying notice explains:

> Biohacking collective The Odlin sell this kit, which enables purchasers to use a technique called CRISPR to edit DNA. The kit, which is sent by post, claims to contain everything needed for CRISPR editing, including *E. coli* bacteria. Kits like this one raise questions: as science moves outside the laboratory and becomes more accessible, who do we trust? How comfortable are we with this freedom?[29]

This is freedom not just to alter our own biology, and indeed those of others, but to change the very code of life itself. CRISPR is an acronym for 'clustered regularly interspaced short palindromic repeats'; it is, as Nessa Carey tells us, 'cheap and easy to obtain, it's alarmingly straightforward to generate the molecular reagents to try this at home. You literally can inject yourself with gene editing materials and absolutely no one can do anything about it'.[30] You can just as easily acquire the genome of others. Artist Heather Dewey-Hagborg sequenced DNA from discarded cigarette butts, gum, and hair, and looked for genetic markers related to appearance—and produced three-dimensional printed portraits. The four letters that represent the genetic code—G, A, T, C—suggest that a genome is nothing more than a text, a 'book of life' we can easily read, edit, change, and manipulate at will. The individual is reduced to nothing more than sequences of code—not unlike computer code.

The 'AI: More than Human' exhibition displayed even more disturbing futures. Among displays of intelligent robots, fibrebots, organ chips, and neural networks, the exhibition told us that

> As AI permeates our lives, it merges with other scientific disciplines and begins to change our idea of the 'natural'. While AI emulates the behaviour of the brain, the related research area of artificial life (A-Life) works with a much wider set of natural processes, including human and animal biology, and environmental science. This gives us the potential to improve our bodies, eradicate illness, produce new food groups and extend life. It is possible to imagine both new futures for our species and the creation of new species. In this scenario, organic life is an expanding process—our form is not fixed at birth. As new body parts, new living environment and new beings are created, it is clear that our world is in endless evolution.[31]

Besides this cheerfully dystopian image of 'endless evolution', a display told us that 'the US, China, Israel, South Korea, Russia and the UK are developing increasingly autonomous weapons', which with the help of AI, would be able to racially profile their targets. What the exhibition did not show was how AI and bio-engineering is being used to revive and promote eugenics, how decisions by algorithms—or 'augmented decision-making'—are leading to the marginalisation and oppression of those considered undesirable, and how data-mining, facial recognition, and social media surveillance are hurling us towards 'Big Brother' states. The exhibition did hint towards the racial bias inherent in AI systems; indeed, AI is so infected with biases that it would be foolish to regard its decision-making process as fair or to put one's trust in it. The work by Australian artists, Latai Taumoepeau and Deborah Kelly, *No Human Being is Illegal*, illustrated the impact rising sea levels would have on small island nations. While at times technological innovation borders on what we might refer to as science fiction, it is important that we take stock of the real-world implications that might result, while also examining what problems we leave as 'left-overs' for future generations, once they have become bloated and unignorable.

Both exhibitions illustrate how our humanity is being compromised; and our lives, and the well-being of future generations, placed in serious, existential danger. The artworks and displays in the 'Being Human' exhibition, in particular, refer to the calamities we may experience in the coming decades. *Flooded McDonalds*, the haunting video by the Danish artistic trio Superflex, shows a life-size replica of a fast-food restaurant slowly filling with water, hinting at the culpability of both corporates and consumers in advancing climate change. As our humanity stands before a precipice, a complex threat ties the problems of our day together in a way that we would be foolish to disregard.

So, our conventional notions of what it means to be human, what is life, what is real, and what is just illusory are being rapidly transformed. And these transformations are inherently connected to digital technologies, advancement in bioengineering, and dominant ideas about progress, freedom, efficiency, management, and control, which in turn are linked to academic disciplines such as economics and development, popular consumption of social media, the ideology of the 'free market', and the power of financial systems in the global economy. Rethinking capitalism requires us to rethink the whole lot. And the whole is one, giant, interconnected, complex system: a self-organising, ever-changing tangle. There are so many dynamic parts in this horrendous Gordian knot that if we try to untangle a single one, the tangle gets worse.

AI and bioengineering have yielded formidable powers. We are converting 'old-style evolution into neo-evolution' and 'we know intuitively', writes environmentalist Al Gore, 'that we desperately need more wisdom than we currently have in order to responsibly wield some of these new powers'.[32] But where will this wisdom come from? How are we going to make the right choices? And, as Gore, asks, 'just who is this "we" who will make the choices?'[33] In the era of techno-feudalism we find ourselves in, it seems to me that choices will be made by a tiny minority that stands to gain all. So, alongside this we must also seek intergenerational justice. Given current trends, the future of bioengineering and AI will certainly be made by what have come to be dubbed the 'tech bros' and bioengineering and pharmaceutical corporations.[34] We are being pushed, at an accelerated pace, towards a new world order where we will have no control over our bodies, lives, or minds and will play no part in shaping our own futures according to our aspirations.

As the age-old questions of what it is to be human have become further complicated and brought to the fore of our concerns, another of what we might call our 'old' problems has lingered in the background so as to be the greatest existential threat we have yet faced. What it means to be human will have little importance on an inhospitable planet. Gore drew our attention to the issue of climate change back in 2006 in his film *An Inconvenient Truth* (he reasserted the message about climate crisis again in *An Inconvenient Sequel: Truth to Power* released in 2017).[35] But it has been a concern going back at least half a century. If we are to properly rethink ourselves, we must consider that for the first time in the history of human existence, our actions and behaviour are having a direct geological impact on the planet. And whatever future we might create together will need a stable planet for that future to take place on. The state of climate change, which is beyond crisis and rapidly appearing to be a catastrophe, adds yet a further dimension to the complexity at play in our very strange present. Finally, most governments around the world have come round to seeing the importance of tailoring climate policy. Noam Chomsky and Robert Pollin's work, *Climate Crisis and the Global Green New Deal*, nicely synthesises the numerous green policies at work, with an awareness of the shortcomings of the 2016 Paris Climate Agreement and how the annual COP conference is becoming a broken record of talk without much walk taking place. But the importance of what Chomsky and Pollin did was that they highlighted that hope remains, but the move must be big: local steps can act like rain on the mountain, but we do not have that sort of time, and our air, water, and atmosphere do not respect national borders.[36] While indeed the game of climate policy is not fair, the world is far from being a fair place; we all must do our part even when those responsible for the greatest impact may not be us. Naomi Klein's brilliant *This Changes Everything* not only took the complexity of the issue to a new level but gave us all a long overdue dressing-down. Our economic and political actions, large and small, have put us in the mess we find ourselves in. The rethink is not only in terms of our personal choices but in democracy, economics, and even in how we respect indigenous peoples and territories.

Klein acts as the doctor who finally tells us that all our ailments are our own fault, and a complete lifestyle overhaul is necessary.[37] Meanwhile, in *The Future We Choose*, environmental advocates and strategists Christiana Figueres and Tom Rivett-Carnac break us out of the impasse of the present and ask us to consider the future. Their analysis is a realpolitik approach to the climate crisis that motivates us to break from the old-world notion of certain things and to actualise what we might sometimes view as utopian or idealistic. While they frame the story of our future around survival, they hope that in embracing the work before us, we can turn the future from becoming a story of survival into one of thriving, a new renaissance for all humanity.[38]

Many of the things we have conventionally cherished—truth, democracy, politics, freedom, free will, the sanctity of life, and the pre-eminence of our own intellect—are being seriously reassessed. Not because they are irrelevant, but because the chasm between the ideal and reality has further widened. It is not just that all that was solid has melted into air, but that what remains has been turned over completely—inverted, polluted, demented. I am reminded of the Indian mystic and poet Kabir. Claimed by both Muslims and Hindus as their own, Kabir wrote thousands of poems, but none can be attributed to him with certainty. Yet his collective voice is so individual, so unique, that it cannot be mistaken for anyone else's. And, of course, there is that signature at the end of many of the poems that leaves little doubt. He wrote a number of 'upside down' poems, a poem that can be read from one direction and then from the other, to convey deeper, richer, even contradictory, meaning. Kabir's poem 'Brother, I've seen some' is particularly apt for our time.

> A tree with its branches in the earth,
> Its roots in the sky;
> A tree with flowering roots.

This said Kabir,

Is your key to the universe.
If you can figure it out.

III

Our futures are trapped in dominant paradigms and their world views, the economic and political institutions they have produced, and the legal and financial regimes they have enforced. We need to dispatch, as German sociologist Ulrich Beck pointed out over two decades ago, the 'Zombie categories' which 'govern our thinking but are not really able to capture the contemporary milieu'.[39] We need to transcend modernity, postmodernism, and associated notions of perpetual growth and progress, the obsession with neoliberal economics and 'free markets', freedom without responsibility, unbridled individualism and consumerism, and 'redefine, reconstruct, restructure our concepts and our view of society',[40] and, I would add, ourselves! We need to unlearn almost as much as we have to learn. We need to give voice to the views of those who have been marginalised and silenced, and to seek out new perspectives to steady our boat as we navigate our way through the ocean of time.

The best place to begin this process is by assessing where we are, looking at how change is being ushered in, examining the forces that are hurling us towards undesirable, destructive futures. Many contemporary researchers and thinkers, not surprisingly, have devoted considerable intellectual and scholarly thoughts to this task. The most notable is the late Polish British sociologist Zygmunt Bauman, who explored the weirdness and 'astonishing sights' of our era in a series of books, some in conversation with other scholars and thinkers, published during the last two decades. Bauman's thesis is that we are living in 'liquid times', dominated by uncertainty and an absence of frames of reference, and created by the passage from solid to 'liquid modernity', transforming a society of producers into a society of consumers. There is an ever-increasing gulf between power and politics, everything is fragmented, society has become myopic, focussed only on short-term goals, concepts like progress and careers have become meaningless, and 'liquid evil' stalks the Earth. We have even lost our faith in happiness—far from working towards fulfilling futures, we idealise and dream of a glorious past, entombed in 'retrotopia'.[41] Byung-Chul Han argues that we are living under the 'dictatorship of capital', dominated by 'neoliberal psycho-politics', where 'freedom itself is bringing forth compulsion and constraint', and society is experiencing a 'burnout'.[42] Shoshana Zuboff suggests we are living in 'the age of surveillance Capitalism' based on a 'parasitic economic logic' and order, where 'human experience is used as free raw material for hidden commercial practices of extraction, prediction, and sales'.[43]

Such powerful analyses shed a much-needed light on our contemporary malaise. But we need a broader, theoretical framework that not only describes the nature of our 'liquid times' and 'burnout society' under constant surveillance, but that also tells us something about the nature of contemporary change and captures the essence of our present with key analytical concepts. I believe that the theory of postnormal times[44] fulfils this requirement.

Postnormal times theory not only describes our present condition with astute observations; it is also a theory of change that aims to provide the capacity to retain some agency for shaping sustainable and viable futures. Ziauddin Sardar first coined the term 'postnormal times' in his final article as editor of *Futures*, a leading journal in the field of futures studies. This article set the stage for a more focussed discourse on futures studies, aimed at resolving the problems in forecasting as well as dangers lurking over the horizon as the twentieth gave way to the twenty-first century.[45] We must first look at the long-held thesis of Sardar's that the future is being colonised—much like the colonisation of the recent past—and futures studies itself, like other disciplines and fields of study, has been dominated by Western thought. The non-Western world was conspicuously absent or orientalised. Even postmodernism, the once revolutionary framework that emerged as an alternative to the malaise of modernity, has turned complicit. Postmodernism not only failed to give voice to the marginalised—one of its major touted principles—but itself became a new form of imperialism. Far from responding to the problems of modernity, postmodernism took us beyond the dark paths modernity had taken our societies down, to rampant consumerism, relativism, despair, suicide, and genocide.[46]

It was not just the world that was changing ever-more rapidly, but that how things changed was changing. That is, change itself was changing. This, Sardar characterised with the 4S's: speed, scope, scale, and simultaneity. Things were moving faster than at any point in history and at an accelerating pace. Small, even microscopic, objects and events were having globe-rattling impacts. Scope was unprecedented, and global events were reaching down to all localities, right down to the individual level, no matter where the individual was located. Indeed, no man is an island as scale blows up. And lastly, there was not just one crisis or event, but several, all happening at the same time: simultaneity. It was these gathering clouds that ushered our interconnected and interdependent world into postnormal times.

At the heart of postnormal change, driven by speed, scope, scale, and simultaneity, Sardar showed, were complexity, chaos, and contradictions—the 3C's of postnormal times. The world is, and is becoming, increasingly complex. Our interconnections and instant communication generate feedback loops that push complexity towards chaos. Much like the feedback loops in a microphone: the microphone picks up sound from a speaker, or speakers, and amplifies it back into the speaker system, thus creating a loop. The end product is a ringing frequency that rapidly increases its volume to horrible, unbearable screeching vibrations—the sound of chaos! Those outliers and seemingly insignificant factors begin to add up and have a tremendous impact on our already untenably complex systems. As a result, contradictions abound, fracturing what we took for granted, what was normal to us. The result is that we find ourselves not quite out of the old, but with nothing truly new to reach for. Or as Sardar put it, 'an in-between period where old orthodoxies are dying, new ones have yet to be born, and very few things seem to make sense'. This in-between, where less and less is making sense, is our postnormal times. To get beyond this interregnum, it is necessary for us to reinvigorate our creativity and resuscitate our imaginations. In doing this we must further excavate the depths of our ignorances and gain a greater appreciation of uncertainty. Greater futures awareness and understanding of postnormal times give us agency to shape what may come tomorrow and to construct more preferred futures. Conceptual reexaminations must be carried out as a continuum together with robust intellectual discourse so that we may successfully navigate this phenomenon.

Postnormal times provides a long overdue divergence that might well cure the slump of desolation that many contemporary postmodern thinkers have found themselves confined to. Such thinkers as Slavoj Žižek, Judith Butler, Nancy Fraser, and other left-wing intellectuals in the Western tradition, find themselves at an intellectual cul-de-sac. But there must be more than nihilism, suicide, and anarchy at the end of the road of our intellectual pursuits. The one overarching sin in Islam is despair; the flame of hope must be kept from being extinguished. Others await collapse as if it is something we should face with some imbecilic bravery. Half of the crowd weeps for the planet, a lost cause in their eyes, the rest seek what they call the next step in human evolution, ironically the end of humanity, in posthumanist utopias of eternal life. But we have been here before and these stances are as old as human thought. There must be another way, one in which we rebalance our relationship with nature, with ourselves and each other, and with the future. As we transit postnormal times, we free ourselves from our collective dark wood, from the winter of our discontent.

IV

In November 2022, I became the prime minister of Malaysia. The impetus to translate ideas into reality took on a greater sense of urgency. I lament the fact that I lost twenty years, more than half of it spent in prison. I could not allow another cycle of Dante's comedy to befall me or the people. The time for reading had ended and the time for critical thought and action was upon me. A basic thesis of postnormal times is that they cannot be managed or controlled. They can only be navigated. So I had to dispense with my old tendency for such things, for 'business as usual' models of management and administration. With a firm eye on the future of Malaysia, noting postnormal times theory, and my intellectual cognitions from the solitude of prison, I set about developing a navigational road map for Malaysia for our ever-changing, turbulent times. I had learned from Antonio Gramsci and other revolutionaries that a total *tabula rasa* revolutionary approach would not do. This was not the time for revolution, but for reform and transformation. We need to grapple with a new set of circumstances, not the least being a power configuration which must be navigated circumspection. One would also have to contend with the intricacies and problems posed by those who had been accustomed to the practices and culture of the past. In this vein, we are looking at a smorgasbord—such as the political elite, robber barons, powerful bureaucrats and elements within the judicial system. In short, it is systemic, fundamental, an almost permanently engrained problem which must perforce warrant a sustained wholistic and even a whole-of-nation approach. Without exception, the rule of law must prevail in order to guarantee certainty, impartiality, and focus in implementing the changes and reform so direly needed in order to take the nation out of this quagmire. While, indeed, the times are changing—and changing fast and furiously—in many cases, ironically, the more things change the more they stay the same—*plus ça change, plus c'est la même chose!* It was essential to balance new ideas with old tried-and-true systems. Some elements of our societies are fine and can be fully actualised with just the right intellectual nudge or ethical motivation. At least for the last two decades, the texture, nature, and velocity of change has been so mired in complexity that it becomes all the more treachous to navigate the contradictions and chaos that confront us every day. Well-thought-out political strategies and development projects are put to the grinder and minced beyond recognition because of the enormous gap that stands between theory and practice. As a multicultural society, Malaysia has had ample experience in navigating the challenges and in learning to adapt to the pluralistic nature of our societies, and yet we have not attained our desired objectives. To do this requires retrospection and critical analysis. And that was what we desperately needed—a through line, an interstitial substance that could draw us together to pursue our common, preferred futures.

I had started discussing what needed to be done with my friends and colleagues a couple of years before I became prime minister. Our meetings generated much debate and heated arguments. Our aim was to develop a philosophy of nationhood. Different suggestions were made to construct an intellectual backbone that would help Malaysia navigate through these turbulant times. As Aristotle stated, we are indeed social animals. And for society to function, what did we need? Some argued for a strong homeland. Various diasporas might beg to differ. Others suggested an emphasis on language. Indeed, Bahasa Melayu serves us well, not just as a lingua franca but, even more significantly, as a pride and joy of our nation and its history. Although the sovereignty of the Malay language is a singular importance to the cultural ethos of the nation, special attention is also being given to the use of English as a commercial and international language. At the same time, the languages of our myriad communities, particularly Mandarin, Tamil, and other indigenous languages in Sabah and Sarawak are protected and upheld as cultural treasures. And we are all the stronger and more united for this effort. Language and love for the nation truly go hand in hand, underpinned by our common shared values.

For nations to progress and thrive, a whole-of-society approach and value system is paramount. It must be one that cuts across social and economic frameworks as well as political strucutres and systems. For without values, even if the economy prospers, the moral compass of the nation would be lost. That said, it would be naive to assume that the assimilation and practice of such values could be taken for granted. On the contrary, by virtue of the law of requisite variety, the dynamics of compleixty is the rule, rather than the exception.

Societal composition in Malaysia is not monolithic. It is comprise of a multiplicity of ethnicities, namely Malay, Chinese, Indian, Dayak, or Orang Asli. Modernity had ridden roughshod on our diversity and if we throw caution to the wind, we run the risk of losing our soul in the pursuit of our collective endeavours. Policymaking and presription must be circumscribed by consideration of values and humanity. With our values as the foundation of policy, we could proceed with the great task of reform needed to build more solid policy and navigate our nation into a future for all.

In the formulation of these values, we examined various religious tenents as a source of inspiration, apart from the humanistic precepts of numerous worldviews and universal morals and ethics. There were/are hundreds of values to choose from. The goal was to focus on shared values; ethics, morals, and ideals that would appeal to our diverse communities and that spoke to the vast array of teachings, principles, and philosophical underpinnings found within them.

Eventually, it came down to six central values: Sustainability, Care & Compassion, Respect, Innovation, Prosperity, and Trust. Together they form the acronym SCRIPT (or MADANI in Malay).[47] Not only are these values cherished by the ethnic and religious communities in Malaysia, and, as such, unite the nation in all its diversity, but they also represent a rich complexity. Viewed singularly, each value appears simple enough. But the beauty of this concept becomes clear when seen in its entirety, where one value seamlessly connects to, and is found within, the others. Take, for example, prosperity. If one wants to build a policy towards prosperity, within that policy must be an accounting for trust-building, mutual respect, advanced care and compassion, and a conception of sustainability. Prosperity without sustainability is meaningless. Mutual respect is essential for building trust; and care and compassion for the poor and marginalised is a building block both for prosperity and sustainability. Moreover, these values are defined in our Malaysian way and comprise the various traditions of Malaysia and how we look at these values. Thus, sustainability is not simply a buzzword or coverall for sustainable development and green policies. While these concepts are a part of our Malaysian definition of the value of sustainability, it is more. This value also stands for developing sustainable relationships between one another; seeking balance in life with nature, and between all things; and sustaining our own continuity into the future and between generations. This is an integral part of our various faiths and cultural traditions. This sophistication is then placed onto our modes of policy- and decision-making, and problem-solving. The final feature is to keep the changing nature of the present in mind, and our eyes open to the hazards and challenges of the future.

As soon as I occupied the office of prime minister, I established the SCRIPT/MADANI framework as the guiding principle of all government policies. It has been implemented as a dynamic, long-range national plan known as 'Malaysia MADANI'. The Malaysia MADANI framework is grounded in humility. While solidly anchored in its foundation, its dynamism lies in its capactiy to adapt and assimilate. This dynamism is essential as a bulwark against the encrustation of time brought on by complasency and contentment.

It should be clear that these SCRIPT/MADANI values are neither culture nor geography bound. Neither are they time bound. By virtue of this, it is my earnest belief that with the courage of conviction and the tenacity of purpose, this philosophy of nationhood, and the method behind it, will enable us to find the right path towards growth, progress, and prosperity. We need these values to bring us together for the sake of all our futures. In practical terms, this calls for mutual respect, tolerance and understanding, as well as care and compassion. These values and principles are the *sine qua non* of a fair and just society. Where ethnic harmony prevails over strife and distrust.

Values-based discourse, having been relegated to near irrelevance during the modern and postmodern era, must regain its rightful place. Modernity has suppressed what is good and wholesome in traditional communities, East and West. The major drawback of postmodernism was the absence of a moral centre and the predominance of relativism that left societies 'lost'. Rethinking ourselves demands greater self-introspection to fathom what has been 'lost', in terms of our spiritual and moral wellbing under the deadweight of material growth on account of unbridled capitalism.

It is up to us to translate theory into practice, ideas into reality. Our recent collective global trauma under the Covid-19 pandemic compels us to rethink what the future may hold. Without a doubt, the impact of the pandemic was devastating. But even more revealing is that it exposed the ills and fissures in the system from the lack of basic amenities to the deplorable state of public health and the gross inequalities found across our societies. The pathos of human suffering were laid bare in Malaysia with households flying *Bendera Putih* (Malay for 'white flag') symbolised families crying out for help in utter desperation. Daily news of scores, even hundreds, of victims succumbing to the disease while loved ones barred from being near them could not fail to pluck at our heartstrings. Yet behind this circumstance of suffering and hopelessness, the acts of sacrifice and dedication from healthcare workers and volunteers served to redeem our humanity. The American philanthropist Melinda French Gates noted in her annual Goalkeepers Report that 'this pandemic has magnified every existing inequality in our society—like systemic racism, gender inequality, and poverty. And it's impossible to pick one issue as more serious because so many people live at the intersection of all of those challenges'.[48] Tragedies have a remarkable ability to bring people together. The pandemic certainly did that; we did our duty, kept ourselves masked and distanced, helped one another out, got our vaccines, flattened the curve, and loved our first responders. But we cannot rely on tragedy to keep us motivated. We may or may not have seen what was magnified by the pandemic, but the lessons are out there; we need only to take the leap and rethink our situation. There is no future in going back to the past, because by returning to normal or business as usual would set ourselves up for failure.

It is a wickedly complex dilemma. We need to resist the urge to run back to the status quo or the false stability it offers. Nostalgia and 'should-haves' will not serve us at this point. What is direly needed is reform in education at all levels to mould generational thinking to ensure the inculcation of knowledge and new technology with the imbuing of values. Reform would include a complete review of the curriculum and pedagogy so that previous objectives can be meet and future objectives can be determined in order to define a robust blueprint for the future. We need to think about how we teach and how we form our students, our future citizens, who will need to be equipped for challenges beyond what we can presently imagine. We need to embody in our pedagogy and culture refreshing and thought provoking learning. We need to move towards a greater appreciation of complexity and chaos. We need methods for transcending contradictions through the enrichment of imagination and creativity. This requires a move from disciplinary approaches (often of a 'zombie' nature) to inter-, multi-, and trans-disciplinary perspectives. While we need to diversify our specialisations and develop new specialists, it is perhaps more important that we simultaneously focus on producing versatile generalists and polymaths. This need not be a contradiction. We must expand our own thinking so that we can enhance the thinking of our pupils. We have got to teach an appreciation and comprehension of uncertainty and ignorance in the multiple and evasive forms it takes. We need to emphasise in our students that we are not just local communities, nation-states, threatened identities, but that we are part of a complex, globalised world. We need to instil our youth with confidence in their own identities and traditions so that they will take them on into the future and allow them to evolve and adjust to changing circumstances.

The pandemic taught us that every day something can be done, a new step, a new direction can be crafted. From the lessons learnt, a value-centric approach to societal reform will set us on a positive trajectory. And this can only come about with a committed and concerted effort, barring none, at rethinking as we move into the future infused with the capacity and agency for change.

V

A number of recent works envisage that the coming decades will force us to undertake some serious soul-searching—such as Fareed Zakaria's *Ten Lessons for a Post-Pandemic World*, Gordon Brown's *Seven Ways to Change the World*, and again in Brown's work with Mohamed A. El-Erian and Michael Spence, *Permacrisis*.[49]

We have to begin with the realisation that *Homo sapiens*, the doubly knowing species that we are, is intrinsically moral. We are the only species that can, and does, exercise free will. We are free to choose. But the choices we make and the actions we take and the positions we adopt on the basis of these choices are inherently moral judgements. Morality is the curse of free will; we are, if you like, destined to be moral. Even those who abdicate all sense of morality and ethics are actually taking a moral position. There is little out there that is value-neutral. Sardar points out that 'modernisation, progress, bureaucracy, science and all the disciplines of modern knowledge emerged complete with a rich sustaining mythology whose most basic tenet was the delusional notion that they were value neutral, universal and inherently good'. Soul-searching requires us to tackle and transcend this 'sustaining mythology'.[50]

All the intractable, interlinked, knotty problems we face, from freedom and authoritarianism, equality and justice, identity and tradition, economy and capitalism, representation and social media, AI and bioengineering, are, at their core, moral and ethical issues. Moral discernment is perhaps the only tool we have to untangle this confounding Gordian knot that sits before us.

Morals are both the exercise of discernment and statements of what is to be discerned as having value. The value derived from morals is the refinement of a coherent vision of a society and culture—and the human condition. Acting morally is discerning how to achieve the greatest refinement of human potential to realise the best possible enjoyment of the human existence. But this abstract approach is really something of an intellectual conceit. As human beings, we are products of history. And in history, all moral worlds emerged and were derived from religion—any and all religions. Secular ideologies and liberal humanism added and subtracted from morality based on religion to produce their own moral schemas. You do not have to be a theist to be moral. But the truth is that all morality has its origins in religion.

Today, we drive our moral sense from a plethora of sources. Even the Highway Code is a moral document concerned with what is best and right for humans to do for the greater good. All societies have laws, and therefore are based on moral precepts, a conception of what life is about. The question is not whether you have morals, but what morals you have and how you prioritise them. And that's exactly where we run into insurmountable problems.

In postnormal times, driven by contradictions, complexity, and chaos, the questions of morality and identity have become interlinked and interdependent. What gives us meaning shapes our experience and defines who we are, and what we are helps determine how we ought to live. And what gives meaning to our lives are the values we cherish. It is our values that define who we are, how we should live, and how we should shape and interact with the world. In other words, Morals R Us. This is why struggles over moral principles are so linked to identity politics; and, in many cases, have become a matter of life and death. It is seen as a battle for the survival of our identity—our very Self.

This moral-based identity politics—from the East as well as the West, from Muslim societies as well as Europe—is the greatest current threat to all morality. Any comprehensive package that is the source of all our morality is dangerous: it often ends up with a tailor-made metaphysics that fits our moral prejudices, or that distorts our morals to fit a false ideology. It turns morality, whether religious or secular, into custom and customary practice. It presumes that all moral questions are settled once and for all; and there are no hard questions and particularly difficult circumstances which will force us to revise our moral outlook. Morality has to be liberated from ideology, for ideology is our greatest enemy. 'The imagination and spiritual strength of Shakespeare's evildoers', writes Aleksandr Solzhenitsyn,

> stopped short at a dozen corpses. Because they had no *ideology*. Ideology—that is what gives evildoing its long-sought justification and gives the evildoer the necessary steadfastness and determination. That is the social theory which helps to make his acts seem good instead of bad in his own and others' eyes ... That was how the agents of the Inquisition fortified their wills: by invoking Christianity; the conquerors of foreign lands, by extolling the grandeur of their Motherland; the colonizers, by civilization; the Nazis, by race; and the Jacobins (early and late), by equality, brotherhood, and the happiness of future generations ... Without evildoers there would have been no Archipelago.[51]

Rethinking ourselves, going forward to viable, plural futures, means freeing ourselves from all types of ideologies—the ideology of economics, the ideology of technological determinism, nationalist ideologies, religious and secular ideologies—and working with age-old moral virtues that have stood the test of change and time: compassion, humility, love, tolerance, equality, truthfulness, fairness, unity, responsibility, modesty, self-control, temperance, justice, dignity, and respect for nature and Others. Some of these virtues may be problematic to pin down theoretically, as, for example, with justice and equality, but none of them are difficult to achieve in practice. But realising these virtues in our individual and collective lives, as communities and nations, necessitates ditching the destructive values we have imbibed from modernity, free-market ideology, and postmodernism: Eurocentrism, individualism, absolute relativism, egocentrism, dogmatism, libertarianism, populism, and a range of associated falsehoods, racisms, and misrepresentations. Those who stand by time-honoured virtues have to stand up against these cancers that afflict our times.

But well-established old virtues also need to be employed to help us navigate our current perilous condition; from simply being discrete to a holistic, integrated, and consciously nurtured universal imperative. They must function as a three-dimensional lens, our basic navigational tool—a new-age sextant and compass—that helps us to negotiate accelerating change, transcend contradictions, orient complexity through profound simplicity, and survive chaos. This matrix of virtues has thus to function on a collective and communal, as well as local, national, and global level. Only then can it enable us to distinguish what is really good and wholesome in a rapidly changing context from an excess of destructive and inhuman options.

That is what I learned in my life of politics, in and out of prison, working to keep hope alive (and may it last well beyond my own lifetime). It is a lesson that began with the last lines of the Epilogue in Shakespeare's final work, *The Tempest*:

Gentle breath of yours my sails
Must fill, or else my project fails,
Which was to please. Now I want
Spirits to enforce, art to enchant,
And my ending is despair,
Unless I be relieved by prayer,
Which pierces so that it assaults
Mercy itself and frees all faults.
As you from crimes would pardon'd be,
Let your indulgence set me free.

EPILOGUE

PREPARING FOR THE NEXT STORM

To borrow roughly from the words of the American novelist E. L. Doctorow, where the historian tells us what happened in the past, the artist tells us how it felt.[1] To the outside world, he is not well known. But in Malaysia, Teuku Zakaria bin Teuku Nyak Puteh, better known by his stage name 'P. Ramlee', is an absolute legend. A creative with no formal training in the fields he mastered, P. Ramlee was an actor, musician, composer, singer, and filmmaker. He flourished between 1945 and 1973, the period when he made his most notable films and wrote and sang his most memorable songs. When we watch his films or listen to his songs, we feel Malaysia's independence, *Merdeka*, in all its anxiety, hope, uncertainty, and excitement. Indeed, the appreciation of the man often derives from a romantic longing for a bygone era. While there is nothing wrong with art and the artist being held as a source of evocative sentimentality, to paint the portrait of P. Ramlee in nostalgia alone is to miss the subject—almost entirely. For he was a revolutionary. But not a revolutionary in the sense we might readily think of when reflecting on postcolonial heroes. He drew no blood with either sword, *keris*,[2] or even the words he penned; the most vehement thing he ever did was melt hearts with his dulcet voice and debonair charm. But

215

with image and sound, he poked fun at and exposed the underlying vestigial feudalist tendencies that carried forward into Malaysian culture and, with clever subtlety, criticised the government and the ruling party UMNO, something not readily done at the time. And his stories championed the values we hold dear as Malaysians, such as social justice and equality. He was a revolutionary in the way that only the artist can be. He helped us engage with change.

What I value the most in P. Ramlee's films is that each story has a core thread of justice running through it. Beyond nostalgia, he captured those universal feelings that we carry through our histories, while also keeping that which we hold most dear, our culture, intact, tapping into and drawing out our most inherent values. Through the laughter and tears conjured, his films have no pontificating heroes but instead we are shown images of what justice looks like. The faults in our society are placed before our eyes. Unobtrusively, we learn where we may have strayed, be it in the social or cultural arenas or even in the realm of politics. And then we wake, to borrow from Kant, 'from our dogmatic slumber',[3] we find new cogitations stirring us. This is at the heart of rethinking ourselves. Taking this one step further, he not only critiques to denigrate; he synthesises.

In the 1958 film, *Sarjan Hassan* (*Sergeant Hassan*), we see P. Ramlee at his pinnacle. The fictional story follows the story of a young orphan, suffering the indignation of his foster brothers, who rises up through the Malayan military as it fought against Japanese occupation.[4] Coming out only a year after Malaya's independence from Great Britain, but set during World War II, the film balances the nascent nation of Malaya between British and Japanese rule when we did not know who we were going to be or where we were going to stand between the rest of Asia and the West. But the true genius is in the music. The hit single from the film, 'Wait a Little While' (*Tunggu Sekejap*), blends

Western motifs with those of other Asian films of the time while retaining a distinct Malayness—the lyrical play of Bahasa Melayu is masterful. If the song had appeared in a Bollywood or Hollywood film, people all over the world would be humming the tune. Such synthesis and integration of styles and motifs demonstrated the rich potential of the independence not just of Malaysia but all the newly independent Asian states.

Independence was a revolutionary change and a moment of great hope. New ideas were in no short supply, and no idea was considered to be mutually exclusive. Islam and modern music lived as cordial neighbours; Islam and democracy were seen as bedfellows. There was no need to look East or West. There was a real opportunity for a new way that went beyond colonialism or anything that fitted nicely into one categorical box or the other. There was a wonderful cosmopolitanism that today seems too good to be real, only the stuff of escapist cinema. Best of all, there was no fear. For what was distinctly Malaysian or Islamic, or Indian, or Asian, was not lost. P. Ramlee demonstrated the ability to play between East and West while also being Asian, Malay, Muslim, and Malaysian, and losing none of the vibrance of any of the parts or the whole in the process. It is a cultural narrative without the affection of scholastic disputation, but it is certainly meritorious and deserves a closer study considering that it was advanced decades earlier than the leading discourses of the day. Speaking of which, one cannot overlook *The Ethics of Identity*, where Kwame Appiah challenges essentialist, hard-and-fast notions of identity, positing them as static. Appiah instead notes that identity is in constant flux and subject to the extraordinary forces of time, including the dynamics of historical developments and language. Rejecting the notion that identities inevitably clash, he calls for dialogue among the world's diverse communities and ethnicities that would foster greater respect and understanding. He champions cosmopolitanism, where ethical considerations are the imperative of connectedness and inclusivity rather than division and isolation.[5]

It is hard to tell whether it was our reticence to change or our accumulated ignorance when faced with change that played a greater role in sidetracking us from crafting our preferred futures. Perhaps it was a combination of both. No doubt our own elites, who drank the Kool-Aid of 'Westernisation', played a major part in the situation that many former colonial states find themselves in; much like Sergeant Hassan's stepbrother who joins the Japanese secret service and then exploits his own people. Yet, the American futurist Alvin Toffler's definition of change as 'the process by which the future invades our lives'[6] is apt here. Without awareness, we appear to be under the constant siege of the future. Indeed, one might say we are being colonised by the future. But as we hone our awareness, we quickly see that that 'future' does not hold up. For it is not our future, but someone else's.

That future, rather, has been influenced and dictated by Western leaders who, ostensibly, preached liberalism, democracy, and the rule of law. However, from Iran to Egypt, Lebanon to Indonesia, Chile to Congo, they have systematically undermined all three. The US has openly accepted interference in elections and the toppling of democratically elected governments that it did not appreciate. Whenever it suits, Western nations support and promote military and authoritarian regimes. For the past fifty years, Western diplomacy has essentially been diplomacy by military might. Politics and economics writ large have come to be a process of perpetuating the present. Even though the theory does not hold, our actions dictate that history has ended and as long as we maintain the status quo, nobody has to get hurt. Yet, we do not realise we are negotiating while we have a gun held against our heads. The very notion of justice seems to have no value. Where so-called justice has been pursued, it has benefited only the privileged few. Even the much-lauded Rawlsian theory of justice as fairness, using the veil of ignorance, has no place for the poor, women, or other marginalised communities, nor much universal value. We are asked to look inward and forget about history and never mind the future. And we live life through that ignorant lens not realising, to borrow from the words of the American memoirist and poet Maya Angelou, that in our ignorance we imprison one another, and also ourselves.[7]

Being able to quickly adapt and respond to change has been the unwritten and incompletable daily work behind my career in politics that has framed most of my life. It took me far too long to consider the future and to look ahead at that beautiful, plural potentiality. Granted, I have always had dreams and desires, but these wishes were often tempered upon the stage of a perpetual present or cloaked in an unwaning fixation on the past. Reflection on the past is necessary, so that we might take wisdom from the lessons ignored or the road less travelled, but we must not let the past linger and limit our capacity to build a better tomorrow. And even with justice as my guide, to not consider what justice looks like in the future held my efforts back. I was trapped between a past that haunted me, both with the threat of subjugation and the false promise of romantic nostalgia, and a future that was unattainable.

The seeds of rethinking ourselves, so that our future could again be ours, were planted the day I was named Malaysia's minister of finance in 1991. While a minister of finance could be said to have done their job if they can balance the budget—a task by no means easy or straightforward—so much more was at stake with my appointment. First, financial failure would not only topple the government come election time, but could doom the whole nation to years of suffering. Second, having seen so many respectable and prominent individuals entering my office and suddenly reduced to begging panhandlers, this was my first chance to demonstrate my own style of executive leadership and to nudge Malaysia's governance structure from one of loosely connected fiefdoms into a cohesive cooperative where efficiency drove common visions dictated by the will of the people. Third, this was my chance to begin, to use the common parlance of the day, to drain the swamp, or to chisel away at the normalised corruption that had been taken for granted in the country. Fourth, my career up until that point was characterised by the struggle for justice in our times; but justice now was not simply the destination, it had to be attained in such a way that it could be sustained into the future. And I was keenly aware of change by this point. Justice in 1991 might not look the same as justice in 1998, in 2018, or in 2025 and beyond. In terms of finance, the trick is not access. Access is always there to be given, but unwisely distributed, it will not last long and may not see out the just ends desired. The trick was making sure that access was equated to agency. The master stroke was making it sustainable. So, while I was under constant pressure to come up with the funds needed, I also needed a solid system to replenish the coffers—something that has not always been of the highest priority in Malaysian history! And this is where a fifth point comes in. Malaysia, being a rather young nation in comparison to the international community, needed to begin thinking about its place in the wider world, as the forces of globalisation were already reaching down to the most local and remote reaches of the planet. We did not have the military or other conventional wherewithal that other nations did with regard to exerting their influence. But we did have a rich history as a trading crossroads, and we do have a renowned culture of hospitality. So it is in the synergy of our financial and economic ministries, both domestic and foreign, bolstered by our well-trained and well-mannered diplomats, that Malaysia engaged with the outside world that, by the end of the twentieth century, was indeed becoming a small place.

EPILOGUE

Out of the gate, it was essential to demonstrate both a loyalty to my government and to show a good face to the globe's economic movers and shakers. As a sociology major in the Malay Studies Department, I had no formal academic training in economics. This of course had its advantages and disadvantages. One advantage was that I was not married to one school of thought or another, nor trying to desperately win one academic war or another. I had always taken a more practical approach. And my experience in running other ministries had me ready for this challenge. The network of intellectuals I had rubbed shoulders with over the prior two decades also came in handy. I knew how to bring in the experts, but also how to be critical and ask the right questions. I had no interest in winning ideological debates; I needed practical results. Of course, as I would learn, some of these ideological debates need to be taken on so that the poorest of the world are able to put food on the table for their families. Furthermore, the Cold War had ended, but I and others knew that while the Washington Consensus was quick to throw up the flag of victory, history had not come to its terminus and the precepts and prescriptions of Western economists were neither divine law nor without their flaws. Indeed, I advocated for market-friendly and pro-growth policies, but the Club of Rome's report, *The Limits of Growth*, was almost two decades old.[8] I also cautioned against the addiction many of us in the 'developing' world had to development, as if it was the key to everything. I opposed our obsession with mega projects that stood mostly as grotesque displays of grandeur. Instead, I stressed spending on education, healthcare, and public housing. At the same time, we needed to balance this with projects that would bring economic returns, attract private investments, encourage an increase in foreign direct investments, and promote small and medium industries. While growth provided opportunities for people to improve their livelihoods, it also opened wider doors to corruption, unless checks and balances were fortified.

Indeed, globally, the great debate over the future of neoliberal economics was the talk of the town. The economic models of Ronald Reagan in the US and Margaret Thatcher in the UK were being both glorified on one side of the aisle and vehemently denounced on the other. I often found myself agreeing with a colourful variety of people, but for very different reasons. I believed that there should be a reduced government involvement in business, but not for the reasons my peers did. My call for the separation of business and state was to prevent a dependency of business on the state. Free enterprise is essential for the growth of the economy. However, where the government could not but be involved was in upholding and continuously re-evaluating regulation. Corporate predators think faster than bureaucrats. But this is a two-sided coin. On one side, you need the corporately minded to have some freedom to innovate and compete, but on the other, the issues of transparency, corporate governance, and the need to get tough on corruption take on even greater urgency. And despite being market-friendly and supportive of the private sector, I believed in the strong role—the duty—the state had as provider of public goods, upholder of political stability, and regulator, levelling the playing field among competing interests.

In the debate between having a government that is interventionist and one that allows unbridled capitalism, conventional wisdom has it is not the business of government to be involved in business. According to this doctrine, government must get out of the way and let the movers and shakers of business and corporate tycoons have absolute free rein to drive the economy forward. But there are, it seems, what some might call exceptions and what others might call contradictions. When it comes to those businesses that are 'too big to fail', allowance must be made for interventionalist policy, especially to bail out failing enterprises such as big banks and insurance companies. This is perverse, as such approval looks very much like a 'socialism for the rich and capitalism for the poor', where state policies ensure that the rich and powerful get to have their cake, and eat it too, while the poor and marginalised will be left to clean up the plates! What I was witnessing through the collusion of business and politics, was the hijacking of the state by vested interests. Competition at home was anything but fair, although those in power continued to complain about the absence of a level playing field on the international front. Between the state and businesses, the people were conspicuously absent.

To overcome such degenerate forms of capitalism, the proper mode of interventionist policies must be people-centric. While the American economist Joseph Stiglitz calls it 'progressive capitalism', I call it the 'humane economy for social justice'. In 2024, Stiglitz had become the new hot topic with the publication of his *The Road to Freedom*.[9] Stiglitz advocates for more government, not less, including the need for environmental regulations: financial and other regulations necessary for the proper functioning of the economy. In order to achieve a productive economy, the government needs to spend money on physical, technological, and social infrastructure. Where 'greed is good' is the mantra of unfettered free enterprise, where moral hazard is allowed to encourage reckless behaviour, and where the onslaught of negative externalities is treated as being inevitable—that is, in fact, the road to serfdom. This calls to mind Isaiah Berlin's famous aphorism, which Stiglitz also reiterates, that 'freedom for the wolves means death to the sheep'.[10]

Recently, economic discourse has become very confusing, producing a well of contradictions. Take, for instance, the collapse of Western capitalism. This collapse was first reported by Stiglitz after the fall of the Berlin Wall. Likewise, we hear the proclamation echoed in the cycle of financial crises triggered by the 2008 sub-prime fiasco and its aftershocks. Yet, others, like the Indian

American economist Jagdish Bhaghwati, have countered that this is a fundamentally flawed analogy. Essentially, the argument is that whereas the fall of the Berlin Wall laid waste to authoritarian politics and the near totalitarian economics of the Soviet states, the crisis in Wall Street and Main Street was merely a consequence of the externalities of market forces and the damage was transitional, neither permanent nor paradigm changing. Both sides of the Western divide remain committed to capitalism as the foundational system, but they continue to clash on the extent of free-market systems. The anti-globalists are inclined towards state intervention while the fundamentalists insist on a hands-off position. Some are even contemplating the resurgence of Keynesian economics and its growing prevalence over the Austrian school, as exemplified by the prescriptions of Friedrich Hayek. In an address soon after the sub-prime crisis unfolded, I postulated the decline, if not demise altogether, of the neoliberal advocates, but it would appear that I was greatly misunderstood as I was reported to be pro-interventionist and anti-free market.

The most glaring misunderstanding is the belief that capitalism is synonymous with democracy because of the assumption that a 'market economy' is the antidote to dictatorship or totalitarian rule, thanks no less to Hayek's treatise on liberty.[11] This was adopted as the Bible of economics by Margaret Thatcher, but the discourse has been somewhat jaundiced by the hardline stance of those who think that the only road to freedom is unadulterated wholesale free-market capitalism. Across another paradigm, commonly said to be the Islamic model, the advocates flay capitalism for its 'inherent flaw in being unable to distinguish between "private money" and "public property"'. The Islamic economic model is able to separate the two.

In this day and age, when the inequities of wealth distribution are so glaring, the term 'perfect competition' has become meaningless because the caveat *ceteris paribus* is purely fictional. In

Islam, the *maqasid al-shariah* dictates that there be checks and balances against the disproportionate accumulation of wealth or the monopolistic control of resources, while monopoly of essential endowments is solely vested in the state, which is the guardian of God's dominion. The scholars argue that the essence of an Islamic model must include a prohibition not just against *riba*, usury, but against greed itself! It is on this basis, among others, that the advocates of the Islamic model launch their assault on the foundations of the capitalistic economic model. The common root of this discontent lies in the excessive profits that can be made. If there is no dispute that profit is a premium paid for risks taken by the seller, the only serious question is what constitutes 'excessive'. This charge about profit is invariably linked to the philosophy of greed, which is said to be the cornerstone of the Smithian rationale for capitalism. This is based on the much-quoted passage in *The Wealth of Nations* concerning 'the butcher, the brewer, or the baker', and that we 'address ourselves not to their humanity but to their self-love'.[12] But Adam Smith is often done a disservice when we only read *The Wealth of Nations*. In his lesser-known work, *The Theory of Moral Sentiments*, we find the ethics that are so often missing from his great intellectual defenders. His stereotyped tone is tempered in the passage where Smith asks us 'to feel much for others and little for ourselves, that to restrain our selfish affections constitutes the perfection of human nature'.[13]

We have seen how the traditional bastions of capitalism in the West were overwhelmed by the 'Occupy Wall Street' movement in the aftermath of the sub-prime crisis. There is a growing call by economists in the tradition of Rawls, through J. K. Galbraith, to Stiglitz, Jeffrey Sachs, and Thomas Piketty, questioning basic economic issues about the control of government by conglomerates, the problem of poverty, and gross inequality. A clear indictment is raised against the concept of the 'invisible hand', another over-inflated idea from Smith divorced from the ethics he wrote of in his earlier writing. The invisible hand is, after all, only mentioned once in the nearly 700-page *Wealth of Nations*. Interestingly, the word 'inequality' is mentioned seventeen times and he spared no opportunity to use the word in his other works, as Emma Rothschild, British historian and wife of Amartya Sen, is always quick to remind me![14] Almost as invisible as it is in Smith's writings, the invisible hand has remained invisible so often that governments in the 'free' world have felt compelled to intervene in situations traditionally left to market forces. There is even an emerging prevalent view that inequality is not necessarily unjust.[15] The ease with which ethics can be sloughed off from economics speaks to a much larger crisis that needs to be urgently addressed.

Islam not only comes to the table with a well-pronounced system of ethics, it also acknowledges the importance of society's need to pursue commerce to its fullest. The concept and sanctity of contracts as well as the requisite principles of justice and fairness in dealings remain the cornerstone by which to judge the validity of transactions. One indicator of the success of the Islamic capital market is how it has weathered the recent financial crisis. However, even in advocating a more Islamic approach to economics as an option for the future of capitalism, I do not present it without criticism. An Islamic model must be conceived beyond mere legalistic compliance. Instead of matching a model to one brand or interpretation of doctrine, the new model before us should have a built-in, overriding concern with catalysing economic development, promoting wider participation, and championing justice.

The inequalities of wealth, power, and status are not exclusive to nations subscribing to 'free' markets. Whatever the system may be, poverty reduction programmes, without which the gap between the rich and the poor will never be narrowed, let alone bridged, are essential. In reality, the present figures point to a dismal situation in Muslim countries where the Gini coefficient is growing along with its attendant social problems of housing, education, and health. But this need not be fate. Thus, a few critical adjustments must be made through instruments which can shelter the poorer groups in a country. The development pathway taken must also be forward-looking in order to serve the well-being of the people, addressing poverty, inequality, and cultivating a mindset of shared responsibility and innovation. There is an urgent need to embrace the spirit of inclusiveness and openness—a readiness to adapt, to innovate, and to constantly push the boundaries of what is possible. And the response must be holistic, coordinated, and, above all, focussed on the long-term well-being of the nation.

It has often been argued that the emphasis on political freedom, liberties, and democracy is a specifically Western priority. I must say the recent political developments in Europe and the US have seen that demagoguery, racism, and the dictates of the far right seem to have taken precedence. And similarly, we need to caution against the argument suggesting that emerging economies are not ready to adopt a democratic system or other 'Western' ideas. Economic development, it is said, must precede freedom. Empty stomachs shout not for liberty, but for food. Development is not a trade-off for unfreedom, and in the name of development, fundamental liberties and dissent should not be stifled. If development is to enlarge freedom, then substantial development enlarges freedom substantially, for 'it is hard to think that any process of substantial development can do without extensive use of markets'.[16] According to Sen, statecraft, which will necessarily warrant social support and public regulation, cannot be precluded when it can enrich—rather than impoverish—human lives. The way forward is neither Western nor non-Western, but it should be a path in which the ideas of all are integrated, tempered by the failures and victories of all who have tried.

In light of the foregoing, it would be a fool's errand to contemplate a magic-bullet formulation for a be-all and end-all system of income distribution. Yet, even though there may be no master key to unlock the secrets of any kind of utopian system of income distribution, some basic prescriptions for the attainment of social justice may be stated. Governments must be committed to the principle that a more equitable distribution of income is a fundamental precept for the realisation of social justice. John Rawls's abiding question on what principles of justice should prevail in order to attain a good society, that is, a society that is fair and egalitarian, awaits our address. Governments should undertake with full conviction integrated plans for poverty reduction, while ensuring a comprehensive support system for the poor and the economically marginalised. This is best summed up as 'the empowerment of and public protection of the powerless'.[17]

And it is not just our conventional, often Western, approaches to economics that are crumbling and in dire need of greater thought. At least since the fall of the Berlin Wall, Western dominance overall has been collapsing in on itself. The lofty promises of the post-war era not only remained unanswered but became demented by the neoliberalism of the 1970 and 1980s, ushering in corruption and hate, misinformation, extreme individualism and fundamentalism, as well as war, devastation, suicide, and genocide. Now that the colonial enchantment with Western moral and democratic superiority has revealed itself to be a total sham, the postcolonial states need to shape their own futures, not in isolation but in collaboration. And even collaboration with what can still be called 'the West'.

This future can only be shaped with an awareness of what has changed. With an appreciation of the stark reality that faces us. The world order has changed. The unipolar structure of the last forty years has now given way to a multipolar world. The old superpowers are no longer super. Middle powers like Turkey, Brazil, Indonesia, and South Africa are coming of age. The intergovernmental arrangement that is BRICS will expand and become a major player in its own right, at least tipping the scales, if not launching a fleet of new ways. In doing this, BRICS acts as the herald of a new paradigm. First, it offers a voice and table to those often silenced or left outside of the room where geopolitical and economic decisions are made. Second, it demonstrates that indeed history did not end, and there is another way, and perhaps that we all need not to be tied to one dominant currency. And lastly, it acts as an economic mode of diplomacy that tears down once-assumed divisions of civilisations or, to put it crudely, 'good guys' and 'bad guys', offering a challenge to our assumed world order. My efforts in pushing Malaysia's acceptance into BRICS have been a point of contention for many. Simply put, BRICS offers substantial opportunities for Malaysian businesses given its diverse resource base, allowing Malaysia to tap into new markets and increase trade and investment opportunities. This expanded market access is likely to benefit the palm oil, rubber, and the electronics sector—areas where Malaysia holds a competitive advantage. More significantly from a geostrategic standpoint, it bears stressing that Malaysia will not shy away from exercising agency and participating in geoeconomic arrangements as we see fit. By participating in BRICS, we aim to diversify our economic diplomacy efforts and enhance our collaboration with member countries through shared initiatives and strategic partnerships. Malaysia's entry into this grouping will not only strengthen economic linkages with the founding members but also open new avenues for cooperation across a broader spectrum of industries and policy areas, as more states join. I have also been asked whether joining BRICS is indicative of 'Malaysia slouching towards China and Russia' and while I take this line of inquiry as being rather condescending, nonetheless, my answer is clear: Malaysia's policy is not about slouching towards or pivoting one way or another, but is one that manifests the principle of collectively shaping our shared futures, the commonality of goals and aspirations, and the overarching ideal of universal peace and prosperity. Not only is BRICS well received by countries in Asia, Africa, Latin America, and throughout the Global South, increasingly we are seeing, and with greater urgency of late, more receptive responses from various EU members. I cannot overstate the importance of this approach as a rampart against the forces of discord and protectionism, demonstrated lately in extreme, perverse fashion. North or South, West or East, there should be no bifurcation when it comes to the imperative of building a community with a shared future to uphold values of humanity and justice, global peace and security, as well as sharing experiences, expertise, and technologies amongst the community of nations. Now, these are not pious platitudes but as Elvis Presley reminds us, perhaps we simply need 'a little less conversation, a little more action, please'. There are alternative futures that can be shaped. The old political orthodoxies, such as the transatlantic alliance and NATO, are dismantling. The European Union is fragmented and deflated, and to paraphrase its description of the nineteenth-century Ottoman Empire, looks like the 'sick man of the West'. The United States has become an old-fashioned transactional imperial power. A world order of this level of complexity presents us with formidable issues.

Yet, we either turn a blind eye or tackle every crisis with half-baked solutions. Then another series of crises emerge and are met in a similar manner. But the human and environmental cost of each crisis continues to increase. Meanwhile, we are stupefied by accelerating change. The hyper-chaotic media cannot process the news cycle, let alone provide a satisfactory response. Chaotic weather events continue to take their toll in a world riddled with acceleratingly despotic climate change. Astronomical levels of inequality between nations and within nations are perpetuated by the worship of an economic model that is grounded on promoting inequality and exclusion. Democracy is undermined by money politics, inefficiency, and inability and failure to adapt to rapid changes and existential threats. The excessive focus on individualism in liberal democracies is ripping societies apart. It is hardly surprising that trust in democracy is evaporating, and not only this, but trust in one another. The ignored drip of moral decadence, often with the complicity of ruling elites, has culminated in an unprecedented trust deficit that threatens the very fabric of society.

The shock of change, seen or not, comes with whiplash. Just as a swift kick to the ribs, whether one is blindfolded or in full vision, hurts all the same. Already, we are working in an incredibly complex space. For lack of a more encompassing term, the world up to the twentieth century gave us one preferred approach to change, summed up nicely by the phrase 'taking the bull by the horns'. However, it is ill-advised to take even the most docile bull by the horns if one values one's safety, let alone one's mortal coil. And change is no docile bull. I tried to take the bull by the horns three times. My body carries the consequences of those choices. And not just did I get thrown down and locked up, but each time I re-emerged from the prison, I found myself in a radically changed world. An innocent arrival lost in future shock. In 1976, I was released into a world where the honeymoon of independence, as well as my youth, were officially history. In 2004, I was released into a new century where the marriage of rapidly advancing technology and the pervasiveness of postmodernism were taking us down a dark and twisted trail. In 2018, I was released into a Malaysia released from the clutches of the dominant political alliance, and into a world where people were spending more time on social media or in the digital space than IRL

(In Real Life). IRL was just one of the new acronyms and words I had to learn, along with selfie, meme, fake news, deep fake, troll, and clickbait! Influencers, I learned, had replaced journalists. And social media had become a formidable weapon in identity politics. And then there was the global trauma of the Covid-19 pandemic! Far from the simple omission of the gaps from my own history, the world itself was undergoing a more radical change than I could imagine.

A common response to postnormal times is a retreat into a dogmatic defence of what worked normally. Uncertainty unhinges; and the unknown cannot be faced and is frightening. The speed of change we are up against is challenging the most adaptive of us—and it is only accelerating, faster and faster. And the complexity of all things has us entangled in a wide and deep spider's web. And the innumerable contradictions arising from what we took as business as usual or standard operating procedure—which are set by largely Western and modern definitions—slap us in the face over and over again as we struggle to hold ourselves up on less and less stable ground. Global warming became climate change became global boiling became climate catastrophe, as one by one planetary boundaries are crossed. The ugly Frankensteinian monster of politics and economics threatens all societies, cultures, and traditions simultaneously as instability breeds uncertainty breeds panic. Technology advances faster than our understanding, driving us to abandon thinking itself as truth appears as opinion and is assigned as mission impossible. Ignorance, identity politics, and xenophobia perpetuate hate towards an unprecedented, destructive trajectory. What we have actually learned in the post-Covid-19 years, is that social media has not just been weaponised, it has in fact become a weapon of bigotry. It has killed the very idea of human empathy. And it is now the chief instrument for propagating and proliferating fascism and the decline of culture into barbarism. Far right parties are the new normal in Europe and could conquer the continent in the coming decade. I see the rise of fascism in Europe, the US, Asia, and Africa as a clear and present danger in general, and for Muslim societies and other marginalised communities in particular. Racism is rife but often unidentified, not least by racists and xenophobes. When examined closely, xenophobia finds its roots in the dehumanisation and devaluation of people of a particular ethnicity, nationality, or faith group and is exacerbated by the perception of threat to one's position in society. This worldview has driven politically dominant societies in the West and the East (or the Global North and South) to raise their guard against any outsider and usurper that dares challenge their natural superiority. The prejudices of politically dominant groups, no matter how big or small they are compared to their perceived enemies, must be recognised and condemned as a threat unto the rights of the latter. This refusal to accept the humanity of others due to their belonging to another place or group constitutes a major stumbling block against resolving this insidious issue. To a xenophobe, an Islamophobe, and a racist, it is unthinkable that another group of people could offer an equally valid perspective on life as they could. Xenophobia and ignorance, particularly in the form of Islamophobia, have now evolved and expanded. At this moment ignorance, a key driver of xenophobia, is the elephant in the room not just in the West, but also, and perhaps more so, in Asia and Africa. The phenomenon has gone global and is now found in various forms across different countries and political spectrums. While our policies struggle to keep up, this is where building futures-aware approaches can be a point of anchor. We need to not only build our knowledge in this area but also find creative policy potential in our education system and from within our societies.

There is no space to try new policies and no time to wait for results and revise our hypotheses. Reform cannot cope. Problems we have not managed to solve up to this point still remain and only fester and ferment. Normal, or at least what's left of it, is the problem, and no alternatives stand in the wings. This is no bull you want to take by the horns. This is postnormal times. But again, awareness is simply not enough.

The non-West, the Global South, cannot remain complacent in the face of these threats. We cannot allow all our futures to be colonised in the interests of Western capital, corporations, or the hegemonic powers. To prevent the powerful from owning our futures, the Global South must actively reclaim futures by developing new paradigms, new ways of knowing, and articulating viable but also visionary political alternatives. A basic methodological precept which needs to be followed in this task is to acknowledge the complexity of today's social and cultural world. We need to bring to the fore open systems and social agency. We need to wrestle freedom from deterministic technology, hateful social media, manipulative corporations, and political expediency, and stand up for true justice and representation. We must remember that truth and justice are two sides of the same coin; one cannot exist without the other. Both need democracy to flourish. We need to ditch reptilian free-market capitalism and move towards humane economics; a pluralistic and practical approach to justice that considers economic and social contexts. And we need to move towards the open and balanced approach inherent in Islamic concepts of justice that advocate for a global *Convivencia* based on the values of diversity and shared human objectives. The ummah too now requires a global moral vision that transcends the sectarian divide and political bickering among Muslim states and other communities. The notion must now include all the 'rest' and marginalised communities. And Islamic fundamentalism must be rejected outright everywhere—loudly and clearly. Politics cannot be based on simple, singular experience, identity, or projects. But we need to explore the plurality of political demands and seek viable synthesis that is good for the people and the planet. And while this navigational balancing act is no utopian fantasy, it can be realised. We are humans with brains, endowed with reason. We can take that step. As we look back at the widening typhoon of change accompanying postnormal times, we can make some observations. That same struggle of good versus evil, or however we like to characterise it, remains the timeless drama of moral conflict. The continuous bending of this arc of conflict towards evil demands that we rethink how we are positioning ourselves. Fundamentally, while it is easy to get lost in the complexity of our contemporary challenges, they boil down to largely moral considerations. Yet this modernity we find ourselves in is ethically bankrupt. Thus, our starting point is a reconsideration of our values, particularly those common values which unite our societies and communities. This is the basic mechanism behind the aforementioned SCRIPT/MADANI framework that stands as Malaysia's navigational road map through postnormal times while promoting unity, sustainable development, and the pursuit of just, better futures for all.[18] In parallel to this framework we are also having to take a new appreciation and approach to the complexity of our contemporary reality. We have no choice but to forestall chaos. Some wish to harness chaos; a most dangerous endeavour, which inevitably always fails, leaving tumultuous calamity in its wake. Some even seek to propagate chaos; the toddler's mantra of 'if I can't have it, then no one else can' displays such action's immaturity. We have to anticipate chaos but also seek to reduce the opportunity for chaos to distract us from our pursuit of sustainable futures. We also have to work with contradictions, transcending these interactions when we can. It is weird when looked at from a distance, but this also means we have to accept other contradictions. In politics, friends and enemies are relative terms. And if you are seeking a more participatory and inclusive future, this means you have to talk to the good guys and those you considered the bad guys, while also trying to shake the neutral from their apathy. But as long as our vantage point is focussed on the future, guided by our values, there is tremendous hope. The futurists often noted that the least likely future is the one in which nothing changes. Never has this been truer than at this moment in history we are all living through. And in that impermanence, there are opportunities for all.

This is how Malaysia and what is commonly referred to as the 'rest', the Global South, carry on into the future, on our own terms. But the point is not just to turn the tables, but to change the game entirely. We must resist the temptation to exert and flex our individuality. The time of destructive nationalisms and winner-takes-all economics, essentially the tyranny of one over another, is over. We must stand against marginalisation or fundamentalism or supremacy. It is time for true plurality and inclusivity; for moral discourse and ethical rationality. It is time to think. Time to pursue truth again, to collaborate and cooperate, to build new things. We must not hide behind false insecurities or seek a return to normal. Normal is what we make it in the future. And perhaps the global shutdown caused by the pandemic showed us that we do not need a capital 'N' Normal. We should transcend normal so that all desired futures are respected and left open for the participation of all. We must learn from one another so that we can know one another. Both the old and the young must look out for one another for the sake of community and continuity. This not only delivers justice but it ensures it for the future, while also building intergenerational justice across time. Maybe then we can have true progress beyond the problematic definitions inherited from modernity. We must be critical in our thinking. Fostering creativity and invigorating our imaginations will ensure our transcendence into better futures.

The unfolding digital transformation of the world represents one of the most radical, eminent changes before us. To prepare for and drive a smooth energy and digital transformation for Malaysia, I launched 'AI for Rakyat', or 'AI for the People'. This is a people-centric digital literacy programme, a powerful first step. This industrial transformation is and will continue to be unlike any other we have experienced. It is not simply about learning new skills and acquiring new technology. This is a true paradigm shift for Malaysia, and the rest of the world, as many of us strive to catch up on the digitalisation frontier, as we simultaneously shift from a software-centric world to one that is AI-centric. Inasmuch as 'the technological zeitgeist of our times is one of exponential progress' and 'our civilisation strives for technological growth', the socio-economic transformation heralded by AI must warrant robust discussion and deep conversations among the various stakeholders. On a global scale, the upward trajectory will be exponential. For the Malaysian economy alone, according to 2023 reports, generative AI has the potential to unlock $113.4 billion in productive capacity, while the digital sector as a whole is expecting to contribute $25.5 billion to GDP in 2025.[19] To ensure its safe deployment and adoption, there is concern about introducing AI with eyes wide shut. Developers and lawmakers are both challenged by the regulatory and legislative maze faced with such issues as culpability on account of accidents involving autonomous cars, or AI diagnoses gone awry. Apart from the legal implications, there are, again, ethical and moral dimensions to the equation. ChatGPT and other similar LLMs have been known to produce fictional court cases and medical prescriptions yet to be tested to confirm bias, that was not accounted for by developers. Even artists and creatives are threatened by AI, the creative realm once thought to be all-too-human for AI to be considered a threat. Our anthropomorphic tendencies provoke questions around whether or not we can trust the machine, AI, whether it can feel or think. Can it be blamed for its missteps or should it be afforded legal rights? All of this and we are only at the level of traditional or narrow AI, which essentially is only really good at computing swathes of data and replicating what is already in the world (including all of our problems). The issue increases exponentially as we move towards generative AI.

Apart from the overriding concerns about governance and establishing checks and balances in an AI-driven society, there is a fundamental issue to be resolved. How would AI sync with values espoused under the Malaysia MADANI philosophy of nationhood? With regard to governance, compliance with international standards and principles is a given, along with the imposition of safeguards and guard rails. Such a dispensation need not be a disadvantage as it opens up the opportunity to project Malaysia's AI platform as an international platform, reflective of Malaysia's values, ethics, and morality. But this requires our people to educate themselves on these matters and engage with the future, which, to our disadvantage, appears to be invading our present. But we are moving from being passive to active participants in this unfolding future. The current vibrant debate among stakeholders, including the public at large, concerning the scope and nature of AI regulation is promising and highly indicative of a healthy development in this field.

While there is no denying the pervasiveness of AI's disruptive impact, viewing it purely through the prism of its problems is rather myopic. Ultimately, granted that building a holistic AI governance ecosystem is no walk in the park, with the requisite engagement of all stakeholders, including leading legal and corporate institutions, domestic and foreign, as well as a thorough understanding of the socio-economic and political dimensions of AI, such an understanding will have greater prospects of fruition. Malaysia is profoundly mindful of this imperative and progressing well in this regard. Our holistic and ethical approach to this change has the big tech corporations of Europe, the US, and China viewing Malaysia positively, regarding us as a preferred destination for their major investments in the digital and AI sectors.

The work ahead is cut out for us. But it is essential that we do not allow fatigue or complacency to steer us off course. Most of all, we can no longer afford to take anything for granted. Everything needs to be rethought, challenged, reformed, reconsidered, looked at under an ethical lens, put into context, reconfigured—possibly lost, but in that loss, perhaps something new can be gained. I hope my reflections here serve as critical starting points for something greater for people to take on—those who are living now, but also those not yet born. Let the future generations judge us, learn from our triumphs and failures, and do better! Regardless of the intention, much of our postcolonial and reformist thought has taken us down alleyways we would be wise to get ourselves out of. Justice discourse needs to be weeded and tended so that new roots and branches may grow, and the beautiful plant is not left to die. I believe in democracy. But if we do not rethink it and bring in new perspectives, then it will fail. More authoritarian and tyrannical systems stand at the ready to take over once its death throes have ceased. The arc of ignorance needs to be curbed, and hate opposed directly. This will only come about through more voices coming to the table, so that knowledge building can happen on equitable ground where our rethought education systems not only survive but thrive. This, however, is not the limit of rethinking ourselves. Multiple world views and ways of thinking awaken our critically creative imaginations. We must envision and build brighter futures beyond contemporary postnormal times. I hope this is a start. May these modest seeds give way to a grand forest of wisdom.

When we truly appreciate change, we realise that nothing is forever. This does not have to be a source of fear or anxiety, for it gives us an opportunity. And one thing human beings have demonstrated again and again is that when things fall apart, as they often do, we can start again and rebuild and craft something better for tomorrow. This is the fuel that lights the eternal flame of hope. And that hope brings me back to the musical films of P. Ramlee. The rich stories held within these films explore the inner turmoil we all face, draped upon the outer conflicts that constantly arise above us, from the wars we see occurring all around the world in daily news updates, to the battling of ideas, philosophies, and moralities that shape our souls and how we interact with one another. I believe we can again adopt the integration that allows for a confluence of ideas to exist in our societies of plentiful diversity, while peace, security, and our historical traditions carry forward untouched. Something like *La Convivencia*, experienced in medieval Al-Andalus, can have its day in the sun again. The budding hope and cosmopolitanism of the days of independence could be nursed to bloom. A future where we love and think and live as caring neighbours with one another and the natural world need not be a fiction for the silver screen. The lyrics of 'Wait a Little While' echo through the last seventy-five years:

> Wait a while, my love,
> Wait till the rain has gone
> Let me sing.[20]

Brighter futures remain ahead. We have the agency and the capacity to shape our tomorrows. There will be more storms ahead, but we will face them with the wisdom we did not have in the past. We have a responsibility to rethink our present for the sake of each other and the sake of our children and children's children. The songs sung in the infinite futures beyond today can ring with the beauty we hear on old recordings.

I look forward with great anticipation and hope for what comes next.

ACKNOWLEDGEMENTS

I would like to thank my friends Professor Ziauddin Sardar, for his guidance—sometime a bit overwhelming—in writing this book; and the late Merryl Wyn Davies, for the inspiration she provided me with for over forty years. Scott Jordan provided invaluable editorial support, editing and re-editing my text, as I revised and then revised again! Thanks are also due to Aasil Ahmad, who has been with me from my exile days in the US, Professor Faiz Abdullah, my speech writer then and now, and Shukri Saad, my trusted personal secretary for the last decade.

NOTES

PROLOGUE: EYE OF THE STORM

1. On 2 September 1998 I was dismissed from cabinet, ending my term as both deputy prime minister and minister of finance under Prime Minister Mahathir Mohamad. The following day, I would be expelled from UMNO, the political party I had been in since entering politics in 1982.

2. The Y2K virus, also known as the 'millennium bug', was the moniker used to express a problem for computers once we moved into the year 2000. Since only two digits were used to represent calendars on computers, and data between the 1900s and 2000s would be indistinguishable, it was anticipated that this would kick off a cascade that might bring down the whole word's computing infrastructure and upend computer-based industry. Many across the globe expected the toll of midnight to usher in a new dark age for the planet and a great deal of basic necessities were hoarded. Panic of such a global nature would not be witnessed again until the days before global shutdowns took place in response to the Covid-19 pandemic in 2020.

3. On 29 September I was taken to the court to have the charge for which I was being incarcerated read to me. Between the door of the courthouse and my transport, I rose my hand to all the masses there to see me and a photograph was snapped. This photo became a symbol of resistance to the government of the day, known as Reformasi, and is now immortalised on the party flag of PKR (Parti Keadilan Rakyat, the People's Justice Party).

4. The Internal Security Act (ISA) was a carry-over from British colonial

law that was enacted into Malaysian law in 1960. It was stated as an 'Act to provide for the internal security of Malaysia, preventive detention, the prevention of subversion, the suppression of organized violence against persons and property in specified areas of Malaysia, and for matters incidental thereto'. In short, the law allowed the Malaysian government to detain individuals without trial or criminal charge under not-so-limited legally defined conditions. For a better account of the horrors of the ISA, I recommend Syed Husin Ali's *Two Faces: Detention Without Trial* (Petaling Jaya, SIRD, 1996) and Kassim Ahmad's *The Second University: Detention Under the ISA* (Petaling Jaya, Media Intelek, 1984).

5. A period in our lives eloquently recounted in Syed Husin Ali's *Two Faces: Detention Without Trial*.

6. *Free Malaysia Today*, 'Najib explains why he told Mahathir "cash is king"', 18 September 2018 (https://www.freemalaysiatoday.com/category/nation/2018/09/18/najib-explains-why-he-told-mahathir-cash-is-king/).

7. For more on 1MDB, I recommend Clare Rewcastle Brown's *The Sarawak Report: The Inside Story of the 1MDB Expose* (Petaling Jaya, Gerakbudaya, 2018); Tom Wright and Bradley Hope's *Billion Dollar Whale: The Man Who Fooled Wall Street, Hollywood, and the World* (New York, Hachette, 2019); and Leslie Lopez's *The Siege Within* (Singapore, Penguin, 2024).

8. The famous quote 'power tends to corrupt and absolute power corrupts absolutely' was originally written by the British historian Lord Acton in a letter to Bishop Mandell Creighton on 3 April 1887.

9. This quote comes from T. S. Eliot's 1925 poem 'The Hollow Men', which is collected in *The Wasteland and Other Poems* (London, Vintage, 2021).

10. Isaiah Berlin, *Four Essays on Liberty* (Oxford, Oxford University Press, 1969).

11. All the quotes from William Shakespeare's opus in this work are taken from G. Blakemore Evans (ed.), *The Riverside Shakespeare* (New York, HarperCollins, 1973).

12. Edward W. Said, *Culture and Imperialism* (London, Vintage, 1994).

13. Syed Hussein Alatas, in his *The Myth of the Lazy Native: A Study of the Image of the Malays, Filipinos and Javanese from the 16th to the 20th Century and Its Function in the Ideology of Colonial Capitalism* (Petaling Jaya, Gerakbudaya, 2023).

14. Antonio Gramsci, *Selections from the Prison Notebooks* (New York, International Publishers, 1989).

15. Ibid.

16. Aleksandr Solzhenitsyn, *The Gulag Archipelago* (London, Vintage, 2003).

17. Colin Tudge, *The Great Re-think: A 21st Century Renaissance* (Siena, Pari Publishing, 2021).

1. POSTCOLONIAL ANGST

1. Just as Malaysia's colonial and pre-colonial histories are a matter of process, so too was Malaysia's independence. While many colonies are famous for hosting revolutionary conflict in order to get their independence, such as Indonesia, Malaysia's struggle, though not without its own violence and strife, was a longer matter of diplomatic negotiation. Following the Japanese Empire's fall, the British returned to their colonial protectorates of Malaya, Singapore, Sarawak, and North Borneo. For the next decades various movements and struggles pushed for Malayan independence. This culminated in the leaders of the three major communities in Malaya, the United Malays Nationalist Organisation (UMNO) Tunk Abdul Rahman, who would become Malaya's first prime minister, the Malayan Chinese Association (MCA) president Tan Cheng Lok, and the Malayan Indian Congress (MIC) president VT Sambanthan, and agreeing to petition London for independence. On 31 August 1957, Malaya gained its independence at Merdeka Stadium and the first Yang di-Pertuan Agong (High King of Malaysia) was installed. Six years later, in 1963, the British Empire could no longer continue in Southeast Asia and the Cobbold Commission was assembled, composed of two Malayans and three Brits to build a plan for the creation of a superstate to be named Malaysia. An agreement, known as the Malaysian Agreement (MA63) was created and came into effect on 16 September 1963. Malaysia, the union of Malaya, Singapore, Sarawak, and North Borneo

(Sabah) was born. Two years later, Singapore was expelled on 9 August 1965, and Malaysia retained its name. Malaysia now celebrates two national holidays, Merdeka Day (31 August) and Malaysia Day (16 September). No shortage of sources exist on these matters, but I would recommend Syed Husin Ali's and Barabara and Lenoard Andaya's books from the last note. Added to this I would recommend Khairudin Aljunied's *Perjuangan: Malaysia's Forgotten Struggles for Freedom* (Cendekia, Petaling Jaya, 2024); Mustapha Hussain's *Malay Nationalism Before UMNO: The Memoirs of Mustapha Hussain* (Utusan Publications & Distributors, Kuala Lumpur, 2004); and Azhar Ibrahim's *Historical Imagination and Cultural Response to Colonialism and Nationalism* (SIRD, Petaling Jaya, 2017).

2. P. Ramlee (1929–1973), the shortened stage name Puteh Ramlee, was born Teuku Zakaria bin Teuku Nyak Puteh and was one of Malaysia's greatest entertainers. His films captured the zeitgeist of Merdeka Malaysia between the 1940s and 1960s. Also a prolific musician, he composed over 350 songs in his short life. He is celebrated today in Malaysia and Singapore as well as the wider Nusantara region.

3. Muhammad Iqbal was a beloved poet, thinker, and political figure in Pakistan, but also one of the great minds of the twentieth century and a champion philosopher of the postcolonial era. He wrote poetry in both Urdu and Persian. He was also instrumental in helping to develop the modern Pakistani state. His seminal work, that was quoted from here, was *The Reconstruction of Religious Thought in Islam* (Stanford University Press, 2012).

4. In 1514, Nicolaus Copernicus published his *Commentariolus*, where for the first time in Europe it was postulated that the Earth revolves around the sun, opposing the old world belief that the Earth was at the centre of the universe with everything revolving around us. *The Copernican Revolution* is well discussed in the American philosopher and historian of science Thomas Kuhn's book of the same name (Harvard University Press, Cambridge, 1957).

5. During a joint session of Congress on 12 March 1947, then US President Harry S. Truman delivered a speech in which he laid out his foreign policy principles that are now known to history as the Truman Doctrine.

In light of Great Britain's withdrawing of assistance to the Greek government in their civil war against the Greek Communist Party, Truman wanted Congress to support the Greeks in their struggle against communism. Truman completely reoriented American foreign policy, which used to be based only on direct threats to American soil, to now giving economic and military assistance to all free peoples fighting the scourge of communism. This policy set the terms for the Cold War between the West (democracy) and the East (communism), but did not come without its own contradictions and hypocrisies.

6. Domino Theory arose out of a speech on 7 April 1954 from then US President Dwight D. Eisenhower, as he traced the fall of China and North Korea to communism and how that was spreading to Indochina. He then projected communism's continued cascade effect throughout Asia, as well as its moving westwards from Eastern Europe. Eisenhower's Domino Theory gave support to Winston Churchill's coinage of the 'Iron Curtain' splitting Europe and also laid the groundwork for the United States's two-decade quagmire in Viet Nam from 1955–1975.

7. This quote comes from the first Inaugural Address of US President Franklin D. Roosevelt on 4 March 1933 at the East Portico of the United States Capitol Building in Washington, D.C.

8. Karl Marx and Friedrich Engels's *The Communist Manifesto* (Penguin, London, 2015).

9. Karl Marx's *Capital Volume 1* (Penguin, London, 1990); *Capital Volume 2* (Penguin, London, 1992); and *Capital Volume 3* (Penguin, London, 1992). These three were intended to be part of a larger opus criticising capitalism, largely the theory put forward by Adam Smith. Marx did not live long enough to complete this work and the three volumes we have are largely a critique of Western capitalism without any alternative proposals in terms of governance or political structuring.

10. When we reflect on the first generation of postcolonial advocates coming out of World War II, it is often underscored that they had a great concern for the proliferation of weapons of mass destruction, like the recently demonstrated atomic bombs dropped on Japan by the US or the repeatedly tested detonations of hydrogen bombs in the US and USSR. Perhaps the Cold War's constant threat of nuclear war and plan-

etary annihilation has numbed us to this old fear, nevertheless it should remain a concern for us even in the present, and of course in the coming futures.

11. Mohandas Gandhi's philosophy is best articulated in his autobiography, *Gandhi, An Autobiography: The Story of My Experiments with Truth* (Beacon Press, Boston, 1993).

12. Toshihiko Izutsu left behind a wealth of books in a variety of fields, but to see his work with Islam, philosophy, and linguistics, the following titles are recommended and have been referenced in this chapter: *God and Man in the Qur'an* (Keio University, Tokyo, 1964); *Ethico-Religious Concept in the Qur'an* (McGill-Queens University Press, Montreal, 2002); and *Sufism and Taoism: A Comparative Study of Key Philosophical Concepts* (University of California Press, Oakland, 2016).

13. While this term comes with a bit of baggage and controversy, upon further thought, it can be a good rallying call for all those today who refuse to be a part of hegemonic power politics. Yet it is important, to retain its authenticity, that the Global South does not become a term referring to a few new players, that it remains a plural identification and that it speaks for the voice of the many, that advocates for participatory actions and open, diverse futures.

14. It is well known that the British style of colonial rule utilised the divide and conquer technique. The British were happy to keep social institutions in place as long as they gave their dues to the colonial administrators at the end of the day. The institutions that divided a country were lauded the most, as the idea was that if the natives were fighting one another, then they would be too busy to oppose the colonial overlords. This is well explored in the Indian intellectual Shashi Tharoor's *Inglorious Empire: What the British Did to India* (Penguin, London, 2018).

15. See John Sydenham Furnivall's *Colonial Policy and Practice: A Comparative Study of Burma and Netherlands India* (Cambridge University Press, 2015).

16. A concept brilliantly dismantled by Syed Husein Alatas in his book *The Myth of the Lazy Native: A study of the image of the Malays, Filipinos and Javanese from the 16th to the 20th century and its function in the ideology of colonial capitalism* (Gerakbudaya, Petaling Jaya, 2023).

17. The Radcliffe Line was the border partition drawn up by the British lawyer Cyril Radcliffe between India, Pakistan, and East Pakistan—a line he drew without having ever visited British India. Yasmin Khan's *The Great Partition: The Making of India and Pakistan* (Yale University Press, New Haven, 2017) gives a detailed account.

18. The Sykes–Picot Agreement was a secret agreement drawn up during World War I by British and French officials to carve up the territories of modern-day Syria, Iraq, Palestine, and Jordan between the two powers to create spheres of influence after the Ottoman Empire collapsed. A good analysis of the men behind this secret treaty and its ramifications is found in Christopher Simon Sykes's *The Man Who Created The Middle East: A Story of Empire, Conflict and the Sykes–Picot Agreement* (William Collins, Glasgow, 2018).

19. Malaysia's first prime minister, Tunku Abdul Rahman, noted that three Cs threaten Malaysia from its birth: colonialism, communism, and communalism. Independence was thought to have at least started the process if not ended the threat of colonialism, while communism was a spectre now in Southeast Asia, and communalism, or the chauvinism and exclusivity expressed by our various communities, was the new threat to the unity of Malaysia.

20. Added to the threatening mask that communism added to Chinese ethnic populations in Malaysia at this time, their population dynamics (including an immigration influx of foreigners of Chinese ethnicity) were rising and projected to equal and possibly exceed Malay ethnic populations threatening the Malay's position as the dominant population of the country.

21. Frantz Fanon, *Black Skin, White Masks* (Grove Press, New York, 2008).

22. The 1963 Malaysia Agreement, which established the modern country of Malaysia as we know it, stated that Malaya (Peninsular Malaysia), Sarawak, and Sabah would all be equal parties in the federation. Reneging on this agreement has created various tensions between East and West Malaysia since the birth of our nation and that since coming to power as prime minister in 2022, I have worked diligently to rectify.

23. Oxford languages dictionary defines equity as 'the quality of being fair and impartial' and equality as 'the state of being equal, especially in

status, rights, or opportunities'. Equality is being equal but blind to history and circumstance, equity is about being fair, and often considers the context.

24. Sukarno's guided democracy was first laid out in his 17 August 1957 Independence Day address, where he presented a manifesto known as *Manipol USDEK* (An acronym laying out the five principles of this new ideology: the 1945 Constitution, Indonesian Socialism, Guided Democracy, Guided Economics, and Indonesian Identity). Guided democracy allowed for localised democracy but under the unification of a strongman leader, something that Sukarno was inspired to create after visiting China in the mid-1950s and inspired by their progress since their own civil war less than a decade prior.

25. An ironic phrasing used for the Abdul Razak administration, especially since many of them were a part of the old government and UMNO of Tunku, but a new administration allows for new branding.

26. For more on King Ghaz's stance on bumiputeraism, see Ghazali Shafie's *Malaysia: Nilai Politik dan Budaya* (Pustaka Antara, Kuala Lumpur, 1981).

27. An insightful analysis of the NEP in its early days comes by way of Toh Kin Woon's *Malaysia's New Economic Policy in its First Decade* (SIRD, Petaling Jaya, 2024).

28. Jean Drèze & Amartya Sen's *An Uncertain Glory: India & Its Contradictions* (Allen Lane, London, 2013). Also see Anthony B. Atkinson's *Inequality: What Can Be Done?* (Harvard University Press, Cambridge, 2016); and Laura D'Andrea Tyson's 'Commentary: how can economic policy strike a balance between economic efficiency and income equality?', Proceedings: Economic Policy Symposium, Jackson Hole, Federal Reserve Bank of Kansas City, 1998, p. 337–43.

29. Jomo K. S. has written extensively on his critique of the NEP, but a good place to begin is Jomo K. S.'s 'The New Economic Policy and Interethnic Relations in Malaysia', Identities, Conflict and Cohesion Program Paper No. 7, United Nation Research Institute for Social Development, September 2004; Edmund Terence Gomez & Jomo K. S.'s *Malaysia's Political Economy: Politics, Patronage and Profits* (Cambridge University Press, 2011); and Jomo Kwame Sundaram &

Wee Chong Hui's *Malaysia@50: Economic Development, Distribution, Disparities* (SIRD, Petaling Jaya, 2014).

30. For more on criticism of the NEP and the development of Malaysia's economy since the NEP, see Shaharuddin Maaruf's *Malay Ideas on Development: From Feudal Lord to Capitalist* (SIRD, Petaling Jaya, 2014); Rogayah Hj. Mat Zain, 'Income Inequality in Malaysia', *Asian Economy Policy Review* (2008) 3, 114–32; A. H. Roslan's 'Income Inequality, Poverty and Development Policy in Malaysia', International Seminar on Poverty and Sustainable Development, Université Montesquieu-Bordeaux IV and UNESCO, Paris, November 2001, pp. 4–10; Hal Hill, Tham Siew Yean, & Ragayah Haji Mat Zin's (editors) *Malaysia's Development Challenges: Graduating from the Middle* (Routledge, Milton Park, 2012); and J. M. Gullick's *Malay Society in the Late Nineteenth Century: The Beginnings of Change* (Oxford University Press, Singapore, 1991).

31. Anthony Reid's *Slavery, Bondage and Dependency in Southeast Asia* (St. Martin's Press, New York, 1983).

32. Mahmud bin Mat's 'The Passing of Slavery in East Pahang', *The Malayan Historical Journal*, vol. 1. 1954.

33. Abdullah bin Abdul Kadir Munshi's *Kisah Pelayaran Abdullah Ke Kelantan dan Kedah*, edited by Kassim Ahmad (Oxford University Press, Kuala Lumpur, 1968).

34. Goenawan Mohamad's *Conversations with Difference: Essays from Tempo Magazine* (NUS Press, Singapore, 2003).

35. For a great history of debt and slavery see David Graeber's *Debt: The First 5,000 Years* (Penguin, London, 2011).

36. Samir Amin's *Capitalism in the Age of Globalization* (Bloomsbury, London, 2014).

37. Samir Amin's *Accumulation on a World Scale: A Critique of the Theory of Underdevelopment* (Monthly Review Press, New York, 1974)

38. Unfortunately, the Royal Malaysian Professor Ungku Abdul Aziz did not write much during his lifetime, but the idea for what would become Tabung Haji, started with the setting up of the Prospective Hajj Pilgrims Savings Corporation (Perbadanan Wang Simpanan Bakal-bakal Haji) (PWSBH) which was triggered by a proposal made by

Ungku Abdul Aziz in December 1959 to the Federal Government of Malaya with cooperation from the Ministry of Rural Development. PWSBH was established under Law No. 34, 1962, in 1963. In 1969, PWSBH merged with the Hajj Affairs Management Office that had been operating out of Penang since 1951. In 1995, the organisation was renamed Tabung Haji (TH).

39. *The Star*, 'Tabung Haji sets 2025 pilgrim fees for B40 at RM15,000 and M40 at RM23,500 per person', 16 December 2024 (https://www.thestar.com.my/news/nation/2024/12/16/tabung-haji-sets-2025-pilgrim-fees-for-b40-at-rm15000-and-m40-at-rm23500-per-person#:~:text=While%20the%202025%20season%20Haj,starting%20Monday%20(Dec%2016).

40. Frantz Fanon's *The Wretched of the Earth* (Penguin, London, 2012).

41. Ashis Nandy's *The Intimate Enemy: Loss and Recovery of Self under Colonialism* (Oxford University Press, New Delhi, 1988).

2. JUSTICE FOR OUR TIME

1. Al-Fatani's *Munyatul Musalli* is available in original Malay and various translations, and extracts from the book, as well as discussion on its contents, can be heard on YouTube. For a more elaborated discussion, see Wan Mohd Shaghir Abdullah's *Mun-Yatul Mushalli Syeikh Daud Abdullah al-Fathani: Pengetahuan Sembahyang Masyhur* (Kuala Lumpur, Khazanah Fathaniah, 1991).

2. Cornel West, *Race Matters* (London, Vintage, 1994).

3. NPR, 'The Rise in Anti-Asian Attacks During the COVID-19 Pandemic', 10 March 2021 (https://www.npr.org/2021/03/10/975722882/the-rise-of-anti-asian-attacks-during-the-covid-19-pandemic).

4. BBC, 'Coronavirus: Islamophobia concerns after India mosque outbreak', 3 April 2020 (https://www.bbc.com/news/world-asia-india-52147260).

5. *New Straits Times*, 'Migrant workers' poor living conditions fuel Southeast Asia's Covid-19 crisis', 24 January 2021 (https://www.nst.com.my/world/world/2021/01/660033/migrant-workers-poor-living-conditions-fuel-southeast-asias-covid-19).

6. Reference to the United States Pledge of Allegiance.

7. Olesya Khromeychuk, '"Ukraine fatigue": why I'm fighting to stop the world forgetting us', *The Guardian*, 25 January 2024 (https://www.theguardian.com/world/2024/jan/25/ukraine-fatigue-why-im-fighting-to-stop-the-world-forgetting-us).

8. UN News, 'No end in sight to "horror" in Gaza, UN official tells Security Council', 25 November 2024 (https://news.un.org/en/story/2024/11/1157436).

9. Mark Twain, *The Adventures of Huckleberry Finn* (London, Penguin, 2003).

10. John Donne, *Selected Prose* (London, Penguin, 2015).

11. Ernest Hemingway, *For Whom the Bell Tolls* (New York, Scribner, 1995).

12. As detailed in Plato's *Republic* (Cambridge, Cambridge University Press, 2012).

13. As elucidated in Aristotle's *The Nicomachean Ethics* (Indianapolis, Hackett, 2024).

14. Gore Vidal, *Creation* (New York, Vintage International, 2002).

15. From *Plato's Complete Works*, edited by John M. Cooper (Indianapolis, Hackett, 1997).

16. See Aristotle's *Nichomachean Ethics*.

17. John Steinbeck, *East of Eden* (New York, Viking, 2003).

18. Just War theory was articulated first by St Augustine of Hippo in *The City of God* (London, Penguin, 2003). St Thomas Aquinas developed the theory further in the medieval period and various thinkers in the Catholic Church carried it forward until modern Western philosophers took it in a variety of directions. In the Catholic Church today, Just War theory holds some connection to evangelical practices in Latin America and the concept of Liberation Theology, a philosophy of theology that has, like many theories, been used for real goods and true evils in the history of its application.

19. The French notion of 'secularism'. It only took them five republics of experimentation to be convinced that it was the only way anyone beholden to democracy ought to conduct themselves.

20. The phrase 'never again' used to be synonymous with the notion of the

possibility that fascism would never again be welcomed in Europe. The phrase was first inscribed at the sight of the Buchenwald concentration camp in Germany by the survivors of the Holocaust after they were liberated by Allied Forces. The phrase actually derives from a Zionist poem from the 1920s. The phrase is used rather loosely in a variety of contexts currently.

21. The 'state of nature' is a common idea found in modern political philosophy and is found in Thomas Hobbes, John Locke, and Jean-Jacques Rousseau. In the contemporary period, John Rawls altered the phrase to 'the original position'. Generally, versions of this phrase refer to a pre-civilisational condition of humanity, a wild state before rules, law, and order existed. Often the Western modernists envision this as the Garden of Eden.

22. Thomas Hobbes, *Leviathan* (London, Penguin Classics, 1982).

23. John Locke, *Second Treatise of Government* (Indianapolis, Hackett, 1980).

24. Jean-Jacques Rousseau, *The Social Contract* (London, Penguin Classics, 1968).

25. John Stuart Mill, *Utilitarianism* (Indianapolis, Hackett, 2002).

26. William MacAskill, *What We Owe the Future* (New York, Basic Books, 2022).

27. Quote from a speech given by Winston Churchill to the House of Commons in London on 11 November 1947.

28. John Rawls, *A Theory of Justice* (Cambridge, MA, Belknap Press, 2005).

29. I spoke extensively on the Rawls-versus-Nozick academic debate in a lecture I gave at the University of Cambridge in the UK on 16 March 2007, titled 'Examining Economic Growth and Social Justice in the 21st Century'.

30. Robert Nozick, *Anarchy, State, and Utopia* (New York, Basic Books, 2013).

31. F. A. Hayek, *The Constitution of Liberty* (Chicago, University of Chicago Press, 1960).

32. John Rawls, *Political Liberalism* (New York, Columbia University Press, 1993).

33. Martha Nussbaum has written several papers in support of and chal-

lenging her teacher John Rawls, but in her work *Frontiers of Justice: Disability, Nationality, Species Membership* (Cambridge, MA, Harvard University Press, 2007) she brings it together. Thomas Nagel's main defence of John Rawls is found in his 'Rawls on Justice', *The Philosophical Review*, 82 (2) April 1973, pp. 220–34.

34. The nigh insanity that is Habermas thought in the last few years is best summed up in Asef Bayat's 'Juergen Habermas Contradicts His Own Ideas When It Comes to Gaza', *New Lines Magazine*, 8 December 2023 (https://newlinesmag.com/argument/juergen-habermas-contradicts-his-own-ideas-when-it-comes-to-gaza/).

35. Amartya Sen, *The Idea of Justice* (Cambridge, MA, Belknap Press, 2009).

36. Khaled Abou El Fadl, *Reasoning with God: Reclaiming Shari'ah in the Modern Age* (Lanham, Rowman & Littlefield, 2014).

37. Abu Nasr Al-Farabi, *On the Perfect State*, translated by Richard Walzer (Chicago, Kazi, 1998).

38. Quote from Alexis de Tocqueville's *Democracy in America and Two Essays on America* (London, Penguin, 2003).

39. Samuel P. Huntington, 'The Clash of Civilizations?' *Foreign Affairs*, 72 (3), 1993, pp. 22–49.

40. Quote from Ziauddin Sardar's 'The Erasure of Islam', *The Philosopher's Magazine*, 42 (3) 2008, pp. 77–9.

41. Marshall G. S. Hodgson, *The Venture of Islam*, 3 vols. (Chicago, University of Chicago Press, 1974).

42. Ibn Rushd, *Tahafut Al-Tahafut*, translated by Simon Van Den Bergh, 2 vols. (London, E. J. W. Gibb Memorial Trust, 1978).

43. For more on the Islamization of Knowledge Project, see Ismail al-Faruqi', *Islamization of Knowledge: General Principles and Working Plan* (Herndon, VA, IIIT, 1982) and Syed Muhammad Naquib Al-Attas, *Islam and Secularism* (Kuala Lumpur, ABIM, 1978).

44. For more on the Integration of Knowledge Project, see Ziauddin Sardar and Jeremy Henzell-Thomas's *Rethinking Reform in Higher Education: From Islamization to Integration of Knowledge* (Herndon, VA, IIIT, 2017).

45. Khaled Abou El Fadl, *Reasoning with God: Reclaiming Shari'ah in the Modern Age* (Lanham, Rowman & Littlefield, 2014).

46. Which existed from approximately 711–1492 when the Reconquista expelled non-Christians from the Iberian Peninsula.

47. *The Bhagavad Gita*, translated by Laurie L. Patton (London, Penguin, 2008).

48. For more on Chinese thought around justice, see David L. Hall and Roger T. Ames, *Dao De Jing: A Philosophical Translation* (New York, Ballantine Books, 2003); David L. Hall and Roger T. Ames, *Anticipating China: Thinking Through the Narratives of Chinese and Western Culture* (New York, SUNY, 1995); and Osman Bakar and Cheng Gek Nai, *Islam and Confucianism: A Civilizational Dialogue* (Kuala Lumpur, University of Malaya Press, 1997).

49. Quote from Syed Muhammad Naquib Al-Attas's *On Justice and the Nature of Man* (Kuala Lumpur, IBFIM, 2015).

50. Roger T. Ames, *The Analects of Confucius: A Philosophical Translation* (New York, Ballantine Books, 1999).

51. 'Tubular Bells' by Mike Oldfield was originally released in 1973 under Virgin Records. While the song was big in the UK, it gained international adoration when it was used in William Friedkin's 1973 horror film, *The Exorcist*. Subsequent versions were released in 1974, 1992, 1998, 1999, 2003, and 2009. The song was also featured as part of the 2012 Summer Olympics opening ceremony in London.

52. Mancur Olson, *The Rise and Decline of Nations: Economics, Economic Growth, Stagflation, and Social Rigidities* (New Haven, Yale University Press, 1982).

53. Amartya Sen, *Development as Freedom* (Oxford, Oxford University Press, 1999).

54. Ibid.

55. John Kenneth Galbraith, *The Good Society: The Humane Agenda* (Boston, Houghton Mifflin, 1996).

56. I first put this forward in Anwar Ibrahim, *The Asian Renaissance* (Singapore, Time Books International, 1996).

57. Rawls, *Political Liberalism*.

58. This was first articulated in Isaiah Berlin's inaugural lecture as Oxford's Chichele Professor of Social and Political Theory titled 'Two Concepts of Liberty', delivered at Oxford University on 31 October 1958, but

was later reproduced in Isaiah Berlin's *Four Essays on Liberty* (Oxford University Press, 1969).

59. *Tolstoy's Letters Volume 1: 1828–1879*, selected and edited by R. F. Christian (New York, Scribner, 1978).
60. Thomas Piketty, *Capital in the Twenty-First Century* (Cambridge, MA, Harvard University Press, 2013).
61. Shoshana Zuboff, *The Age of Surveillance Capitalism* (New York, PublicAffairs, 2019).
62. Mimi Sheller, *Mobility Justice: The Politics of Movement in the Age of Extremes* (London, Verso, 2018).

3. LIBERATING DEMOCRACY

1. Andrew Adonis, 'For the sake of democracy, we need to get the young voting again. Here's how', *The New Statesman*, 18 July 2013 (https://www.newstatesman.com/politics/2013/07/sake-democracy-we-need-get-young-voting-again-heres-how).
2. For their criticisms of democracy, see Plato's *Republic* (Cambridge, Cambridge University Press, 2012) and Aristotle's *Politics*, translated by Carnes Lord (Chicago, University of Chicago Press, 2013).
3. Jean-Jacques Rousseau, *The Social Contract* (London, Penguin Classics, 1968).
4. Plato, *Republic*.
5. John Stuart Mill, *On Liberty* (London, Penguin, 1982).
6. Alexis de Tocqueville, *Democracy in America and Two Essays on America* (London, Penguin, 2003).
7. Karl Marx and Friedrich Engels, *The Communist Manifesto* (London, Penguin, 2015).
8. According to the US Federal Election Commission, 'presidential candidates raised $1.6 billion and spent over $1.3 billion in the first 21 months of the 2023–2024 election cycle, according to campaign finance reports filed with the Federal Election Commission that cover activity from 1 January 2023 through 30 September 2024. Congressional candidates collected $3.3 billion and disbursed $2.8 billion, political parties received $2.1 billion and spent $1.8 billion, and political action committees (PACs) raised $12.3 billion and spent $10.9 billion, according to

campaign finance reports filed with the Federal Election Commission that cover activity from 1 January 2023 through 30 September 2024. Disbursements for independent expenditures and electioneering communications reported in this period totalled $2.2 billion and $7 million, respectively. Communication costs reported to the Commission totalled $11.3 million.' From 'Statistical Summary of 21-Month Campaign Activity of the 2023–2024 Election Cycle', 28 January 2025 (https://www.fec.gov/updates/statistical-summary-of-21-month-campaign-activity-of-the-2023–2024-election-cycle/).

9. Quote from Bhikhu Parekh's *Rethinking Multiculturalism: Cultural Diversity and Political Theory* (Cambridge, MA, Harvard University Press, 2002).

10. Francis Fukuyama, *The End of History and the Last Man* (New York, Free Press, 1992).

11. *Al-Jazeera*, 'Italy's far-right leader Meloni forms new government', 21 October 2022, (https://www.aljazeera.com/news/2022/10/21/italys-far-right-leader-meloni-forms-new-government).

12. Jon Henley, 'Support for Eurosceptic parties doubles in two decades across EU', *The Guardian*, 2 March 2020 (https://www.theguardian.com/world/2020/mar/02/support-for-eurosceptic-parties-doubles-two-decades-across-eu).

13. Brian Osgood, 'What are swing states, and why are they critical? What to know in 500 words', *Al-Jazeera*, 13 September 2024 (https://www.aljazeera.com/news/2024/9/13/what-are-swing-states-and-why-are-they-critical-what-to-know-in-500-words).

14. George Makdisi, *The Rise of Humanism in Classical Islam and the Christian West* (Edinburgh, Edinburgh University Press, 1990).

15. Abdul Rahman Al-Kawakibi, *The Nature of Tyranny and the Devastating Results of Oppression* (London, Hurst, 2021).

16. Rifa'a Rafi' al-Tahtawi, *An Imam in Paris: Account of a Stay in France by an Egyptian Cleric (1826–1831)* (London, Saqi Books, 2011).

17. Taha Hussein, *The Future of Culture in Egypt*, translated by Sidney Glazer (New York, American Council of Learned Societies, 1954).

18. Raden Adjeng Kartini, *From Darkness to Light*, translated by Agnes Louise Symmers (New York, Alfred A. Knopf, 1986).

19. Rokeya Sakhawat Hossain, *Sultana's Dream and Padmarag* (New Delhi, Penguin, 2005).

20. Eric Hobsbawm, *The Age of Extremes: A History of the World, 1914–1991* (London, Penguin, 1996).

21. Khaled Abou El Fadl, *Islam and the Challenge of Democracy* (Princeton, Princeton University Press, 2004).

22. Ibid.

23. Ibid.

24. Ziauddin Sardar, 'The smog of ignorance: Knowledge and wisdom in postnormal times', *Futures*, 120, June 2020, 102554. This paper also appears as a chapter in *The Postnormal Times Reader Volume 2*, edited by Ziauddin Sardar, Shamim Miah, and C. Scott Jordan (London, CPPFS & IIIT, 2024), pp. 219–44.

25. Tocqueville, *Democracy in America and Two Essays on America*.

26. Jacques Rancière, *Hatred of Democracy* (London, Verso, 2014).

27. Daniel J. Fiorino, *Can Democracy Handle Climate Change?* (Cambridge, Polity, 2018).

28. Madeleine Carlisle, 'How 9/11 Radically Expanded the Power of the U.S. Government', *Time*, 11 September 2021 (https://time.com/6096903/september-11-legal-history/).

29. Editors, 'Declaration of emergency in our history', *Malaysiakini*, 23 October 2020 (https://www.malaysiakini.com/news/547827).

30. Gordon Brown, Mohamed A. El-Erain, Michael Spence, and Reid Lidow, *Permacrisis: A Plan to Fix a Fractured World* (London, Simon & Schuster, 2023).

31. James C. Scott, *Seeing Like a State* (New Haven, Yale University Press, 1998).

32. Mimi Sheller, *Mobility Justice: The Politics of Movement in the Age of Extremes* (London, Verso, 2018).

33. Neil Postman, *Technopoly: The Surrender of Culture to Technology* (New York, Vintage Books, 1993).

34. Shoshana Zuboff, *The Age of Surveillance Capitalism* (New York, PublicAffairs, 2019).

35. See both Byung-Chul Han's *Psycho-Politics: Neoliberalism and New*

Technologies of Power (Verso, London, 2017) and Byung-Chul Han's *The Burnout Society* (Stanford, Stanford University Press, 2015).

36. Rancière, *Hatred of Democracy*.

4. RECONSIDERING THE UMMAH

1. My reflections on the 11 September 2001 terrorist attacks against the United States were first published as Anwar Ibrahim, 'Who Hijacked Islam?' *Time*, 15 October 2001.

2. Ibid.

3. *Vox*, 'The mistake that toppled the Berlin Wall', 8 November 2019, YouTube (http://youtube.com/watch?v=Mn4VDwaV-oo).

4. The details of this event are more eloquently put in Ziauddin Sardar's *Desperately Seeking Paradise* (London, Granta, 2004).

5. Peter F. Drucker, *The New Realities* (Oxford, Heinemann, 1989).

6. Quote from Francis Fukuyama's 'The "End of History" debate', *Dialogue*, 89, 1990, pp. 8–13.

7. Samuel P. Huntington, *The Clash of Civilizations and the Remaking of World Order* (London, Simon & Schuster, 2002).

8. Edward W. Said, 'The Clash of Ignorance', *The Nation*, 22 October 2001 (https://www.thenation.com/article/archive/clash-ignorance/).

9. Anwar Ibrahim, *The Asian Renaissance* (Singapore, Times Books International, 1996).

10. BRICS is a rising alternative intergovernmental organisation comprised of Brazil, Russia, India, China, and South Africa, now grown to include Egypt, Ethiopia, Indonesia, Iran, and the United Arab Emirates. Malaysia, at the time of writing, is in talks to become a full member of BRICS.

11. The full text of UN Secretary General António Guterres's speech is available online from the World Economic Forum, 'Davos 2025: Special Address by António Guterres, Secretary-General, United Nations', 22 January 2025 (https://www.weforum.org/stories/2025/01/davos-2025-special-address-by-antonio-guterres-secretary-general-united-nations/).

12. Ibid.

13. Aristotle's theory concerning political change is found in his *Politics*,

translated by Carnes Lord (Chicago, University of Chicago Press, 2013); *anacyclosis* is discussed in Polybius's *The Histories* (Oxford: Oxford University Press, 2010); Sima Qian discusses dynastic cycle theory in his *Records of the Grand Historian* (New York, Columbia University Press, 1996).

14. Ibn Khaldun, *The Muqaddimah: An Introduction to History*, translated by F. Rosenthal (London, Routledge & Kegan Paul, 1967).

15. Quote from Malik Bennabi's *Islam in History and Society*, translated by Asma Rashid (Islamabad, Islamic Research Institute, 1988).

16. Ibid.

17. Ibid.

18. Muhammad Iqbal, *The Reconstruction of Religious Thought in Islam* (Stanford, Stanford University Press, 2013).

19. Ibid.

20. Frantz Fanon, *The Wretched of the Earth* (London, Macgibbon and Kee, 1965).

21. Cemil Aydin, *The Idea of the Muslim World* (Cambridge, MA, Harvard University Press, 2017). Chandler Barton's review of *The Idea of the Muslim World* in *Maydan* (https://themaydan.com/2017/12/book-review-cemi-aydin-idea-muslim-world-global-intellectual-history/) offers good comment and insight as well.

22. Ziauddin Sardar, *Science, Technology and Development in the Muslim World* (Abingdon, Routledge, 1977).

23. Aydin, *The Idea of the Muslim World*.

24. Faiz Abdullah, *The Province of Shari'ah Determined: Fundamental Rethink of the Shari'ah* (Petaling Jaya, The Islamic Book Trust, 2016).

25. Al-Ghazali, *The Incoherence of the Philosophers*, translated by Michael E. Marmura (Provo, Brigham Young University, 2002).

26. Ibn Rushd, *Tahafut Al-Tahafut*, translated by Simon Van Den Bergh, 2 vols. (London, E. J. W. Gibb Memorial Trust, 1978).

27. Sarah Stroumsa, *Freethinkers of Medieval Islam* (Leiden, Brill, 2016).

28. Barton's review of *The Idea of the Muslim World* in *Maydan*. For more on the population dynamics of Muslims, see the Pew Research Center's 'The Future of the Global Muslim Population', 27 January 2011 (https://www.pewresearch.org/religion/2011/01/27/the-future-of-the-global-muslim-population/).

29. From T. S. Eliot's 'Burnt Norton' in *Four Quartets* (London, Faber & Faber, 1944).

30. Shahab Ahmed, *What is Islam?* (Princeton, Princeton University Press, 2016).

31. Hadith.

32. H. A. R. Gibb and C. F. Beckingham's translation of *The Travels of Ibn Battuta* (London, Hakluyt Society, 1994).

33. See Hasan Moinuddin's *The Charter of the Islamic Conference and Legal Framework of Economic Co-operation Among Its Membership States* (Oxford, Clarendon Press, 1987) and Abdullah Al Ahsan's *OIC: The Organization of the Islamic Conference* (Herndon, VA, IIIT, 1988).

34. Bertrand Badie, 'The Impact of the French Revolution on Muslim Societies: Evidence and Ambiguities', *International Social Science Journal*, 41 (119), 1989, p. 15.

35. Ziauddin Sardar, Jordi Serra, and Scott Jordan, *Muslim Societies in Postnormal Times: Foresight for Trends, Emerging Issues and Scenarios* (Herndon, VA, IIIT & CPPFS, 2019).

36. See Ismail al-Faruqi's *Islamization of Knowledge: General Principles and Work Plan* (Herndon, VA, IIIT, 1982) and Ziauddin Sardar and Jeremy Henzell-Thomas's *Rethinking Reform in Higher Education: From Islamization to Integration of Knowledge* (Herndon, VA, IIIT, 2017).

37. AbdulHamid A. AbuSulayman, *Crisis in the Muslim Mind* (Herndon, VA, IIIT, 1993).

38. Abdelwahab El-Affendi, *Who Needs an Islamic State?* (Peterborough, Upfront, 2008).

39. Said, 'The Clash of Ignorance'.

40. While President of Türkiye Recep Tayyip Erdoğan has noted his famous saying, 'the world is bigger than five', on various platforms, he reiterated it in Malaysia when I hosted him as prime minister during a speech he gave while receiving an honorary doctorate in international relations from the University of Malaya on 18 February 2025.

5. THE ARC OF IGNORANCE

1. Frank J. Klingberg, 'The Historical Alternation of Moods in American Foreign Policy', *World Politics*, 4 (2), January 1952, pp. 239–73.

2. See Arthur Schlesinger, Sr., *Paths to the Present* (New York, Macmillan, 1949); Arthur Schlesinger, Jr., *The Cycles of American History* (Boston, Houghton Mifflin Harcourt, 1999); Gore Vidal's whole *Narratives of Empire* series (1973–2000), as well as his collection *Armageddon? Essays, 1983–1987* (New York, HarperCollins, 1989); and Samuel P. Huntington, *American Politics: The Promise of Disharmony* (Cambridge, MA, Belknap Press, 1981).

3. George Santayana, *The Life of Reason: Introduction and Reason in Common Sense* (Cambridge, MA, MIT Press, 2011).

4. Thomas Kuhn, *The Structure of Scientific Revolutions* (Chicago, University of Chicago Press, 1996).

5. Karl Marx, *The German Ideology* (Amherst, Prometheus, 1998).

6. G. W. F. Hegel, *Phenomenology of Spirit* (Oxford, Oxford University Press, 1997).

7. Ibn Khaldun, *The Muqaddimah: An Introduction to History*, translated by F. Rosenthal (London, Routledge & Kegan Paul, 1967).

8. Jose Rizal, 'The Indolence of the Filipinos' in *Selected Essays and Letters of Jose Rizal*, translated and edited by Encarnacion Alzona (Manila, Rangel & Sons, 1964).

9. Abdullah bin Abdul Kadir Munshi, also known as Munshi Abdullah (1796–1854) was a translator and teacher of Malay to colonial officials. His autobiography, *Hikayat Abdullah*, published in 1849, was the first book in Malay to be published commercially.

10. Senu Abdul Rahman, *Revolusi Mental* (Kuala Lumpur, Utusan Publication, 1971).

11. Mahathir Mohamad, *The Malay Dilemma* (Kuala Lumpur, Asia Pacific Press, 1970).

12. Edward W. Said, *Orientalism* (London, Routledge & Kegan Paul, 1978).

13. Edward W. Said, *Culture and Imperialism* (London, Vintage, 1994).

14. Fred Halliday, 'Orientalism and Its Critics', *British Journal of Middle Eastern Studies*, 20 (2), 1993, pp. 145–63.

15. See R. W. Southern's *Western Views of Islam in the Middle Ages* (Cambridge, MA, Harvard University Press, 1962); and Norman Daniel's *The Arabs and Mediaeval Europe* (London, Longman, 1979), *Islam, Europe and Empire* (Edinburgh, Edinburgh University Press,

1966), *Heroes and Saracens* (Edinburgh, Edinburgh University Press, 1984), and *Islam and the West* (Oxford, Oneworld, 1993; original edition, 1960).

16. See A. L. Tibawi's *Arabic and Islamic Themes* (London, Luzac, 1976) and *English-Speaking Orientalists* (London, Luzac, 1964).

17. Hichem Djait, *Europe and Islam* (Berkeley, University of California Press, 1985; original French edition, 1978).

18. Syed Hussein Alatas, *The Myth of the Lazy Native* (London, Frank Cass, 1977).

19. Anouar Abdel-Malek, *Civilisations and Social Theory* (London, Macmillan, 1981).

20. Said, *Orientalism*.

21. Michael Richardson, 'Enough Said: Reflections on Orientalism', *Anthropology Today*, 6 (4), August 1990, pp. 16–19.

22. Ernest Gellner, 'Culture and Imperialism', *Times Literary Supplement*, 19 February 1993.

23. Richardson, 'Enough Said'.

24. Ziauddin Sardar, *Orientalism* (Milton Keynes, Open University Press, 1999).

25. See Wilfred Cantwell Smith, *Islam in Modern History* (Princeton, Princeton University Press, 1977); H. A. R. Gibb, *Modern Trends in Islam* (Chicago, University of Chicago Press, 1947); and Philip K. Hitti, *Islam and the West* (Malabar, Krieger Publishing, 2003).

26. Cantwell Smith, *Islam in Modern History*.

27. Samuel P. Huntington, 'The Clash of Civilizations?', *Foreign Affairs*, 72 (3), 1993, pp. 22–49.

28. Bernard Lewis's foray into clashing civilisations, which inspired his student Samuel P. Huntington, was his article 'The Roots of Muslim Rage', *The Atlantic*, September 1990 (https://www.theatlantic.com/magazine/archive/1990/09/the-roots-of-muslim-rage/304643/), but Lewis's ignorance only developed further with his books *What Went Wrong? The Clash Between Islam and Modernity in the Middle East* (New York, Harper Perennial, 2003) and *The Crisis of Islam: Holy War and Unholy Terror* (New York, Random House, 2004).

29. Edward W. Said, 'The Clash of Ignorance', *The Nation*, 22 October 2001 (https://www.thenation.com/article/archive/clash-ignorance/).

30. Akbar S. Ahmed, *Postmodernism and Islam: Predicament and Promise* (Abingdon, Routledge, 1992).

31. Ian Almond, *The New Orientalists: Postmodern Representation of Islam from Foucault to Baudrillard* (London, I. B. Tauris, 2007).

32. Ibid.

33. Andrew Brown, 'The New Atheists', in *Critical Muslim 17: Extreme*, edited by Ziauddin Sardar (London, Hurst, 2016).

34. Tom Holland, *In the Shadow of the Sword: The Battle for Global Empire and the End of the Ancient World* (London, Little, Brown and Company, 2012).

35. Ibid.

36. Anas Al-Shaikh-Ali, *Bias in Popular Culture: The Power of Visual and Linguistic Narratives* (Istanbul, Mahya, 2023).

37. Fernando Bravo López, 'Towards a Definition of Islamophobia: Approximations of the Early Twentieth Century', *Ethnic and Racial Studies*, 34 (4), 2011, pp. 556–73.

38. The Runnymede Trust, 'Islamophobia: A Challenge for Us All' (1997) is available online (https://www.runnymedetrust.org/publications/islamophobia-a-challenge-for-us-all).

39. For more on Brian Klug's discussion of Islamophobia, see his 'Islamophobia: A Concept Comes of Age', *Ethnicities*, 12 (5), 2012, pp. 665–81; and 'The Limits of Analogy: Comparing Islamophobia and Antisemitism', *Patterns of Prejudice*, 48 (5), 2014, pp. 442–59.

40. See Antony Lerman's *Whatever Happened to Antisemitism? Redefinition and the Myth of the 'Collective Jew'* (London, Pluto Press, 2022) and Shlomo Sand's *The Invention of the Land of Israel: From Holy Land to Homeland* (London, Verso, 2014) and *The Invention of the Jewish People* (London, Verso, 2010).

41. Geert Wilders, *Fitna*, a 17-minute short film distributed by LiveLeak in the Netherlands, 27 March 2008.

42. See Emmanuel Todd's *Who is Charlie?* (Oxford, Polity, 2015).

43. Paul Owen, Matthew Weaver, and agencies, 'Qur'an burning day to go ahead despite death threats', *The Guardian*, 8 September 2010 (https://www.theguardian.com/world/2010/sep/08/hillary-clinton-plan-to-burn-quran-disrespectful).

44. Adam Taylor, 'How the Quran burners got the global attention they wanted', *The Washington Post*, 3 August 2023 (https://www.washingtonpost.com/world/2023/08/03/sweden-quran-burning-denmark-islam-stunt-global-attention/).

45. Bernama, 'Distribution of Copies of Al-Qur'an Important to Enhance Understanding of Islam—Pm Anwar', 15 September 2023 (https://bernama.com/en/news.php?id=2225997).

46. Liz Fekete, *Integration, Islamophobia and Civil Rights in Europe* (London, Institute of Race Relations, 2008).

47. Ibid.

48. See both Sindre Bangstad's *Anders Breivik and The Rise of Islamophobia* (London, Zed, 2014) and 'Researching Islamophobia', in *Critical Muslim 15: Educational Reform*, edited by Ziauddin Sardar (London, Hurst, 2015).

49. Sophie Arie, 'Anti-Islamic books' success fuel fears of racism in Italy', *The Guardian*, 7 August 2004 (https://www.theguardian.com/world/2004/aug/07/italy.sophiearie). This review concerns Oriana Fallaci's *The Force of Reason*, the third volume of her Islamophobic Eurabia trilogy.

50. Bat Ye'or, *Eurabia: The Euro-Arab Axis* (Madison, Fairleigh Dickinson University Press, 2005).

51. Abigail Hauslohner, 'How a series of fringe anti-Muslim conspiracy theories went mainstream—via Donald Trump', *The Washington Post*, 5 November 2016 (https://www.washingtonpost.com/national/how-a-series-of-fringe-anti-muslim-conspiracy-theories-went-mainstream--via-donald-trump/2016/11/05/7c366af6-8bf0-11e6-bf8a-3d26847eeed4_story.html).

52. Douglas Murray, *The Strange Death of Europe: Immigration, Identity and Islam* (London, Bloomsbury Continuum, 2017).

53. An approximation of the theory put forward by the German Nazi Party Chief Propagandist Joseph Goebbels in his article 'Aus Churchills Lügenfabrik' ('From Churchill's Lie Factory') published in *Die Zeit ohne Beispiel*, 12 January 1941.

54. Anas Al-Shaikh-Ali, *Bias in Popular Culture*.

55. A phrase first used by UN Secretary General António Guterres in the

speech 'Secretary-General's opening remarks at press conference on climate', from 27 July 2023. Available online (https://www.un.org/sg/en/content/sg/speeches/2023–07–27/secretary-generals-opening-remarks-press-conference-climate).

56. *Al-Jazeera* maintains a live tracker on 'Israel-Gaza war in maps and charts' that has been tracking the devastation since 7 October 2023. Available online (https://www.aljazeera.com/news/longform/2023/10/9/israel-hamas-war-in-maps-and-charts-live-tracker).

57. For more on future plans and trajectories for Gaza, see Lorenzo Tondo, 'Benjamin Netanyahu considering mass clearance of northern Gaza', *The Guardian*, 23 September 2024 (https://www.theguardian.com/world/2024/sep/23/israel-benjamin-netanyahu-plan-northern-gaza-palestinian-civilians-hamas); *Al Jazeera*, 'What was Netanyahu's map and "plan for Gaza" all about?', 5 September 2024 (https://www.aljazeera.com/news/2024/9/5/what-was-netanyahus-map-and-plan-for-gaza-all-about); *Middle East Eye*, 'Satellite images show Israel paving new road along Philadelphia Corridor: Report', 7 September 2024 (https://www.middleeasteye.net/news/satellite-images-show-israel-paving-new-road-philadelphi-corridor); and Rashid Khalidi, *The Hundred Years' War on Palestine* (New York, Metropolitan Books, 2021).

58. For more information on these Islamophobia reports, see Türkiye's Foundation for Political, Economic and Social Research (SETA), *Annual European Islamophobia Report*, available online (https://www.setav.org/en/tag/european-islamophobia-report); the Council on American-Islamic Relations (CAIR) Annual Civil Rights Reports, available online (https://www.cair.com/resources/cair-civil-rights-reports/); and the Tell MAMA (Measuring Anti-Muslim Attacks) website (https://tellmamauk.org/).

59. Henri Pirenne, *Mohammed and Charlemagne* (Cleveland, Meridian Books, 1965).

60. Merryl Wyn Davies, *Knowing One Another: Shaping an Islamic Anthropology* (Manchester, Beacon, 2023).

61. Ziauddin Sardar and Jeremy Henzell-Thomas, *Rethinking Reform in Higher Education: From Islamization to Integration of Knowledge* (Herndon, VA, IIIT, 2017).

62. Ziauddin Sardar (ed.), *Emerging Epistemologies: The Changing Fabric of Knowledge in Postnormal Times* (Herndon, VA, IIIT & CPPFS, 2022).

63. For more on emerging studies of ignorance, see Robert N. Proctor and Londa Schiebinger (eds.), *Agnotology: The Making and Unmaking of Ignorance* (Stanford, Stanford University Press, 2008) and the insightful articles contained within *Critical Muslim 43: Ignorance*, edited by Ziauddin Sardar (London, Hurst, 2022).

64. Matthias Gross and Linsey McGoey (eds.), *Routledge International Handbook of Ignorance Studies* (Abingdon, Routledge, 2023).

65. Rokhaya Diallo, 'What has 20 years of banning headscarves done for France?' *The Guardian*, 12 April 2024 (https://www.theguardian.com/commentisfree/2024/apr/12/ban-headscarves-france-secularism-exclusion-intolerance).

66. Tim LaHaye and Jerry B. Jenkins's Left Behind series of books were released by Tyndale House Publishers from 1995 to 2007.

67. Brian Fung, 'UK riots show how social media can fuel real-life harm. It's only getting worse', *CNN*, 9 August 2024 (https://edition.cnn.com/2024/08/09/tech/uk-protests-social-media/index.html).

68. Matthew Smith, 'Facebook Wanted to Be a Force for Good in Myanmar. Now It Is Rejecting a Request to Help With a Genocide Investigation', *Time*, 18 August 2020 (https://time.com/5880118/myanmar-rohingya-genocide-facebook-gambia/).

69. Kunal Purohit, 'India's Hindu-Muslim hate crimes are being tracked, by self-exiles Modi's BJP want silenced', *South China Morning Post*, 14 August 2023 (https://www.scmp.com/week-asia/people/article/3230868/indias-hindu-muslim-hate-crimes-are-being-tracked-self-exiles-modi-supporters-wants-silenced).

70. Reuters, 'ICJ ruling: Key takeaways from the court decision in Israel genocide case', 27 January 2024 (https://www.reuters.com/world/middle-east/key-takeaways-world-court-decision-israel-genocide-case-2024-01-26/).

71. Francesca Albanese, *Anatomy of a Genocide—Report of the Special Rapporteur on the situation of human rights in the Palestinian territory occupied since 1967 to Human Rights Council—(A/HRC/55/73)*, United Nations Human Rights Council, 24 March 2024 (https://www.un.

org/unispal/document/anatomy-of-a-genocide-report-of-the-special-
rapporteur-on-the-situation-of-human-rights-in-the-palestinian-ter-
ritory-occupied-since-1967-to-human-rights-council-advance-
unedited-version-a-hrc-55/).

72. For a sampling of Germany's anti-Palestinian protest policies, see Tom
Wills, 'Germany: Police admit people detained under "protest ban" just
looked Palestinian', *Middle East Eye*, 16 March 2023 (https://www.
middleeasteye.net/news/germany-police-admit-protest-ban-people-
detained-looked-palestinian); Ruairi Casey, 'Punched, choked, kicked:
German police crack down on student protests', *Al-Jazeera*, 25 May
2024 (https://www.aljazeera.com/features/2024/5/25/punched-choked-
kicked-german-police-crack-down-on-student-protests); and Reuters,
'Anti-Semites cannot be granted German citizenship under new law—
minister', 25 October 2023 (https://www.reuters.com/world/europe/
anti-semites-cannot-be-granted-german-citizenship-under-new-law-
minister-2023-10-25/).

73. Karl Jasper, *The Question of German Guilt* (New York, Capricorn Books,
1961).

74. Adnan Delalić, 'German Redemption Theology', in *Critical Muslim
50: Halal*, edited by Ziauddin Sardar (London, Hurst, 2024).

75. A. Dirk Moses, 'The German Catechism', *Geschichte der Gegenwart*,
23 March 2021 (https://geschichtedergegenwart.ch/the-german-cat-
echism/).

76. Delalić, 'German Redemption Theology', quoting Amnon Raz-
Krakotzkin, 'Secularism, the Christian Ambivalence Toward the Jews,
and the Notion of Exile', in *Secularism in Question: Jews and Judaism
in Modern Times*, edited by Ari Joskowicz and Ethan B. Katz
(Philadelphia, University of Pennsylvania, 2015), pp. 276–98.

6. RETHINKING OURSELVES

1. George Santayana, *Three Philosophical Poets: Lucretius, Dante, and Goethe*
(Cambridge, MA, Harvard University Press, 1910).

2. Alison Flood's 'Divine Comedy is "offensive and discriminatory", says
Italian NGO', *The Guardian*, 14 March 2012, https://www.theguardian.
com/books/2012/mar/14/the-divine-comedy-offensive-discrimantory

3. John Milton, *Paradise Lost* (London, Penguin, 2003).

4. An approximation of the theory put forward by the German Nazi Party Chief Propagandist Joseph Goebbels in his article 'Aus Churchills Lügenfabrik' ('From Churchill's Lie Factory') published in *Die Zeit ohne Beispiel*, 12 January 1941.

5. A line roughly translated from Charles Baudelaire's 'Le Joueur Généreux' ('The Generous Gambler'), *Le Figaro*, in 1864.

6. A quote that was possibly said by J. Robert Oppenheimer, but he was likely quoting from James Branch Cabell's 1926 novel *The Silver Stallion*.

7. Harold Bloom, *Shakespeare and the Invention of the Human* (New York, Riverhead, 1998).

8. Dorothy Hewlett, *Adonais: A Life of John Keats* (New York, The Bobbs Merrill Company, 1938).

9. T. S. Eliot, 'Hamlet and His Problems', in *Selected Essays* (London, Faber & Faber Ltd, 1932).

10. The Collected Works of Samuel Taylor Coleridge, *Lectures 1808–1819: On Literature I*, edited by R. A. Foakes (Abingdon and Princeton, Routledge & Kegan Paul, Princeton University Press, 1987).

11. Martin Lings, *To Take Upon Us the Mystery of Things: The Shakespeare Lectures*, edited by Ira B. Zinman (London, The Matheson Trust, 2014). Lings is better known in the Muslim community as Shaikh Abu Bakar Siraj al-Din, the writer of the highly popular modern biography of the Prophet, *Mohamed, His Life Based on the Earliest Sources* (Dar Al Wahi Publications).

12. Lings, *To Take Upon Us the Mystery of Things*.

13. Rudyard Kipling's poem 'The Ballad of East and West' is collected in *Kipling: Poems*, edited by Peter Washington (London, Everyman's Library Pocket Poets Series, 2007).

14. This section echoes a plenary paper titled 'Between Tyranny and Freedom: A Brief Voyage with the Bard', that I delivered during the VIII World Shakespeare Congress at Brisbane City Hall, Queensland, Australia, 16–21 July 2006.

15. Walt Whitman, *Leaves of Grass* (New York, Modern Library, 1993).

16. John Milton, *Areopagitica and Other Writings* (London, Penguin, 2016).

17. Isaiah Berlin, 'Two Concepts of Liberty', in *Four Essays on Liberty* (Oxford, Oxford University Press, 1969), pp. 118–72.

18. Rosie Gray, 'Trump Defends White-Nationalist Protesters: "Some Very Fine People on Both Sides"', *The Atlantic*, 15 August 2017 (https://www.theatlantic.com/politics/archive/2017/08/trump-defends-white-nationalist-protesters-some-very-fine-people-on-both-sides/537012/).

19. Ziauddin Sardar and Robin Yassin-Kassab (eds.), *Critical Muslim 1: The Arabs Are Alive* (London, Hurst, 2012).

20. From David Simon's 'There are now two Americas. My country is a horror show', *The Guardian*, 8 December 2013 (https://www.theguardian.com/world/2013/dec/08/david-simon-capitalism-marx-two-americas-wire).

21. The following economic works have given capitalism a long overdue dressing down: Shoshana Zuboff, *The Age of Surveillance Capitalism* (New York, PublicAffairs, 2019); Naomi Klein, *The Shock Doctrine* (London, Penguin, 2014); Guy Standing, *The Corruption of Capitalism* (London, Biteback, 2016); Grace Blakeley, *Stolen: How to Save the World from Financialisation* (London, Repeater, 2019); Matt Stoller, *Goliath: The Hundred-Year War Between Monopoly Power and Democracy* (London, Simon & Schuster, 2020); Andrew Manno, *Toxic Masculinity, Casino Capitalism, and America's Favorite Card Game: The Poker Mindset* (London, Macmillan, 2020); Kimberly Kay Hoang, *Spiderweb Capitalism: How Global Elites Exploit Frontier Markets* (Princeton, Princeton University Press, 2022); and Thomas Piketty, *Capital in the Twenty-First Century* (Cambridge, MA, Harvard University Press, 2013).

22. Syed Hussein Alatas, *The Problem of Corruption* (Petaling Jaya, The Other Press, 2015).

23. Joris Luyendijk, 'Our banks are not merely out of control. They're beyond control', *The Guardian*, 19 June 2013 (https://www.theguardian.com/commentisfree/joris-luyendijk-banking-blog/2013/jun/19/banking-britain-beyond-control).

24. Michael Jacobs and Mariana Mazzucato (eds.), *Rethinking Capitalism: Economics and Policy for Sustainable and Inclusive Growth* (Hoboken, Wiley-Blackwell, Hoboken, 2016).

25. Liliann Fischer, Joe Hasell, J. Christopher Proctor, and David Uwakwe (eds.), *Rethinking Economics: An Introduction to Plural Economics* (London, Routledge, 2017).

26. Joe Earle, Cahal Moran, and Zach Ward-Perkins, *The Econocracy* (London, Penguin, 2017).

27. Wolfgang Sachs, 'The Age of Development: An Obituary', *New Internationalist*, January–February 2020.

28. John Gray, *Heresies* (London, Granta, 2004).

29. From the Wellcome Collective's exhibition *Being Human*, which opened in London on 5 September 2019.

30. Nessa Carey, *Hacking the Code of Life* (London, Icon, 2019).

31. From the Barbican International Enterprise's *AI: More than Human*, which opened in London's Barbican on 16 May 2019..

32. Al Gore, *The Future* (London, W. H. Allen, 2013).

33. Ibid.

34. Amy Webb, *The Big Nine* (New York, PublicAffairs, 2019).

35. Al Gore, *An Inconvenient Truth*, directed by Davis Guggenheim, Paramount Classics, 2006; and *An Inconvenient Sequel: Truth to Power*, directed by Bonni Cohen and Jon Shenk, Paramount Pictures, 2017.

36. Noam Chomsky and Robert Pollin, *Climate Crisis and the Global Green New Deal* (London, Verso, 2020).

37. Naomi Klein, *This Changes Everything* (London, Penguin, 2014).

38. Christiana Figueres and Tom Rivett-Carnac, *The Future We Choose: Surviving the Climate Crisis* (London, Manilla Press, 2020).

39. From 'Interview with Ulrich Beck', *Journal of Consumer Culture*, 1 (2), 2001, pp. 261–77.

40. Ibid.

41. See Zygmunt Bauman's *Liquid Modernity* (Oxford, Polity, 2000) and *Liquid Times* (Oxford, Polity, 2007); Zygmunt Bauman and Leonidas Donskis's *Liquid Evil* (Oxford, Polity, 2020); and Zygmunt Bauman's *Retrotopia* (Oxford, Polity, 2017).

42. See Byung-Chul Han's *Psycho-Politics: Neoliberalism and the New Technologies of Power* (London, Verso, 2017) and *The Burnout Society* (Stanford, Stanford University Press, 2015).

43. See Zuboff, *The Age of Surveillance Capitalism*.

44. See Ziauddin Sardar (ed.), *The Postnormal Times Reader* (London, CPPFS & IIIT, 2017) and Ziauddin Sardar, Shamim Miah, and C. Scott Jordan's *The Postnormal Times Reader Volume 2* (London, CPPFS & IIIT, 2024). For more information visit the website postnormaltim.es

45. Ziauddin Sardar's 'Welcome to Postnormal Times', was originally published in *Futures*, 42 (5) 2010, pp. 435–44. It is also found in *The Postnormal Times Reader*, edited by Sardar.

46. For more on Sardar's earlier work on critical futures, see Ziauddin Sardar (ed.), *Rescuing All Our Futures: The Future of Futures Studies* (Westport, Praeger Publishers, 1998); Ziauddin Sardar, Ashis Nandy, and Merryl Wyn Davies (eds.), *Barbaric Others: A Manifesto on Western Racism* (London, Pluto Press, 1993); and Ziauddin Sardar, *Postmodernism and the Other* (London, Pluto Press, 1998).

47. Anwar Ibrahim, *SCRIPT for a Better Malaysia: An Empowering Vision and Policy Framework for Action* (Shah Alam, IDE & CPPFS, 2022). Prior to the completion of this work, the following other works looked at the postnormal situation and challenges posed in Malaysia and beyond: Ziauddin Sardar, Jordi Serra, and Scott Jordan, *Muslim Societies in Postnormal Times: Emerging Issues and Scenarios* (London, IIIT & CPPFS, 2019) and Ziauddin Sardar (ed.), *Emerging Epistemologies: The Changing Fabric of Knowledge in Postnormal Times* (Herndon, IIIT & CPPFS, 2022). Other references to these topics in the quarterly literary magazine *Critical Muslim* can be further explored at criticalmuslim.com; see, too, the websites postnormaltim.es and cppfs.org.

48. Bill Gates and Melinda French Gates, 'Covid-19: A Global Perspective', 2020 *Goalkeepers Report*, September 2020, (https://www.gatesfoundation.org/goalkeepers/report/2020-report/#GlobalPerspective).

49. See Fareed Zakaria's *Ten Lessons for a Post-Pandemic World* (New York, W. W. Norton, 2020); Gordon Brown's *Seven Ways to Change the World* (London, Simon & Schuster, 2021); and Gordon Brown, Mohamed A. El-Erian, Michael Spence, and Reid Lidow's *Permacrisis: A Plan to Fix a Fractured World* (London, Simon & Schuster, 2023).

50. See Sardar, 'Welcome to Postnormal Times'.

51. Aleksandr Solzhenitsyn, *The Gulag Archipelago* (London, Vintage, 2003).

EPILOGUE: PREPARING FOR THE NEXT STORM

1. The quote appears in E. L. Doctorow's *Ragtime* (London, Penguin, 2007).

2. The *keris* (sometimes spelled *kris*) is an asymmetrical dagger distinguished for its curved blade found throughout Nusantara. It is an object of spiritual value that is also used as a weapon. It is a common accessory for traditional wear throughout the Malay Archipelago.

3. Immanuel Kant, *Prolegomena to Any Future Metaphysics*, translated and edited by Gary Hatfield, (Cambridge, Cambridge University Press, 2004).

4. *Sarjan Hassan*, written by Ralph Modder and P. Ramlee, directed by Lamberto Avellana and P. Ramlee, distributed by Shaw Brothers Ltd, released 28 August 1958.

5. Kwame Anthony Appiah, *The Ethics of Identity* (Princeton, Princeton University Press, 2007).

6. Alvin Toffler, *Future Shock* (New York, Bantam, 1984).

7. These words borrow from the phrasing used by Maya Angelou in an interview with Greg Jackson in the independent series 'One-On-One' from 1983.

8. Donella H. Meadows, Dennis L. Meadows, Jorgen Randers, and William Behrens III, *The Limits of Growth: A Report for The Club of Rome's Project on the Predicament of Mankind* (New York, Universe Books, 1972).

9. Joseph E. Stiglitz, *The Road to Freedom: Economics and the Good Society* (London, Allen Lane, 2024); this work was also extensively discussed during the 2024 Kazanah Megatrends Conference in Kuala Lumpur.

10. Isaiah Berlin, *Four Essays on Liberty* (Oxford, Oxford University Press, 1969).

11. Friedrich A. Hayek, *The Constitution of Liberty* (Chicago, University of Chicago Press, 1987).

12. Adam Smith, *An Inquiry into the Nature and Causes of the Wealth of Nations*, edited by Edwin Cannan (London, Methuen, 1904).

13. Adam Smith, *The Theory of Moral Sentiments*, edited by A. L. Macfie (Oxford, Clarendon Press, 1976).

14. Emma's making of this point occurred during a meeting with the French economist Michel Camdessus and myself in Bilbao, Spain in the noughties. The moment is detailed in Anwar Ibrahim's 'The Last Word: On Sympathy for Mr Smith', in *Critical Muslim 46: Capital*, edited by Ziauddin Sardar (London, Hurst, 2023).

15. I have dealt extensively on this issue in the lecture 'Examining Economic Growth and Social Justice in the 21st Century' at the University of Cambridge, 16 March 2007.

16. From Amartya Sen's *Development as Freedom* (Oxford, Oxford University Press, New York, Alfred A. Knopf, 1999).

17. Václav Havel, *The Power of the Powerless* (London, Vintage Classics, 2018).

18. Anwar Ibrahim, *SCRIPT for a Better Malaysia: An Empowering Vision and Policy Framework for Action* (Shah Alam, IDE & CPPFS, 2022).

19. Marcus Ng, Gayathri Haridas, Evelyn Teoh, and Jing Ting Toh's 'The Economic Impact of Generative AI: The Future of Work in Malaysia', Malaysia Centre for the Fourth Industrial Revolution, September 2023, (https://www.ai.gov.my/media/thought-leadership/Reports-06-EN-Economic-Impact-of-Generative-AI-MY-1.pdf).

20. 'Tunggu Sekejap', lyrics by P. Ramlee, performed by P. Ramlee, in the film *Sarjan Hassan*, 1958.

INDEX

INDEX

INDEX

INDEX

INDEX

INDEX

INDEX

INDEX

INDEX

INDEX

INDEX

INDEX

INDEX